The Life and Works of Works of Arthur Schnitzler

A Biography

ARTHUR C. RAUSCHER

OVID PUBLISHING GROUP

Rediscover the timeless wisdom of classical literature with Ovid Publishing Group. We breathe new life into classic masterpieces, making them accessible and engaging for modern readers. Our editions are enhanced with comprehensive introductions, insightful chapter notes, and thought-provoking essays.

https://ovidpublishing.com/

Contents

Introduction   1

Part I: Formation (1862-1893)

  1. The Physician's Son (1862-1871)   7

  2. The Reluctant Doctor (1879-1886)   23

  3. Impertinent Sensuality (1886-1890)   31

  4. Young Vienna (1890-1893)   38

  5. Father's Death (1893)   43

Part II: Breakthrough (1893-1902)

  6. Liberation (1893-1894)   49
    Anatol, Das Märchen

  7. Triumph (1894-1895)   62
    Liebelei

  8. The Great Love (1895-1899)   70
    Paracelsus, Die Gefährtin, Der grüne Kakadu

  9. Scandal (1896-1900)   84
    Reigen

10. Innovation (1896-1900)   98
  Leutnant Gustl

11. A Younger Woman (1899-1902)   112

Part III: The Domestic Years (1903-1921)

12. Early Marriage (1903-1909)   120
  Der einsame Weg, Zwischenspiel, Der Ruf des Lebens

13. The Road into the Open   125
  Der Weg ins Freie

14. The Villa on the Sternwartestraße: The Years Before the War (1910–1912)   135
  Das weite Land

15. Professor Bernhardi and the Jewish Question (1912–1913)   146
  Professor Bernhardi, Frau Beate und ihr Sohn

16. The War Years and Jugend in Wien (1914–1918)   155
  Jugend in Wien, Doctor Gräsler, Badearzt, Casanovas Heimfahrt

17. Divorce & The Reigen Scandal (1920 & 1921)   165
  Reigen

Part IV: Eyes Wide Open (1921-1931)

18. Alone on Sternwartestraße, 1921–1923   179

19. Late Masterpieces: Fräulein Else (1924)   184
  Fräulein Else

20. Traumnovelle and Its Enduring Legacy (1925-1926)   196
  Traumnovelle

21. Lili (1926-July 1928)   207

22. The Last Few Years (1928-1931)   212
     Therese: Chronik eines Frauenlebens

Part V: Epilogue

23. The Archive, the Burnings, and the Long Recovery   221

24. Film, Scholarship, and the Second Life of the Work   225

25. Cultural Relevance   229

The Works of Arthur Schnitzler (1862-1931)   233

More Books by Arthur Schnitzler by Ovid Publishing   243

Chapter Notes (1-10)   249

Chapter Notes (11-25)   278

Chapter Notes (21-25)   305

Bibliography of Sources   319

About the Author   334

Introduction

ON JULY 16, 1999, Stanley Kubrick's final film *Eyes Wide Shut* premiered in theaters worldwide, four months after the legendary director's death. The movie—starring Tom Cruise and Nicole Kidman as a married couple navigating jealousy, desire, and the hidden depths of their relationship—introduced millions of viewers to a story that had obsessed Kubrick for three decades. But few in those audiences knew that the film was based on a 1926 novella called *Traumnovelle* by an Austrian physician-turned-writer named Arthur Schnitzler, who had died sixty-eight years earlier. Fewer still knew that this same writer had invented stream-of-consciousness narration in German literature twenty-two years before James Joyce, or that his works had been condemned as "Jewish filth" and burned by the Nazis in 1933.

This book tells the story of that writer—a man more famous in death than in life, whose biggest cultural moment arrived nearly seven decades after his passing, and whose insights into power, sexuality, marriage, and identity speak more urgently to our era than to his own.

Arthur Schnitzler (1862-1931) lived through the twilight of the Austro-Hungarian Empire, documenting with clinical precision the sexual hypocrisy, antisemitism, and psychological depths of fin-de-siècle Vienna. He was stripped of his military commission for exposing the absurdity of the honor code, branded a pornographer for depicting the circular chain of desire across social classes, and banned from Austrian stages for dramatizing institutional antisemitism. Every scandal proved his point: the truth hurt because it was true.

But Schnitzler was more than a provocateur. He was a technical innovator whose 1900 novella *Leutnant Gustl* pioneered interior monologue in German fiction, a psychological explorer whose work prompted Freud to write that Schnitzler had learned "through intuition everything that I have had to unearth by laborious work," and a prophet whose themes—sexual consent, power dynamics, the impossibility of truly knowing another person—resonate more powerfully today than they did a century ago.

This biography is structured in five parts, followed by extensive appendices and literary essays on Schnitzler's major works.

Part I: Formation (1862-1893) traces Schnitzler's early years as the son of Vienna's most prominent laryngologist, his reluctant medical training, his emergence into the literary circles of Young Vienna, and the death of his father—a loss that paradoxically liberated him to pursue writing full-time.

Part II: Breakthrough (1893-1902) covers his first major successes (*Anatol, Liebelei*), the scandalous *Reigen*, his groundbreaking *Leutnant Gustl*, and his relationship with the actress Adele Sandrock and the singer Marie Reinhard—experiences that would fuel his most penetrating insights into love, power, and self-deception.

Part III: The Domestic Years (1903-1921) examines Schnitzler's marriage to Olga Gussmann, the birth of his children Heinrich and Lili, his major middle-period works (*Der Weg ins Freie, Professor Bernhardi, Das weite Land*), the trauma of World War I, the 1920 *Reigen* riots, and his divorce—eighteen years that saw both his greatest professional triumphs and deepest personal struggles.

Part IV: Eyes Wide Open (1921-1931) follows Schnitzler's final decade: his relationship with Clara Katharina Pollaczek, his late masterpieces (*Fräulein Else, Traumnovelle*), his daughter Lili's marriage to the Italian fascist Arnoldo Cappellini, her devastating suicide in 1928, and Schnitzler's own death in 1931—two years before the Nazis would burn his books.

Part V: Epilogue traces Schnitzler's posthumous journey from the Nazi book burnings through postwar rediscovery, the 1999 *Eyes Wide Shut* phenomenon, and his enduring cultural relevance to contemporary discussions of consent, power, antisemitism, and marriage.

The appendices provide essential context: a complete chronological bibliography of Schnitzler's works; an examination of Young Vienna and fin-de-siècle culture; and an analysis of Jewish identity in his writing—crucial for understanding how a secular, assimilated Jewish physician became one of the most penetrating chroniclers of Austrian antisemitism.

Finally, the literary essays offer in-depth explorations of nine major works: *Anatol* (1893), *Liebelei* (1895), *Reigen* (1897), *Leutnant Gustl* (1900), *Der Weg ins Freie* (1908), *Das weite Land* (1911), *Professor Bernhardi* (1912), *Fräulein Else* (1924), *Traumnovelle* (1926), and *Therese* (1928). These essays examine not just plot and theme, but historical context, technical innovation, censorship history, and contemporary relevance.

Why does Schnitzler matter now? Three reasons compel this claim:

First, **he saw what others refused to see**. While his contemporaries waltzed and drank wine, Schnitzler documented an empire in denial—the sexual exploitation masked as romance, the antisemitism lurking beneath cosmopolitan civility, the psychological abysses beneath polished surfaces. He kept his eyes wide open to uncomfortable truths, and he paid the price.

Second, **he invented techniques that changed literature**. Stream-of-consciousness in *Leutnant Gustl* (1900), perfected in *Fräulein Else* (1924). Circular episodic structure in *Reigen*. Interior monologue that makes visible the invisible workings of consciousness. Schnitzler was doing in fiction what Freud was doing in therapy—making the unconscious conscious, the unspoken spoken.

Third, **his themes are our themes**. *Fräulein Else*'s examination of sexual coercion and consent speaks directly to the #MeToo era. *Professor Bernhardi*'s portrait of institutional antisemitism feels urgently relevant as antisemitism rises globally. *Traumnovelle*'s exploration of marriage and fantasy resonates with anyone who has wondered if they truly know their partner. *Reigen*'s exposure of power dynamics in sexual relationships remains as provocative as ever.

Schnitzler wrote, "I write of love and death. What other subjects are there?" This biography shows how one man's unflinching examination of these eternal subjects created a body of work that grows more relevant with each passing decade—a writer who saw the future because he refused to look away from the present.

Arthur C. Rauscher February 2026

Part I: Formation (1862–1893)

"IN THOSE DAYS WE thought we knew what was true, good and beautiful; and all life lay ahead of us in grandiose simplicity."
—Arthur Schnitzler, *My Youth in Vienna*

CHAPTER ONE

The Physician's Son (1862–1871)

ON THE FIFTEENTH OF May, 1862, in a second-floor apartment at 16 Jägerzeile, a boy was born to Johann and Louise Schnitzler.[1] The street would soon be renamed Praterstraße, part of a general modernizing impulse that was remaking the face of Vienna, but for now the old name still held—a hunters' lane, recalling a time when the nearby Prater had been the private game reserve of the Habsburgs rather than the public park it had become a century earlier. The district was Leopoldstadt, Vienna's Second, a large low-lying island between the Danube Canal and the unregulated arms of the river itself, and it was here, in a neighborhood layered with ironies that the infant could not yet appreciate, that Arthur Schnitzler entered the world.

Schnitzler's birthplace (chapter note 30)

Leopoldstadt carried its history in its name. Emperor Leopold I had expelled the Jews from this area—then called the Unterer Werd—in 1670, and the district's inhabitants, in a gesture that mingled gratitude with something harder to name, had rechristened the place in the emperor's honor.[2] Two centuries later, the ironies had compounded. Jews had returned, slowly at first and then in a great tide after Joseph II's Edict of Tolerance in 1782 opened Vienna's doors again. By 1862, the district was well on its way to becoming the center of Jewish life in the imperial capital. Viennese wits had already begun calling it the Mazzesinsel—Matzo Island—a nickname that carried, depending on who spoke it, either affection or contempt.[3]

The neighborhood Arthur was born into was a place of contrasts. Eleven Orthodox prayer houses—*shtieblach*, as they were known—served the recently arrived immigrants from Galicia, men in dark coats and side curls who spoke Yiddish and kept to the old ways. But there was also the magnificent Leopoldstadt Temple at Tempelgasse 5, completed in 1858 to the designs of Ludwig Förster in a Moorish Revival style, its seating for over two thousand worshippers reflecting the growing confidence of an established community.[4] It stood as a declaration: these Jews were not merely tolerated visitors but permanent participants in the life of the capital. The district's Jewish population, which would swell to tens of thousands by 1870, encompassed the whole spectrum—from peddlers who had arrived at the Nordbahnhof station with little more than a bundle and a prayer to prosperous families like the Schnitzlers, who had already made the leap from the margins to the professions.

Vienna in 1862 was the capital of an empire that still stretched across much of Central Europe, though the strains that would soon reshape it were already visible. The Austrian defeat at the hands of France and Piedmont-Sardinia in 1859 had shaken confidence in the old order; five years hence, the compromise of 1867 would transform the Austrian Empire into the Austro-Hungarian dual monarchy, a constitutional arrangement that promised equality before the law and, for the empire's Jews, something approaching full citizenship. These were years of cautious optimism, of fortifications being torn down—literally, in the case of the old city walls, whose demolition had begun in 1857 to make way for the Ringstraße, the grand circular boulevard that would become the physical expression of liberal Vienna's self-image. Into this atmosphere of construction and aspiration, Arthur Schnitzler was born.

The two families that converged in his parents' marriage told a story about the possibilities of Jewish life in the Habsburg lands, and about its limits. His father, Johann Schnitzler, had been born on April 10, 1835, in Groß-Kanizsa (Nagy-Kanizsa in Hungarian), a market town in western Hungary.[5] Johann's father, Joseph, was a carpenter who at some point took the step of changing the family name from Zimmermann to Schnitzler—both names evoking the craft of woodworking, but the shift carrying a certain ambition, as though the family were carving a new identity from the old material.[6] Joseph married Rosalie Klein, and together they raised a son who would leave carpentry far behind.

Johann Schnitzler 1875 (chapter note 31)

Johann's rise was the stuff of nineteenth-century self-invention. The carpenter's son shed Yiddish and Magyar for German, the language of culture and advancement in the empire, and made his way to the univer-sities of Budapest and Vienna to study medicine. In 1860, at twenty-five, he received his medical degree from the University of Vienna.[7] It was an achievement that, a generation earlier, would have been nearly unthinkable for a Jewish boy from a Hungarian trade family. But Johann Schnitzler was a man of his moment, and his moment was one in which the old barriers were falling, or at least seemed to be.

What Johann Schnitzler did not become—what he might, in differ-ent circumstances, have been—was a writer. He had harbored literary ambitions as a young man, even producing a few dramatic works, but abandoned them for the security and respectability of a medical career.[8] It was the practical choice, the rational choice, the choice that a son of poverty would have been expected to make. And it proved spectacularly successful. Johann would go on to become one of the pioneers of modern laryngology, a specialist in diseases of the throat and larynx who developed new techniques and who built a reputation that reached well beyond the medical profession. Yet the abandoned dream did not simply disappear. It lingered, an unfinished sentence in the story of Johann Schnitzler's life, and it would cast a long shadow over the childhood of his firstborn son.

Arthur's mother, Louise Ludovica Markbreiter, came from an altogeth-er different stratum.[9] Her father, Philipp Markbreiter, was a renowned Viennese physician from a family of court jewelers—a lineage that spoke of generations of established standing in the capital. Her mother, Amalia, was born a Schey von Koromla, a Hungarian Jewish family distinguished enough to hold a baronial title. Where Johann had climbed, Louise had been born to a certain height. She brought to their marriage not only the social connections of a well-placed Viennese family but a sense of belong-ing to the city's cultivated class that no amount of professional success could quite replicate.

The match between Johann and Louise united, in miniature, two cur-rents of Jewish experience in the empire: the striving of the newly emancipated and the settled confidence of the already arrived. Philipp Markbre-iter and Johann Schnitzler were not merely father-in-law and son-in-law but professional collaborators; in 1860, the same year Johann received his medical degree, Markbreiter founded the *Wiener Medizinische Presse,* a medical journal to which Johann was soon attached as co-editor and which he would ultimately lead for over two decades.[10] The partnership cement-ed the bond between the families and gave the young doctor a platform. It also hinted at the pragmatism beneath the romance: this was a marriage of compatible ambitions as much as of hearts, though what passed between Johann and Louise in private remains largely unrecorded.

Arthur, their first child, arrived into a household already charged with the energy of a career in ascent. Johann was twenty-seven, freshly creden-tialed and soon to begin his clinical training under the renowned Johann von Oppolzer at the Vienna General Hospital.[11] Louise was twenty-two. Whatever private hopes they invested in the birth of a son—and for a Jewish family in the Habsburg Empire, a firstborn son carried a particular freight of expectation—they could not yet know that this child would spend a lifetime excavating the very world they were so industriously build-ing.

The family grew quickly. In 1864, Louise gave birth to a second son, Joseph Emil. He lived only a few weeks.[12] The records preserve the fact but not the grief, and one can only speculate about what the death of an infant did to the emotional life of a household with a two-year-old boy. Child mortality was common enough in the 1860s to be expected, but common enough is not the same as painless, and the loss of Joseph Emil almost certainly deepened the family's investment in Arthur, the surviving firstborn, the son who would be expected to carry everything.

A third child, Julius, arrived in 1865. He would grow up to become a surgeon and professor—a career that followed his father's path into medicine without any of the ambivalence that would torment his older brother.[13] In 1867, a daughter, Gisela, completed the family. She would eventually marry Markus Hajek, himself a specialist in laryngology, extending the medical dynasty into the next generation.[14] The household at its full strength was a portrait of the Jewish professional class at its most successful: a prominent father, a well-connected mother, three surviving children, and an atmosphere in which education and achievement were not merely valued but assumed.

Arthur occupied a particular position within this constellation. As the eldest, and as the first surviving son after Joseph Emil's death, he bore the concentrated weight of the family's expectations. Julius, by the accident of birth order, would enjoy the relative freedom of the second son—free to follow their father into medicine as a genuine choice rather than an obligation. For Arthur, the path had been laid before he was old enough to question it. He would be a doctor. The only question was what kind.

In 1868, when Arthur was six, the family left Leopoldstadt. Their new address—Giselastraße 11, in the First District—was more than a change of apartments; it was a statement of arrival.[15] The First District was the heart of imperial Vienna, the center of political power and cultural authority, the address of the Hofburg Palace and the great institutions of state. To move from the Second District to the First was to cross a boundary that was geographic, social, and, for a Jewish family, deeply symbolic. Leopoldstadt, for all its vitality, was the Jewish quarter; the First District was where Jews went when they had succeeded enough to leave.

The move coincided with—and reflected—the acceleration of Johann Schnitzler's career. He was building a reputation as a laryngologist of uncommon skill, and the apartment on Giselastraße served a double purpose: it was both the family home and Johann's medical practice.[16] This arrangement, common enough among Viennese physicians of the period, meant that Arthur's childhood unfolded in the peculiar atmosphere of a household that was also a place of work, where the boundary between domestic life and professional life was porous, and where the sounds and rhythms of medicine—the consultations, the instruments, the voices of patients—formed a constant backdrop to the ordinary business of growing up.

The patients themselves were extraordinary. Johann Schnitzler's specialty was the throat, and the throat was the instrument of the stage. His reputation drew the leading performers of the age: actors from the Burgtheater, singers from the Court Opera, men and women whose voices were their livelihood and whose names were known to every Viennese theatergoer. Adolf von Sonnenthal, the great tragedian, was among Johann's patients; so was Charlotte Wolter, the reigning dramatic actress of her generation.[17] These were not distant cultural figures for young Arthur. They were people who passed through his home, who sat in his father's consulting room, who could be glimpsed and overheard in the ordinary course of a day.

It is difficult to overstate what this meant for a child of Arthur's temperament. The theater, which for most Viennese children was a world of magic and illusion encountered only from the velvet seats of an auditorium, was for him a daily reality seen from its most unromantic angle. He witnessed the performers not in their glory but in their vulnerability—hoarse, anxious, submitting their most essential instrument to the clinical authority of his father. He saw the human machinery behind the art. The interplay between performance and reality, between the self presented to the world and the self laid bare, would become the great theme of Arthur Schnitzler's literary career. Its origins lay in this childhood, in a consulting room on Giselastraße where famous voices came to be healed.

Johann Schnitzler was, by any measure, a remarkable man. From a carpenter's workshop in provincial Hungary to a professor's chair at the University of Vienna was a distance that required not merely talent but an unrelenting will. By the early 1870s, his ascent was well under way. In 1872, he became co-founder and head of the laryngological department at the newly established Vienna General Polyclinic.[18] In the years that followed, he received the title of associate professor in 1880, and in 1884 became medical director of the Polyclinic, accumulating titles and positions with the steady momentum of a man who understood exactly what the world required of him.[19]

His published work was substantial: treatises on pneumatic therapy for lung and heart disease, a manual of laryngoscopy and rhinoscopy, and the *Klinischer Atlas der Laryngologie*, a clinical atlas that would be published posthumously in 1895.[20] He was a pioneer in the use of hypnosis as a medical tool, an early practitioner in a field that would soon intersect with the work of another Viennese Jewish physician, Sigmund Freud, whose trajectory through the city's medical institutions ran in curious parallel to the Schnitzler family's own. Johann's journal gave him a voice in the profession that extended beyond his own practice, and his network of patients and colleagues placed the family at the intersection of Vienna's medical and cultural worlds.

To his eldest son, this formidable career presented itself as both inspiration and burden. A father who has succeeded magnificently in his chosen field sets a standard that can feel less like an invitation than a command. And Johann was, by the scattered evidence available, a demanding figure—not cruel, but exacting, a man whose own rise from poverty had left him with firm ideas about discipline, duty, and the obligations of talent. That he had once dreamed of becoming a writer himself added a dimension to the father-son dynamic that neither man may have fully understood. Johann had surrendered his literary ambitions for medicine. His son would be expected to embrace what the father had chosen—but the son would also inherit, as though by some ironic law of compensation, the very impulse the father had suppressed.

None of this would have been articulated in the household of a six- or seven-year-old boy. These were subterranean currents, felt rather than spoken, shaping Arthur's sensibility before he had language for what was happening. What he did have was a daily demonstration of what a successful life looked like: it looked like his father, efficient and authoritative, moving between patients and publications, respected by the famous and the powerful, building something solid in the great meritocratic project of liberal Vienna. The question of whether this was the only way a life could look—whether there might be other forms of seriousness, other kinds of achievement—was still far in the future.

In 1870, when Arthur was eight, a new figure entered the household. Berta Lehmann was engaged as governess to the Schnitzler children, and her influence on the eldest would prove disproportionate to her station.[21] Where Johann embodied the claims of science and professional ambition, Berta Lehmann represented something else: permission. She encouraged Arthur's interest in literature and theater, nurturing a side of the boy that the household's medical atmosphere might otherwise have left untended. It was her brother who inspired Arthur to attempt his first dramatic work, a play with the arresting title *Aristokrat und Demokrat*—Aristocrat and Democrat.[22]

The title alone is suggestive. At eight or nine years old, Arthur Schnitzler was already drawn to the fault lines of social and political life, to the tensions between classes that animated the world around him. The play itself has not survived as a significant work, but its existence matters: it tells us that the literary impulse was present from an early age, that the child was already reaching for the dramatic form, and that he was doing so with the encouragement of a woman employed to look after his education rather than with the direct sanction of his father. Literature and theater, for the young Arthur, were associated with a feminine encouragement that existed alongside, and slightly apart from, the masculine world of medicine that dominated the household.

Before Berta's arrival, and continuing alongside her influence, Arthur's education had been entrusted to a series of private tutors. This was the standard arrangement for children of the upper middle class, a mark of status that also served a practical function: it ensured that a child entered formal schooling already equipped with the fundamentals of a classical education. Arthur learned his letters and his numbers in the private, cushioned environment of a prosperous home, surrounded by books and the conversation of educated adults, absorbing the textures of a world that took learning seriously—not as a means to an end, but as an expression of civilized life.

The world the Schnitzler family inhabited during Arthur's early childhood was shaped by an idea—the idea that progress was real, irreversible, and available to all who were willing to work for it. This was the creed of Viennese liberalism, and for the city's Jewish population it carried the force of revelation. The constitutional reforms of 1867, which granted Jews full legal equality throughout the empire, seemed to confirm what the optimists had always believed: that the barriers of the past were crumbling, that merit would triumph over prejudice, and that the future belonged to reason, science, and culture.

The statistics bore out the optimism, at least on the surface. Jewish Viennese were entering the professions in extraordinary numbers—dominating law and medicine, commanding a disproportionate share of the city's financial and journalistic life, and contributing to the arts and sciences with an energy that seemed to vindicate every promise of emancipation. Families like the Schnitzlers were the embodiment of this success. Johann, a carpenter's son who had become a university professor, was a walking proof of the liberal proposition. His children were being raised in the First District, educated by private tutors, surrounded by the conversation of cultivated people. The old world of the ghetto, of restriction and exclusion, was receding into memory.

Or so it appeared. Schnitzler would later reflect on the atmosphere of his childhood with a wariness that suggests the seeds of doubt were present even in the years of greatest confidence. The liberalism of the 1860s and 1870s produced a world in which certain values were taken for granted as unassailable, in which young people were directed toward clearly defined goals and encouraged to believe they could build their lives on a stable fou ndation.[23] The error, as he came to see it, was not in the values themselves but in the certainty with which they were held. The foundation was not as stable as it looked.

Even in Arthur's childhood, there were signs for those willing to read them. The stock market crash of 1873, which devastated Vienna's financial markets and ruined thousands, would be blamed in many quarters on Jewish financiers—a foretaste of the scapegoating that would intensify in the decades to come. Karl Lueger, who would ride a wave of populist antisemitism to the mayoralty of Vienna, was already building his political career on resentments that the liberals preferred to believe were relics of a less enlightened age. The nationalism that was rising across the empire threatened the cosmopolitan ideals that Jewish Viennese had embraced as their own. These were distant rumbles in the early 1870s, barely audible above the sounds of construction and celebration, but they were there.

The Schnitzler family's own geography traced the arc of assimilation's promise. From Leopoldstadt to Giselastraße to, in 1871, an apartment at Burgring 1—each address more prestigious than the last, each move a step closer to the center of imperial power.[24] The Burgring address placed the family on the Ringstraße itself, the great boulevard that was Vienna's proudest achievement, lined with the monumental buildings—the Opera, the museums, the Parliament—that embodied the liberal belief in progress, culture, and the public good. To live on the Ring was to live at the symbolic heart of everything the era stood for. It was also, for a Jewish family, to live in a place where belonging was always, at some level, conditional—a fact that the confident façades of the new buildings could obscure but never quite erase.

In the autumn of 1871, at nine years old, Arthur Schnitzler was enrolled at the Akademisches Gymnasium.[25] The school occupied a handsome neo-Gothic building at Beethovenplatz, designed by Friedrich von Schmidt, the same architect who would later produce Vienna's City Hall—a coincidence that nicely captured the school's position at the intersection of civic ambition and intellectual aspiration. Founded by the Jesuits in 1553, it was the oldest secondary school in Vienna, and by the time Arthur entered its doors it had been transformed from a bastion of Catholic instruction into something closer to the opposite: a humanistic institution with a progressive reputation, shaped by the Enlightenment's confidence in reason and the liberal era's faith in education as the engine of social advancement.

The transformation had been gradual. When Pope Clement XIV dissolved the Jesuit order in 1773, the school passed to the Piarists and began to loosen its religious character. Latin remained central, as did Greek, but the curriculum expanded to include history, mathematics, geography, modern languages, and literature. By the 1860s, the Akademisches Gymnasium had become known as a rather liberal institution compared to other traditional secondary schools—a place where intellectual curiosity was encouraged and where the student body reflected the aspirations of Vienna's educated bourgeoisie, and particularly of its Jewish families, who saw in the school precisely the kind of meritocratic environment in which their children could flourish.

The school's alumni list reads like a catalog of Viennese cultural achievement. The playwright Johann Nestroy had studied there; so, in a much earlier era, had Franz Schubert. In the years around Arthur's enrollment and those that followed, the school would count among its students a concentration of future luminaries that seems, in retrospect, almost implausible: the writer Peter Altenberg, the poet Hugo von Hofmannsthal, the dramatist Richard Beer-Hofmann—both of whom would become close friends and collaborators of Schnitzler's in the Young Vienna circle—and, in later generations, the physicist Erwin Schrödinger, the economist Ludwig von Mises, and the nuclear physicist Lise Meitner.[26] It was, in the fullest sense, a school for the formation of an intellectual elite, and the Jewish character of that elite was unmistakable: by the twentieth century, roughly half the student body would be Jewish, a proportion that reflected both the community's passionate investment in education and its concentration in the liberal professions.

For a nine-year-old boy, of course, the school was something more immediate than a historical institution or a gateway to intellectual distinction. It was a world of corridors and classrooms, of teachers and schoolmates, of Latin declensions and the small dramas of daily life among children. Arthur arrived carrying the equipment his background had given him: the confidence of a child raised in comfort and stimulation, the seriousness of a firstborn son in a family that did not take achievement lightly, and, somewhere beneath the surface, the stirrings of a sensibility that was not entirely suited to the path that had been prepared for him. He could write a play at eight, and he would be expected to become a doctor. The tension between these two facts would take years to resolve itself, and the resolution, when it came, would be neither clean nor painless.

In the spring of 1875, at the age of thirteen, Arthur experienced his first infatuation—with Franziska ("Fännchen") Reich, the daughter of neighbors. The attraction was mutual, but the disapproval of both families and the Reich family's move brought an end to it. The episode would linger: after an intermission of nearly two years, the two would meet again in September 1878 and briefly resume their adolescent romance.[27] These youthful attachments, recorded later in the diary he began in March 1879, already hint at the emotional patterns—the intensity, the ambivalence, the fascination with the mechanics of desire—that would run through his mature work.

On July 8, 1879, Schnitzler passed his Matura examination with distinction.[28] As a reward, the family traveled that autumn to Amsterdam, where Arthur accompanied his father to a medical congress. Johann arranged for his son's first publication—a travel report titled *Von Amsterdam nach Ymuiden*, which appeared in the *Wiener Medizinische Presse*.[29] The piece was slight, but its appearance in a professional journal under paternal auspices was itself revealing: even in encouraging his son's writing, Johann channeled it toward medicine. Arthur enrolled at the University of Vienna's medical faculty that autumn, driven more by family expectation than personal conviction. In the diary he had begun keeping that March—the diary that would eventually comprise over sixteen thousand entries spanning more than half a century—he had already begun to articulate the central tension of his young life.[30]

But that resolution lay far ahead. In the autumn of 1871, Arthur Schnitzler had stood at the beginning of eight years of humanistic education, in a school that would expose him to the best that the tradition of *Bildung*—the ideal of self-cultivation through learning—had to offer. He was the son of a physician who had risen from nothing and a mother who had been born to standing, a child of Leopoldstadt and of the First District, of the consulting room and of the theater, of a tradition that was ancient and a freedom that was new. He was entering an institution that would place him among the future architects of Viennese modernism, though neither he nor they could know it yet.

Behind him lay the world his parents had made: secure, purposeful, governed by the belief that hard work and education could overcome any obstacle. Ahead of him lay the world he would eventually make for himself—a world of literature and psychological complexity, of characters caught between desire and duty, of surfaces that concealed depths. The boy who walked through the doors of the Akademisches Gymnasium on that autumn day in 1871 did not yet know that the stable foundation his parents stood upon was already shifting beneath their feet, that the certainties of the liberal age would not survive the century, and that his life's work would be, in large part, a reckoning with their collapse. He knew only what a nine-year-old can know: that school was beginning, that much was expected of him, and that somewhere inside him, alongside the obedient physician's son, another self was stirring—restless, watchful, and drawn to stories.

Chapter Two

The Reluctant Doctor (1879–1886)

"I FEEL IT ALREADY, science will never mean to me what art already does."
—Arthur Schnitzler, diary, 27 October 1879[1]

Arthur Schnitzler (chapter note 26)

In the autumn of 1879, as a reward for passing his Maturitätsprüfung at the Akademisches Gymnasium on the eighth of July, Arthur Schnitzler was taken on a two-week trip to Amsterdam. He was seventeen years old, a graduate of Vienna's most distinguished secondary school, and his father's gift carried, like so many of Johann Schnitzler's gestures, a double meaning. The trip was also a medical conference. Johann was attending in his professional capacity, and he assigned his son a task: Arthur was to write a travel account of the journey. The resulting essay, "From Amsterdam to Ymuiden," appeared under Arthur's name in the *Wiener Medizinische Presse*—the journal Johann had co-founded in 1860 with his father-in-law, Philipp Markbreiter.[2]

It was Arthur Schnitzler's first publication. He was the author; the words were his. But the venue was his father's journal, the occasion was his father's conference, and the subject was his father's profession. The pattern would hold for longer than he could have imagined.

That same autumn, Arthur enrolled in medical school at the University of Vienna—not because he felt called to medicine, but because not enrolling was, in the Schnitzler household, unthinkable. He would later describe the decision, in his autobiography, as one made "more out of habit than inclination."[3] And in the private pages of his diary, on 27 October 1879, he had written the sentence that would serve as the quiet epigraph to the next fourteen years of his life: "I feel it already, science will never mean to me what art already does."[4]

He enrolled anyway. And within six months, in a passage of self-inventory that reveals both the scale of his secret ambition and the compulsiveness that would mark everything he did, he noted in his diary that he had "accordingly completed to the present day 23 dramas and begun writing 13, as far as I can recall."[5] He was eighteen. He had written more plays than most people read in a lifetime, and he was studying to become a doctor.

The University of Vienna's medical faculty was among the most prestigious in the German-speaking world, and the years of Arthur's enrollment coincided with a period of extraordinary distinction. Billroth was revolutionizing surgery; Nothnagel was redefining internal medicine; Meynert was probing the anatomy of the brain.[6] The six-year curriculum was rigorous and empirical, built on direct observation, detailed case notes, and the methodical study of the body in health and disease. It was, in its way, excellent training for a writer—though no one, least of all Arthur, would have described it in those terms at the time.

The double life established itself quickly and completely. By day, he attended lectures in anatomy and physiology, took notes, prepared for examinations. By night, he wrote—plays, sketches, fragments, dialogues, the outpouring of a mind that could not stop composing even as it dutifully memorized the structures of the body and the pathways of the nervous system. The two pursuits existed in parallel, scarcely touching. Medicine was obligation; literature was need. He fulfilled the first and concealed the second, and the strain of the concealment became a defining feature of his young manhood.

Johann Schnitzler, born in 1835, was now in his mid-forties and at the height of his authority. By 1880 he had been named associate professor of laryngology at the University of Vienna; by 1884 he would become medical director of the Polyclinic he had helped to found in 1872.[7] He published prolifically, treated the celebrated actors and singers of the Court Opera, and ran both a thriving private practice and a medical journal.

His career was a monument to the principle that talent, discipline, and the right profession could carry a carpenter's son to the summit of Viennese respectability. Johann's father had been Joseph Zimmermann—the name itself means "carpenter"—a man who had later taken the name Schnitzler.[8] That Arthur might look at this monument and feel something other than admiration—that he might feel, alongside the admiration, a kind of suffocation—was not a possibility Johann's worldview could easily accommodate.

The tension between them was, in one sense, ancient and unoriginal: a son who wants something different from what his father has planned. But it was complicated, in the Schnitzler household, by the fact that Johann himself had once harbored literary ambitions before turning to medicine.[9] Now the physician's son harbored them again, and the father's response was shaped by everything he had sacrificed and everything he had gained. To Johann, Arthur's literary yearnings may have looked like an extravagance that only privilege could afford—the dream of a boy who had never known poverty, who could be impractical because his father had been practical enough for both of them. Whether Johann also recognized in his son's ambition the ghost of his own abandoned dreams, and whether that recognition brought grief or anger or a complicated mixture of both, the available evidence does not allow us to say with certainty.[10]

On November 25, 1881, two years into his medical studies, Arthur met a young woman he later called Gusti in his diary. She was a singer in a theater chorus, living in the suburbs, and what struck him about her was not merely attraction but a kind of recognition.[11] He would later identify this encounter as his first meeting with a figure who already existed, half-formed, in his imagination—the type of the "sweet young girl," the *süßes Mädel*.

The *süßes Mädel* was a social reality before it became a literary type. She was the working-class girl—the seamstress, the shop girl, the chorus singer—who was sexually accessible to young men of the bourgeoisie in ways that women of their own class were not. The arrangement was understood by everyone and acknowledged by no one. A young doctor or lawyer might spend his evenings with a girl from the Vorstadt, the outer suburbs, in a relationship that was tender and temporary and governed by an unspoken contract: she would give him companionship and pleasure; he would give her presents and, eventually, a farewell. Marriage was out of the question. The class divide that made the affair possible also made it impermanent, and the girl was expected to accept this with good grace, as though the transience were a feature rather than a wound.

It was not until September 1887, however, when Schnitzler began his relationship with Jeanette Heeger—a young woman from the suburbs who did sewing work for luxury shops—that he first wrote the term "süßes Mädel" in his diary.[12] Looking back in his autobiography, he recalled the morning after a night with Heeger as the occasion when he first set down the phrase, "without suspecting," as he put it, "that it was destined to become, in a way, literary."[13] The passage is characteristic in its blend of self-awareness and self-exoneration. He knew, even in retrospect, that he was turning life into material. He would not have said he was turning people into material, though the distinction, for the women involved, may have been less clear.

In October 1882, midway through his medical studies, Schnitzler reported for his year of military service at Garrison Hospital No. 1 in Vienna.[14] The *Einjährig-Freiwilliger*—the one-year volunteer system—was a standard obligation for educated young men, a way of fulfilling military duty while training in one's profession. For a medical student, it meant a year of military medicine: treating soldiers, navigating the rigid hierarchies of the officer caste, and absorbing the culture of honor, dueling, and rank that structured life in the Habsburg army.

Schnitzler passed his officers' examination in October 1883 and, as the biographical record notes, promptly turned his back on the military.[15] He received his commission as a reserve officer in the medical corps and returned to his studies with something more than relief. The experience had given him material he did not yet know how to use. Some seventeen years later, in *Leutnant Gustl*—his groundbreaking interior monologue of a vain, honor-obsessed army officer—he would deploy that material with devastating precision. Published on Christmas Day 1900 in the *Neue Freie Presse*, the novella caused an immediate scandal. In June 1901, a military disciplinary committee formally stripped Schnitzler of his reserve officer's rank, finding that he had damaged the honor and standing of the Austro-Hungarian army.[16] The satire was taken, correctly, as an indictment of the officer class. Schnitzler had spent a year among them, and he had been watching.

At the end of May 1885, at twenty-three, Arthur Schnitzler received his degree as a doctor of general medicine.[17] The event was less a culmination than a checkpoint: a line crossed, a duty discharged, a father's expectations met. He had spent six years in a discipline he respected but did not love, and now the question was what to do with the credentials he had earned. The answer, for the time being, was what Johann Schnitzler expected: clinical training, hospital work, the long apprenticeship that would prepare him for a medical career.

He began as an assistant doctor at the Vienna General Hospital—the massive teaching complex where Freud had trained just a few years earlier—while simultaneously working as an aspirant at the Polyclinic.[18] The hospital provided him with a room. He would give it up in 1888, not because he had found better accommodation but because he wanted privacy—space for the parts of his life that could not be conducted under institutional observation.

The triple existence had become unsustainable: trainee doctor by day, his father's deputy in private practice by evening, and playwright by night. Something had to give, and what gave, characteristically, was not any of his obligations but the walls between them. He would find ways to write in the interstices, to carry on affairs in the hours between shifts, to be doctor and writer and lover in rapid succession. It was exhausting, and it would continue for years.

CHAPTER THREE

Impertinent Sensuality (1886–1890)

IN APRIL 1886, LESS than a year after graduating, Schnitzler developed symptoms that suggested tuberculosis. He was sent to Merano, the fashionable spa town in South Tyrol, for the standard cure: mountain air, rest, the recuperative idleness of the invalid. Whether the diagnosis was correct remains uncertain; what is certain is that the trip changed his life. In Merano he met Olga Waissnix.[1]

She was his exact contemporary—born, like him, in 1862—and she was nothing like the working-class girls who had occupied his erotic life. Olga Waissnix, born Schneider, had married Karl Waissnix in 1881 and was now the hostess of the Hotel Thalhof in Reichenau an der Rax, a fashionable establishment near Vienna frequented by members of the upper classes.[2] She was beautiful, worldly, educated, and profoundly unfulfilled by her provincial life. She had three sons and a husband who could not give her the intellectual companionship she craved. Into this void stepped Arthur Schnitzler, twenty-three years old, frightened of tuberculosis, and desperate for someone who would take seriously the part of him that his father could not see.

They spent five days together in Merano. The intensity of the connection astonished him; he later described it as an experience whose depth he had not thought himself capable of reaching. Olga, writing to him afterward, compared Merano to the legendary sunken city of Vineta, rising before her whenever she thought of it.[3] The language was romantic, but the relationship would never become a physical affair. She was married, a mother, a woman whose position in the social order of the Austrian provinces could not survive a scandal. They would maintain their connection for eleven years, through a correspondence of remarkable intelligence and emotional depth, meeting regularly at the Thalhof and in Vienna, building a friendship that was also a love that was also something more difficult to name.

What Olga gave Arthur was something no one else in his life could offer: she took his literary ambitions seriously. She read his work with the attention of a sophisticated critic, discussed his ideas with genuine intellectual engagement, and believed—unequivocally, without the hedging or condescension he encountered elsewhere—that he was a writer. Not a doctor who happened to write, not a dilettante amusing himself between hospital shifts, but a writer. "Never do I speak with a woman as intelligently as with her," he told his diary,[4] and the remark, though it says something unflattering about his estimation of the other women in his life, captures the singularity of the bond. Hans Weigel, in his foreword to the published correspondence, would go so far as to claim that without Olga, Schnitzler might never have become a writer—or at least not the writer he became.[5] It is a large claim, but the evidence supports it. She was the first person to see him whole, and to insist that the half he was hiding was the half that mattered.

The relationship's unconsummated quality was part of its power. Olga existed beyond the erotic economy that governed Schnitzler's dealings with other women—the *süße Mädel* with their temporary pleasures, the fleeting affairs that satisfied the body but left the mind untouched. With Olga, everything was reversed. The mind was engaged; the body was held in abeyance. She became a confidante to whom he told everything—his literary plans, his daily struggles, his other women—and she responded with intelligence, sympathy, and judgment. That she remained forever just out of reach, married and unattainable, only deepened the hold she had on his imagination. She would die in 1897, at thirty-five, and for decades afterward she was largely lost to history, until the publication of their correspondence in 1970 under the title *Liebe, die starb vor der Zeit*—Love That Died Before Its Time.[6]

The same years that produced the Olga Waissnix correspondence also produced the affair with Jeanette Heeger, and the contrast between the two relationships illuminates something essential about Schnitzler's character—or, less charitably, about the compartments into which he divided his emotional life. Olga was mind; Jeanette was body. Olga was the muse; Jeanette was the material. The arrangement was not unusual for a bourgeois man of his era, but Schnitzler's self-consciousness about it—his compulsive need to observe, record, and analyze his own behavior—made it something more than a conventional double standard.

He met Jeanette in September 1887. She was a *Kunststickerin*—an art embroiderer—living with four siblings in a modest apartment, in weak health, unable to work steadily at the salon and reduced to taking piecework at home. According to his diary, their meeting was casual—he and a companion noticed her at the Pferderennbahn, the horse racing track, and struck up an acquaintance.[7] She accompanied them back to his hospital room, and promised to return. She did. The visits became regular—two or three times a week, dinner first, then the night—and for a time something genuine seems to have existed between them. Schnitzler fell in love, which was, by his own account, unusual for him.

By 1888, when he gave up his hospital room, he had rented separate quarters for Jeanette. She waited there for him, embroidering, while he worked at the clinic or the hospital. He came to her afterward. The arrangement had an almost domestic quality, tender and habitual, except that it rested on a foundation both parties understood: marriage between a bourgeois doctor and a working-class embroiderer was unthinkable. The tenderness was real, but it existed within a structure of class and power that predetermined its outcome. He could leave; she could not. He was collecting experience; she was living her life.

What distinguished Schnitzler's conduct from that of other men in similar arrangements was the clinical precision with which he documented it. Over a period of several years, he kept meticulous records not merely of his affairs but of their most intimate dimensions, tallying orgasms with the methodical thoroughness of a bookkeeper—initials, monthly totals, running sums.[8] The impulse was not prurient, or not only prurient. It was the expression of a mind trained in clinical observation that could not stop observing, even—especially—in the bedroom. He was studying himself, as a doctor studies a patient, and the data he collected would feed a body of literary work that made its reputation by exposing exactly this kind of intimate truth.

The affair with Heeger deteriorated after roughly two years, as such affairs did.[9] His love cooled; hers did not. She clung; he pulled away. He was unfaithful continuously, and he was jealous of her fidelity—the classic asymmetry of the man who demands loyalty he will not give. When he finally tried to end the relationship, she threatened suicide. The separation, by his own account, involved months of mutual suffering.

The frankness of his diary was genuine, but it is worth pausing to note what it accomplished. By confessing his cruelty in writing, Schnitzler performed a kind of absolution that cost him nothing. The self-reproach was real, but it changed no behavior. The *süße Mädel* who would populate his plays—Christine in *Liebelei*, the unnamed girls of *Anatol* and

Reigen—would carry a sympathetic charge that their real-life models did not always receive. The literary imagination that could conjure their inner lives with such tenderness was housed in a man who, in life, was capable of treating them with the detached curiosity of a researcher and the carelessness of a class to which consequences did not fully apply.

He knew this about himself. In his diary, in a passage from 1890 that reveals the writer's mind at work even in the act of self-examination, he asked: "I have a strange need to capture myself psychologically. Why? To bring a bit of order to my tortured nervous system? Out of self-love? Out of literary interest?"[10] The question was characteristically honest and characteristically unanswered. All three motives were probably at work, and the inability to disentangle them was itself the subject.

In 1887, Schnitzler joined the editorial team of his father's medical journal, the *Internationale Klinische Rundschau*.[11] Johann had by this point made his position clear: Arthur's literary efforts, such as they were, must not jeopardize his medical credentials. Publishing fiction under his own name, Johann warned, could endanger the young physician's professional standing. The message was unmistakable. Arthur could write if he must, but medicine came first, and medicine's dignity must not be compromised by association with the frivolity of literature.

Arthur complied—and subverted the compliance in the same gesture. As editor of the *Rundschau*, he was expected to review medical literature, and he did, but he steered his attention toward the work that interested him most: the writings of the forerunners of psychoanalysis. He engaged with the work of the French hypnotists—Jean-Martin Charcot's studies of hysteria, Hippolyte Bernheim's investigations of suggestion and the unconscious.[12] The subject matter was, technically, medicine. It was also the territory where medicine shaded into psychology, where the observable body gave way to the hidden workings of the mind, and where the questions Schnitzler cared about—What do people conceal? What drives them beneath the surface of their social performances?—were being asked in the language of science.

Schnitzler and Freud were near-contemporaries, products of the same medical Vienna, both Jewish doctors drawn to the mysteries of the psyche. They never became close. Schnitzler seems to have kept a certain distance, as though proximity to Freud might collapse a distinction he needed to maintain: Freud was the scientist of the unconscious; Schnitzler was its artist. But the parallels were striking enough that Freud himself would eventually acknowledge them. In a letter of May 14, 1922, written on the eve of Schnitzler's sixtieth birthday, Freud confessed that he had long avoided meeting Schnitzler out of a kind of "fear of the double"—*Doppelgängerscheu*—because in Schnitzler's literary creations he kept finding the same assumptions, interests, and conclusions he knew as his own.[13]

The path, in Schnitzler's case, ran through his father's consulting room. In the late 1880s, working in Johann's laryngology department at the Polyclinic, Arthur began treating patients whose voice disorders had no organic cause—functional aphonia, as it was called, the loss of speech in the absence of any physical damage to the throat. These were psychosomatic conditions, ailments of the mind expressed through the body, and they called for a kind of medicine that was still more art than science. Schnitzler treated them with hypnosis and suggestion, and in 1889 he published the results: "Über funktionelle Aphonie und deren Behandlung durch Hypnose und Suggestion."[14] It was serious medical work, grounded in clinical observation, and it stood at the exact boundary between the worlds of father and son—Johann's laryngology and Arthur's psychology, the visible throat and the invisible mind.

By 1888, Arthur Schnitzler was twenty-six years old and formally employed as an assistant at the Allgemeine Poliklinik—his father's institution, his father's department, his father's direct supervision. The arrangement was professionally defensible and personally devastating. He should have been establishing an independent practice, building a reputation of his own, separating from the gravitational pull of a father whose success made independence feel like ingratitude. Instead, he was assisting, deputizing, orbiting. He lived at home. He worked in his father's clinic. He edited his father's journal. He was, at twenty-six, twenty-seven, twenty-eight, still recognizable as Johann Schnitzler's eldest son.

The frustration of these years is visible everywhere in the diaries, though it rarely surfaces as direct rebellion. In May 1886 he had already written: "It was arrant foolishness of mine to become a doctor, and sadly foolishness that cannot be made good."[15] Schnitzler was not a rebel by temperament. He was an evader, a compartmentalizer, a man who managed conflict by maintaining parallel lives rather than forcing a confrontation. He did not tell his father he wanted to abandon medicine. He did not refuse to work at the Polyclinic. He simply continued to write, in the evenings and the early mornings and the stolen hours between shifts, building a body of work that existed in a kind of quarantine from his official life. The plays accumulated. The *Anatol* cycle—a sequence of one-act dialogues about a Viennese philanderer and his various liaisons—took shape between 1888 and 1891. It was brilliant, witty, psychologically acute, and unpublished. Arthur was approaching thirty with a medical career he did not want and a literary career that did not yet exist.

CHAPTER FOUR

Young Vienna (1890–1893)

THE VIENNA INTO WHICH Schnitzler matured was a city of dazzling contradictions. On the surface, it was the glittering capital of an ancient empire, adorned with the monumental architecture of the Ringstrasse and animated by the waltzes of Johann Strauss. Beneath that surface, however, profound anxieties churned. The liberal bourgeois culture that had dominated Viennese public life since the constitutional reforms of the 1860s was in retreat. The rise of mass politics—Karl Lueger's anti-Semitic Christian Social movement, Georg von Schönerer's Pan-German nationalism, and the gathering force of Czech, Hungarian, and South Slavic nationalisms within the empire—threatened the cosmopolitan, rationalist ideals on which the educated middle class had built its identity.[1]

He came of age during the final, febrile decades of the Habsburg Empire, and his literary career tracked almost precisely with the era historians would later call *Fin-de-Siècle* Vienna.

Around 1890, he found his tribe. Café Griensteidl stood at the Michaelerplatz, in the Palais Dietrichstein—a smoke-filled room where the young writers who would define Viennese modernism gathered to talk, argue, and exchange manuscripts.[2] The group called itself, or was called, *Jung-Wien*—Young Vienna. If *fin-de-siècle* Vienna was the ocean, Young

Vienna was the particular current in which Schnitzler swam as a young writer.

The group coalesced around the critic and cultural impresario Hermann Bahr, who had returned from travels through Berlin and Paris afire with new literary ideas—French Symbolism, the psychological novels of Paul Bourget, the philosophy of Ernst Mach.[3] Bahr became the group's chief theorist and polemicist. In 1891 he published *Die Überwindung des Naturalismus*—"Overcoming Naturalism"—a manifesto arguing that German-language literature needed to move beyond the social realism associated with writers like Gerhart Hauptmann and Emile Zola. What Bahr championed instead was a literature of subjective experience: impressionism in prose, the registration of fleeting moods and sensations, an attention to the inner life that anticipated and paralleled the work Freud was doing in the same city.

The circle included some of the most gifted writers of the generation. Richard Beer-Hofmann, a lyric poet of exquisite refinement who had studied law at the University of Vienna, joined the group in 1890 and would become one of Schnitzler's closest lifelong friends.[4] Felix Salten—later, improbably, the author of *Bambi*—was the group's versatile critic. Peter Altenberg, the bohemian prose poet who would later become so identified with Viennese coffeehouse culture that his official address was said to be Café Central, embodied the coffeehouse aesthetic in its purest form.[5]

And there was Hugo von Hofmannsthal, still a gymnasium student when he was introduced to the group in late 1890, already publishing verse of astonishing maturity under the pseudonym "Loris."[6] His talent was so evident and so precocious that even the older writers treated him with something approaching reverence. Hofmannsthal would become Austria's greatest lyric poet and, later, the librettist for Richard Strauss. He and Schnitzler would maintain a friendship and a literary dialogue that lasted decades. By October 1891, Schnitzler could note with evident pride in his diary: "Loris, Salten, Beer-Hofmann and I are already being viewed as a clique."[7]

The café was not, strictly speaking, a workspace—little sustained writing got done amid the conversation and the cigarette smoke. Its function was different and, for Schnitzler, more urgent. It offered him an identity. At the Polyclinic he was Dr. Schnitzler, his father's assistant, a competent and joyless practitioner of a profession he had never chosen. At Griensteidl, he was Schnitzler the playwright, a man whose work was read and discussed by his intellectual peers, whose opinions on literature and theater carried weight, and who belonged to a community that valued exactly the qualities his medical career had no use for. The café gave him an audience, connections to publishers and theaters, and—perhaps most important—the conviction that he was not a dilettante. He was part of a movement. In February 1891, he noted the shift in his diary with characteristic brevity: "Literary recognition is beginning."[8]

Yet Schnitzler's relationship with the Griensteidl legend was more complicated than it appeared. Years later, in a joint interview from 1903 preserved in the Müller collection, both Bahr and Schnitzler pushed back sharply against the mythology that had accrued around the café. When the interviewer raised the subject of the "legendary coffeehouse literature," Bahr smiled and Schnitzler intervened.[9] Bahr declared that he had been in the Griensteidl with Schnitzler and Hofmannsthal together only twice in his life. Schnitzler, for his part, was visibly irritated that magazines still referred to him as a "coffeehouse poet." The interviewer concluded drily that the great slogans supposedly issued by Bahr at the Griensteidl were "invention and foolishness."

The debunking was characteristic of Schnitzler. He was never entirely comfortable with group identities, even ones that served him. He valued the friendships—Beer-Hofmann and Hofmannsthal would remain central to his life—but he kept the movement at arm's length. His diary records a telling remark: "I can't stand the Griensteidl; the atmosphere..."[10]

And around 1894–95, in a satirical novella called *Später Ruhm* ("Late Fame"), he turned the Jung-Wien circle itself into literary material, gently mocking the coffeehouse literati from the inside. The novella remained unpublished in his lifetime; it was finally brought out from the archive in 2014.[11]

Not everyone within the group's orbit was as self-aware. Karl Kraus, the young satirist who hovered at the circle's edges before turning against it with characteristic ferocity, would later dismiss the Griensteidl writers as indolent poseurs who mistook conversation for creation. When the café was demolished in January 1897, Kraus published his essay *Die demolirte Literatur*—"The Demolished Literature"—a savage farewell that used the building's destruction as a metaphor for the literary movement's hollowness.[12] According to Schnitzler's diary, on the group's last evening at the café, Felix Salten—angry over a negative review Kraus had given him—physically attacked the young journalist.[13] The members continued to meet at the nearby Café Central, but the Griensteidl era was over.

There was bite in Kraus's criticism. The line between a literary movement and a coffeehouse clique could be thin, and some of the Young Vienna writers produced more talk than work. But the charge could not stick to Schnitzler. He had the manuscripts to prove it—a drawer full of plays, years of accumulated effort, a body of work that needed only an opening to reach the public.

A Danish journalist visiting Vienna described Schnitzler as "surely at present the most prominent man of young Austria, in the narrower sense of young Vienna," a writer who had learned from both the French and the Scandinavians but was above all a *Vollblut-Wiener*—a full-blooded Viennese. "Light-hearted and sentimental, an elegant man of the world and a rebellious mocker."[14] The article noted that Schnitzler had recently traveled to Copenhagen with Beer-Hofmann and the journalist Paul Goldmann, three friends bound by what the interviewer called "a blind, almost schoolboy-like devotion to one another."

Schnitzler had told his diary, in a passage from an interview he gave that same year, something that reveals how conscious he was of his literary aesthetic. The art of suggestion, he explained, was "not only a consequence of our finer nerves, but also a reaction against naturalism."[15] The remark is revealing. It places Schnitzler exactly where he belonged: not as a naturalist documenting social conditions, but as a psychological impressionist registering the inner tremors that the naturalists missed. The audience, he argued, must be allowed to complete the picture in their imaginations. The era of broad gestures and theatrical shouting was over.

The opening Schnitzler needed was coming. Hermann Bahr, who used his position as theater critic to champion the group's work, would help see to that. But the opening would arrive, with the particular cruelty of timing that seemed to govern Schnitzler's life, only after his father was no longer alive to see it.

CHAPTER FIVE

Father's Death (1893)

J OHANN S CHNITZLER DIED ON the second of May, 1893.[1] He was fifty-eight years old. At the end of April, he had developed erysipelas—an acute bacterial infection—in his face, which progressed rapidly to blood poisoning. Arthur was thirty.

The death released what the life had constrained. In August, three months after his father's burial, Arthur left the Polyclinic.[2] He continued to see a limited number of private patients, but the pretense of a full medical career was over. He moved in with his mother at her Frankgasse address and devoted himself to writing with the single-mindedness he had been denied for fourteen years. *Anatol*, the cycle of one-act plays he had been composing since 1888, had already appeared in book form the previous autumn—published in late 1892, though pre-dated to 1893 on the title page—with a verse prologue by Hugo von Hofmannsthal, writing under his pseudonym "Loris."[3] The literary career that had existed only in drawers and diaries and the conversations at Griensteidl was about to become public. Everything Arthur had wanted was, at last, within reach.

And yet the timing was brutal. Johann had died just before his son's breakthrough—before the theater world recognized what the Griensteidl circle had known for years, before the name Schnitzler meant anything in literature.

The father who had wanted to be a writer and had chosen medicine instead never saw his son succeed as the writer the father had never become.[4] The irony was almost too neat, almost too perfectly shaped for the kind of play Arthur himself might have written: the stern patriarch who suppresses his own literary ambitions, imposes his chosen path on his son, and dies at the threshold of the son's liberation, taking to his grave whatever he might have felt—pride, envy, vindication, regret—had he lived to see what Arthur would accomplish.

The year 1893 was one of upheaval on every front. In March, before Johann's death, Schnitzler's relationship with Marie "Mizi" Glümer had come to a crisis. Her confession of infidelity left him furious—even though he had been unfaithful to her on multiple occasions—and the emotional turmoil fed directly into his first major work for the stage, *Das Märchen* ("The Fairy Tale").[5] That play premiered in early December 1893 at the Deutsches Volkstheater in Vienna, with Adele Sandrock—a formidable actress who would shortly become his lover—in the lead role of Fanny Theren. The production was curtailed after only two performances, the subject matter having provoked a theater scandal. But the trajectory was set. In the space of a single year, Schnitzler had lost his father, abandoned his medical career, and seen his first play staged and shouted down. He was now a working dramatist, however controversial.

The guilt would linger. Arthur Schnitzler had spent his twenties in a state of concealed mutiny, writing in secret, pursuing women his father would not have approved of, building a literary identity behind the façade of the dutiful physician. He had never confronted Johann directly, never forced the crisis that might have led to either a rupture or a reconciliation. Instead he had waited—waited for time to resolve what courage could not, waited for the tyranny of expectation to lift of its own accord. And it had lifted, in the only way it could: not through understanding, but through death.

The relationship between father and son had always been entangled with the diary. In 1879, when Arthur was seventeen, Johann had secretly read his son's journal and discovered the sexual episodes recorded there; he responded with a stern lecture on venereal disease.[6] The betrayal of trust left its mark. Arthur continued to keep the diary—he would maintain it for over fifty years, until two days before his death—but the early notebooks survived only in fragments. The habit of guarded self-disclosure, of saying everything while concealing the essential, became not just a personal instinct but a literary method. Schnitzler's characters are forever failing to say what they mean, deferring the crucial conversation, substituting wit for honesty. He had learned how that worked at home.

Schnitzler was free now, free to be the writer he had always been, but the freedom carried a weight that no amount of success could entirely discharge. He would spend the rest of his life writing about fathers and sons, about duty and desire, about the things that go unsaid between people who love each other imperfectly. The subject was inexhaustible because it was, in the deepest sense, his own.

And yet the reluctant doctor never entirely disappeared. Years later, in an interview in Copenhagen, Schnitzler reflected on the inescapability of his medical inheritance. He had been young, he said—just past thirty—when he first entered public life as a writer. "Before that I was a doctor," he told his interviewer, "and in a certain sense I still am, as my father and my grandfather were, and as my brother and my brother-in-law and several of my relatives are. We constitute an entire family of physicians, and I have never entirely escaped medicine."[7] When a guest at the same gathering asked why he wrote his books, he smiled. It was very difficult to answer, he said. He did not consciously write tendentious books that pursued a specific purpose. He wrote in order to depict people and to shape characters.

In 1922, when Schnitzler turned sixty, the *Wiener Medizinische Wochenschrift* published a tribute that captured this duality with precision.[8] The connection between Schnitzler's medical training and his literary work, the journal argued, was not a biographical coincidence but something essential. The physician's way of seeing—the clinical gaze turned upon human nature—was woven into the fabric of his writing. Even if one did not know that the author was a doctor, the tribute suggested, one might conclude from the works alone that he could have been one, because his entire manner of apprehending the human being recalled the physician's standpoint. The affinity between medicine and art was not incidental: the physician's work was itself a kind of art, and those who practiced it naturally stood close to the other arts as well.

In 1912, nearly twenty years after Johann's death, Arthur would publish *Professor Bernhardi*—a play about a Jewish doctor navigating the politics of a Viennese medical institution modeled, unmistakably, on the Polyclinic.[9] It was a work of admiration as much as critique, a son's attempt to understand the world his father had built and the compromises it required. The play was censored in Vienna—the authorities refused to permit its performance—and premiered instead at the Kleines Theater in Berlin. It was Schnitzler's only major dramatic work without a sexual theme, and perhaps his most directly autobiographical: a portrait of a principled physician surrounded by colleagues whose principles bend to political expedience. In 1918, rereading the play, Schnitzler confided to his diary: there were works of his that he preferred, but there was none in which he liked himself better than in *Bernhardi*.[10]

By then Arthur Schnitzler was one of the most celebrated dramatists in the German language, the author of works that had scandalized and thrilled Vienna, the man who had done what Johann had dreamed of and abandoned. But the clinical eye, the habit of precise observation, the instinct to diagnose what lay beneath the surface—these were his father's gifts, absorbed in the years of unwilling apprenticeship, and they were what made him the writer he became. Johann Schnitzler had tried to make his son a physician. He had succeeded, in ways neither of them intended, in making him an artist.

Part II: Breakthrough (1893–1902)

"AT 4 THE BOY comes into the world. — [...] At 5 began the novel."
—Arthur Schnitzler

CHAPTER SIX

Liberation (1893–1894)

ANATOL, DAS MÄRCHEN

THE YEAR 1893 BROKE Arthur Schnitzler's life in two.

On the second of May, his father died. By autumn, *Anatol* was in the world—published the previous year but predated 1893, and now gathering the attention that would transform its author from a doctor who wrote plays into a playwright who had once been a doctor.[1] The symmetry was too neat, too cruel, too much like something Schnitzler himself might have devised for the stage: the father who had forbidden literature dying at the precise moment the son's literature arrived. Johann Schnitzler was buried in the Zentralfriedhof. Arthur Schnitzler, thirty years old, walked out of the Polyclinic and into a life he had been rehearsing in secret for more than a decade.

He never officially relinquished his medical practice—he would stress this point in later biographical sketches, as though the credential still mattered, as though the physician's authority lent weight to the writer's observations. But the practice became vestigial, a few patients seen out of habit or obligation, while writing consumed everything else.

The decision to turn professional was made, he later said, in 1893 and 1894, and the factors were clear enough: his father's death had removed the primary obstacle; his disillusionment with medical colleagues had deepened; and he had come to feel that laryngology, his father's specialty, had been the wrong choice all along. What remained was the pen, and the question of whether the pen could sustain a life.

He was also, by this time, distancing himself from the café society that had nurtured him. "Café Griensteidl no longer exists for me," he had written to Richard Beer-Hofmann the previous year. "I want to try to become a virtuoso of solitude."[2] It was a characteristically self-dramatizing declaration, but it contained a genuine intention. Schnitzler would never again attach himself to a literary circle.

The Young Vienna group had given him an audience and an identity; now he wanted independence. The plays he was writing—psychological, intimate, built on the close observation of human self-deception—were the work of a solitary mind, not a committee. He would need friends, publishers, actresses. He would not need a movement.

Anatol was a cycle of seven one-act plays about a wealthy Viennese bachelor and his romantic entanglements, each scene a miniature drama of seduction, self-deception, and the failure of intimacy. Anatol—charming, melancholy, incapable of honesty with women or with himself—was accompanied by his friend Max, a cooler intelligence who served as confidant and skeptical chorus. The structure was loose, episodic, more mosaic than narrative, and its power lay not in plot but in the precision with which Schnitzler rendered the psychology of a man who could not stop performing even in his most private moments.

But this description barely suggests the formal innovation Schnitzler achieved. The dialogue cycle was a hybrid form that belonged to no established genre: not a conventional play, not a novel, not a sequence of short stories. Each episode was self-contained, complete in its own dramatic logic, yet connected by a recurring protagonist and an accumulating psychological portrait. The paradox was deliberate: the more episodes one witnessed, the less one felt one truly knew Anatol. Each scene revealed a new facet—his romanticism, his cowardice, his vanity, his capacity for genuine tenderness—only to have that facet undercut or complicated by the next.

Schnitzler was making the form perform the content. Life, particularly erotic life, did not unfold in the shapely arcs of conventional plotting; it consisted of moments, encounters, episodes whose significance could not be assessed until they were over—and even then, assessments remained unreliable. The gaps between episodes—the temporal ellipses, the unstated transitions from one woman to the next—were as expressive as anything spoken. They enacted Anatol's fundamental inability to grow or change.

The individual scenes traced a pattern of escalating humiliation disguised as romantic experience.

In "The Question to Fate," Anatol discovered he could hypnotize his lover Cora into speaking only the truth, but could not bring himself to ask whether she was faithful. The terror was not of betrayal but of knowledge itself—of encountering Cora as an autonomous subject with her own desires rather than as a screen for his projections. Better the beautiful uncertainty of not-knowing than the devastating clarity of truth.

In "Christmas Shopping," he encountered a woman from his own aristocratic circle while buying gifts for his current "sweet girl" mistress, and the collision of Vienna's "big world" and "small world" in a single scene exposed the strict social segregation on which his romantic life depended.

In "Episode," he treasured mementos from a two-hour affair that the woman, Bianca, could not even remember—what had been for Anatol a defining emotional experience had been, for her, literally nothing. The asymmetry was devastating: his romantic self was built on foundations that existed only in his imagination.

Most cutting was "Keepsakes," where on his wedding day to Emilie he discovered she had kept tokens from her own erotic past—a ruby and a black diamond from lovers she could barely recall. His response was to call her a whore. The hypocrisy was spectacular: surrounded by his own sentimental hoards, he had never considered that the women he loved might have histories, memories, attachments of their own.

In "Farewell Supper," his elaborate theatrical scenario of ending an affair with the dancer Annie collapsed when she announced she was leaving him to marry another man.

In "Agony," Anatol and Max discuss his fading love for Else, his married lover. He admits the relationship is agonizing but clings to fleeting moments of passion. Max advises him to end it or leave town. He resists, fearing the loss of emotional depth. Else arrives late, and their brief reunion turns bitter. He accuses her of coquetry and claims their affair was inevitable but meaningless. Else pleads for forgiveness, but Anatol declares it over. She leaves heartbroken as he remains motionless by the window.

In "Wedding Morning," he was in bed with a woman picked up the previous night at a masquerade—on the morning of his wedding. The cycle's movement was not toward growth or self-knowledge but toward an ever-more-refined demonstration of Anatol's incapacity for either.

The figure of Max deserved attention as more than a structural device. His consistent presence lent the cycle a frame-like stability, orienting the audience amid the shifting cast of women, but he was a genuine character whose detachment was itself a philosophical position—perhaps the only tenable one in a world of chronic disenchantment. His sardonic wit did not exempt him from the melancholia that permeated the cycle; it was his adaptation to it. The pairing of romantic sufferer and ironic observer constituted one of the work's subtler achievements.

The cycle was also socially diagnostic. The women divided, broadly, into two types corresponding to Schnitzler's own later formulation: women of the "big world"—the aristocracy and upper bourgeoisie—and women of the "small world," the suburban lower-middle-class, the working girls, the dancers. The "sweet girl" archetype belonged to the second category.

Years later, in his autobiography, Schnitzler would define the type with characteristic ambivalence—a young woman who was somehow both worldly and innocent, sexually experienced yet morally uncompromised, not quite respectable as a bourgeois daughter but utterly devoted as a lover.[3] The definition performed exactly the split consciousness it described: the woman was praised for a paradoxical combination of sexual availability and emotional selflessness that conveniently relieved the man of confronting the social conditions that produced such women, or his own role in those conditions. The sweet girl was idealized precisely because she seemed to offer warmth and devotion without the complications aristocratic women might deploy. She was a projection of male desire for a femininity both sexually available and emotionally unthreatening.

Contemporaries recognized the author in his creation; Schnitzler appeared to many as the living embodiment of Anatol, a resemblance he did little to discourage and much to deserve. This identification was both commercially useful and artistically limiting—it helped establish what one critic later called the "standard image of Schnitzler as decadent aesthete" that would shadow him for decades. Yet the identification was not entirely wrong. The work did celebrate a certain aestheticized surface, a certain melancholic detachment, a certain refusal of moral earnestness. But it did so critically, or at least with enough ironic distance that a careful reader could detect the critique beneath the glitter. Schnitzler was not endorsing Anatol; he was dissecting him.

The book's success owed something to its content and something to its timing, but a great deal to the verse prologue contributed by Hugo von Hofmannsthal, writing under his pseudonym "Loris." Hofmannsthal was still a teenager—a prodigy whose lyric gifts had astonished literary Vienna—and his imprimatur carried a force that Schnitzler's name alone could not yet command.

The prologue situated *Anatol* within the modernist ethos of Young Vienna—the circle that included Hofmannsthal, Hermann Bahr, Peter Altenberg, and Felix Salten—lending it the authority of a generational statement. The group represented the Austrian wing of European literary modernism, sharing its preoccupations: psychological interiority, the critique of bourgeois conventions, the aestheticization of everyday life, and fascination with the erotic as a domain of both liberation and entrapment. *Anatol's* emphasis on psychological introspection over external action, its detached melancholic humor, its precise evocation of social atmosphere placed it among the founding documents of Austrian literary modernism.

Sigmund Freud, reading Schnitzler's work, would later confess that Schnitzler had arrived through intuition at insights Freud himself had reached only through laborious research on other people—a recognition of kinship that pleased the author more, one suspects, than any purely literary compliment could have done.[4] It confirmed what he had always believed: that his work was not mere entertainment but a form of inquiry, a way of knowing what science could not reach. What Freud recognized was not merely Anatol's cowardice but a more general epistemological condition: the ego's vested interest in maintaining its own illusions. To know would be to lose the romantic projection that made the relationship bearable. Ignorance was not merely tolerated but actively cultivated, defended, preferred. This was narcissism in the properly psychoanalytic sense: the beloved encountered not as a separate person but as a screen for the lover's own fantasies, needs, self-images.

The full cycle would not be staged until December 3, 1910—eighteen years after publication—when simultaneous productions opened at the Lessing Theater in Berlin and at the Volkstheater in Vienna.[5] The delay was partly because its frank treatment of sexuality and psychological candor made censors uneasy. By the time it reached the stage, Freud had transformed the intellectual landscape of Vienna, and *Anatol* read, retroactively, like a dramatic illustration of concepts Freud was developing in his consulting rooms. But *Anatol's* impact on Schnitzler's career was immediate. Individual scenes had appeared in periodicals since 1890, building an audience among readers who recognized in Schnitzler's Viennese philanderer something more than a comic type: a diagnosis.

The international reception testified to the work's significance. English-language adaptations helped establish Schnitzler's reputation beyond the German-speaking world.[6] A 1912 Broadway production, titled "The Affairs of Anatol," introduced American audiences to Viennese literary culture. That these adaptations were possible at all spoke to the universality of the psychological types Schnitzler created: the narcissistic romantic male, the autonomous woman whose feelings are persistently misread, the ironic observer who sees clearly but cannot act.

The book made Schnitzler's name. It established the template from which much of his later work would derive: the one-act form, the psychological comedy of manners, the alternation of social surface and erotic subtext, the "sweet girl" archetype. The epistemological anxiety about knowing other people, dramatized in the hypnosis scene, would recur throughout his career in more complex forms: in the married couple's inability to read each other in *Liebelei*, in the radical anonymity of sexual encounter in *Reigen*, in the late *Traumnovelle*, where a husband's erotic fantasies about his wife's inner life lead him through a dreamlike nocturnal odyssey. The theme of the male ego's construction and defense of romantic illusion threaded through the entire oeuvre. *Anatol* was not a departure but its first, confident statement.

Yet *Anatol* endured not merely as a historical document of fin-de-siècle Vienna but as a study in self-deception that transcended its moment. The title figure achieved the status of genuine archetype: charming, shallow, self-aware enough to know he is shallow but not strong enough to be otherwise. He was a precise articulation of a perennial tendency—the tendency to prefer the beautiful image of another person to the actual person, to love in the imperfect indicative rather than the challenging present tense. In anatomizing this tendency with such elegance and psychological precision, Schnitzler created a figure at once historically specific and universally recognizable, charming and deeply troubling, comic and quietly tragic.

The book made Schnitzler's name. It did not yet make him a living.

Into the exhilaration of these months stepped Adele Sandrock, and the relationship that followed was, like everything Sandrock touched, operatic in scale and exhausting in execution.[7] She was the daughter of a Prussian officer and a Dutch stage actress, born in Rotterdam in 1863, already famous at thirty for her work in tragic and modern roles on the Viennese stage. Schnitzler had first seen her perform and recorded his impressions with characteristic ambivalence: the play was "pathetic," the actress was "horrible"—and yet, he admitted in the same breath, she had made him weep bitterly during the second act. "I hate this woman," he wrote in November 1892, in a sentence that anyone familiar with the grammar of romantic obsession could have translated without difficulty.[8]

The contradiction was telling. Schnitzler's response to Sandrock's performance contained in miniature the entire trajectory of their coming relationship: repulsion and attraction, critical detachment and overwhelming emotion, the instinct to flee and the compulsion to surrender. That he could hate and weep simultaneously suggested the presence of precisely the psychological complexity he had been anatomizing in *Anatol*—the inability to experience feeling purely, the constant interior division between observing self and feeling self. He was responding not simply to an actress but to a force that threatened to overwhelm the careful defenses he had constructed against exactly this kind of intensity.

They met personally on October 24, 1893.[9] Felix Salten, the Young Vienna critic and fellow member of the literary circle, had told Schnitzler that Sandrock was "delighted" by his play *Das Märchen* (The Fairy Tale), and the flattery of a famous actress's interest was not something Schnitzler was equipped to resist. The meeting was arranged with the sort of casual inevitability that marked Vienna's small theatrical world, where writers and performers moved in overlapping orbits and personal connections determined artistic fortunes as much as talent did. But there was nothing casual about what followed.

The affair that ensued was, by all accounts, notoriously stormy—two years of volcanic intensity between a woman whose dramatic talent extended seamlessly into her private life and a man whose instinct for psychological observation made him both a compelling lover and an impossible one. Sandrock brought to the relationship everything she brought to the stage: passion without restraint, emotional immediacy without filter, a complete inability to distinguish between performance and authenticity because for her there was no distinction. She lived at the pitch of high drama. Schnitzler, by contrast, could never stop analyzing even his own emotions as they occurred, could never surrender to feeling without simultaneously documenting and dissecting it. The combination was combustible.

She was, in many ways, the anti-Anatol woman—not a "sweet girl" who could be safely idealized and discarded, not an aristocratic figure who maintained the social distance that permitted romantic fantasy, but a professional woman of formidable will and artistic stature who demanded to be encountered as an equal. She was also, paradoxically, the perfect Anatol woman: tempestuous, possessive, capable of theatrical jealousy and dramatic scenes that simultaneously exhausted and fascinated him. The affair became a kind of laboratory for the very dynamics Schnitzler had been exploring in his work. He was living his own diagnosis.

He wrote roles for her. She encouraged his playwriting, recognizing in him not merely a lover but a potential collaborator whose work could serve her artistic ambitions. The relationship operated on multiple registers simultaneously: erotic, professional, psychological. He longed, he confided to his diary in December 1893, for "a female friend" who could enter "the cooler and more sublime realms of your mind, and who would feel at home there"—a remark that captured, with inadvertent precision, both his intellectual snobbery and his genuine need.[10] Sandrock inflamed him; she did not satisfy the part of him that wanted to be understood. She was passion without the intellectual companionship he craved, intensity without the meeting of minds he believed himself to require. The longing he expressed was not for someone different from Sandrock but for Sandrock transformed into someone she could never be—or perhaps for permission to want someone else while still possessed by her.

The impossibility of the relationship had a familiar structure. Schnitzler wanted to be consumed by feeling while maintaining his observational distance. Sandrock wanted total possession, complete emotional availability, the kind of surrender that Schnitzler's psychological makeup made impossible. She accused him, with considerable justice, of always watching himself even in their most intimate moments. He accused her, with equal justice, of demanding a form of devotion he could not give without ceasing to be himself. Both were right. The affair was doomed by a mismatch of temperaments so fundamental that the only mystery was why it lasted as long as it did.

The answer, in part, was that each needed what the other represented. Sandrock needed the validation of a serious literary figure's attention, the prestige of inspiring and collaborating with a writer whose reputation was rising in Vienna's cultural circles. Schnitzler needed the experience of being with a woman who could not be relegated to the categories—"sweet girl," society woman, fleeting episode—that structured his romantic imagination. Sandrock exceeded those categories. She was too substantial, too accomplished, too insistent on her own reality to be reduced to a projection. The relationship forced him to confront the limitations of his own emotional repertoire, even if he could not ultimately transcend them.

Their correspondence, which Schnitzler preserved with his usual archival thoroughness, documented the escalating pattern of rupture and reconciliation that characterized the affair. Sandrock's letters were effusive, demanding, sometimes verging on the hysterical. His were measured, psychologically astute, and—one suspects—maddeningly evasive. She wanted certainty; he offered nuance. She wanted commitment; he offered analysis. The asymmetry was built into the structure of their personalities. When she left Vienna temporarily for theatrical engagements elsewhere, the separation intensified rather than relieved the tension. Distance permitted Schnitzler to idealize what presence made difficult; proximity forced confrontations his temperament was designed to avoid.

The affair also intersected, in complicated ways, with Schnitzler's ongoing involvement with other women. He had not, despite Sandrock's possessive expectations, become monogamous. His diary recorded encounters, flirtations, and liaisons that ran parallel to the central drama with Sandrock. This was not simple infidelity—or rather, it was not only that. It was also a form of psychological self-preservation, a way of maintaining the emotional flexibility that Sandrock's intensity threatened to foreclose. He needed the escape routes. She experienced them, understandably, as betrayals. The pattern repeated: scenes, accusations, temporary ruptures, passionate reconciliations, and then the cycle beginning again.

Das Märchen, the play that had brought them together, became Schnitzler's first full-length failure and, in retrospect, an inadvertent commentary on the relationship that had inspired it.[11] Sandrock had been drawn to its modern, norm-breaking heroine—a woman who defied conventional morality and insisted on her right to love freely. She saw herself in the role, and Schnitzler had written it with her in mind, or at least with her approval as a goal. The play premiered in December 1893 at the Deutsches Volkstheater to poor reviews. Critics found it structurally weak, its psychology unconvincing, its resolution arbitrary. The fairy-tale elements that gave the play its title sat uneasily alongside its aspirations to psychological realism. It was, the reviews suggested, neither one thing nor the other—a problem that might have described the relationship between its author and its leading actress as well.

The failure was necessary, even salutary. *Anatol's* success had come in the shorter forms—the one-act, the sketch, the dialogue—where Schnitzler's gift for psychological observation and verbal precision could operate without the burden of sustained dramatic architecture. *Das Märchen* taught him that his gifts did not automatically transfer to the larger structure of a three-act play. Plot, in the conventional sense, did not come naturally to him. He was a miniaturist, a master of the scene and the moment, not a builder of grand narrative arcs. The full-length play required a kind of artifice—an acceptance of theatrical convention, a willingness to manipulate event and coincidence—that ran counter to his commitment to psychological authenticity.

The lesson would take time to absorb, and he would struggle with the demands of the full-length form for years, but it was real, and it tempered the confidence that *Anatol's* reception might otherwise have inflated beyond usefulness. The failure also carried a professional cost that exceeded the immediate disappointment. A failed premiere at a major theater was not merely an artistic setback but a mark against one's commercial viability. Theater managers remembered failures more vividly than they remembered successes, and Schnitzler would find, in the years to come, that *Das Märchen's* poor reception complicated his ability to place subsequent work.

By late 1894, the relationship with Sandrock had become unsustainable. The pattern of conflict and reconciliation was exhausting both of them, and Schnitzler's emotional resources were increasingly diverted toward managing her expectations rather than toward his work. The affair had become, in the language he might have used in *Anatol*, an episode that had outlived its natural duration but could not be cleanly ended because the participants were too entangled, the feelings too genuine despite their destructiveness. When the final break came in 1895, it was messy, painful, and left scars on both sides. Sandrock's subsequent letters—pleading, accusatory, theatrical even in their grief—testified to the depth of her feeling and to the impossibility of the relationship's continuation.

For Schnitzler, the affair confirmed what he had intuited and dramatized in his work: that he was fundamentally unsuited to the kind of total emotional surrender that great passion demanded, that his observational instinct would always interpose itself between himself and experience, that he was condemned to be Anatol—perpetually divided, perpetually performing, perpetually incapable of the very authenticity he claimed to value. The recognition did not change him. It rarely does. But it deepened his self-knowledge and enriched the psychological complexity of the work that followed.

/ CHAPTER SEVEN

Triumph (1894–1895)

LIEBELEI

THE TRIUMPH, WHEN IT came, arrived through persistence rather than inspiration. Schnitzler had written the first act of what would become *Liebelei* (Affair) in the autumn of 1893, originally setting it in a suburban dance school and showing the first meeting of Fritz and Christine.[1] After criticism from his closest literary friends—Richard Beer-Hofmann, Hugo von Hofmannsthal, Felix Salten, and Gustav Schwarzkopf—he discarded it. He tried to rewrite it three times in the following months, failing each time. On his fifth attempt, beginning on 13 September 1894, he finally sketched out the three-act form that would become his most celebrated play. It was complete by mid-October.

The subject was one he knew intimately: a young man of the bourgeoisie, entangled with both a married woman and a working-class girl—a *süßes Mädel*—whose genuine love he cannot reciprocate because his class and his vanity will not permit it. When the young man dies in a duel, the girl is left not merely bereaved but revealed: she had given everything to a man for whom she was, in the end, a diversion. The word that titled the play—*Liebelei*, a diminutive of *Liebe* (love), suggesting something between flirtation and dalliance—contained the entire ethical architecture of what

Schnitzler was examining. It was a term that described, from the outside and from the privileged position, an institution that functioned smoothly only if both parties understood the terms in the same register. But what happened when one party invested genuine emotional weight in what the other regarded as a stylized social form? The play was constructed around this asymmetry, and its devastating trajectory demonstrated with theatrical precision that the asymmetry was not accidental but structural—determined by class, by gender, by the entire social logic of fin-de-siècle Vienna.

What Schnitzler had achieved was a fundamental revision of the bourgeois tragedy tradition. The genre had been established in German literature by Lessing's *Emilia Galotti* and Schiller's *Kabale und Liebe*—plays in which young women of non-aristocratic origin were destroyed by the sexual appetites and social machinations of powerful men. But those earlier works required villains: aristocratic predators who abused power, fathers who sacrificed daughters. Schnitzler's innovation was to eliminate the villain entirely. Fritz Lobheimer was not a cynical seducer. He was a young man of genuine, if diffuse, feeling—capable of tenderness, troubled by his situation, beginning by the second act to experience something that might become real love for Christine Weiring. His tragedy, and it was in some sense his tragedy too, was that his social formation had rendered him incapable of acting on better impulses. The honor code demanded he fight the duel; his class position made marriage to Christine unthinkable; his psychology, shaped by that position, made it impossible for him to be fully present in a relationship that crossed social boundaries. He was not evil. He was simply inadequate—morally, emotionally, imaginatively inadequate to the demands that Christine's love placed on him.

This shift from villainy to structural inadequacy was Schnitzler's most significant contribution. The play did not require a villain because the social order itself played that role. The duel that killed Fritz was not the result of individual malice; it was the mechanical operation of an honor code that functioned independently of anyone's wishes. The challenge from the Baroness's husband was, within the logic of his world, entirely legitimate. Fritz's inability to refuse was not personal weakness but the product of socialization so deep that alternatives could not be imagined. The tragedy was systemic, and this made it more disturbing than the tradition's individual villains. Villains could be condemned; systems were harder to name and impossible to prosecute.

The play's three-act structure was not conventional scaffolding but a precisely calibrated mechanism for generating and withholding information. Schnitzler arranged his acts in three distinct spatial settings—Fritz's elegant apartment, Christine's modest suburban lodgings, Christine's lodgings again—and the movement between these spaces enacted the movement between social worlds that was the play's subject. The opening act established the terrain through contrast. Fritz's apartment bespoke ease and cultivation: furniture that spoke, without ostentation, of money, taste, leisure. Christine and her friend Mizi Schlager were present as guests whose presence carried specific implications about the nature of their relationships to their hosts.

The contrast between the two women was among the play's most accomplished characterizations. Mizi approached the situation with pragmatic clarity: she understood the terms of the arrangement, expected nothing more than offered, and was, within those terms, genuinely content. There was no sentimentality in her involvement with Theodor Kaiser; she inhabited it with matter-of-fact ease that looked, from one angle, like sophistication and, from another, like self-protective refusal of vulnerability. Christine was immediately and fatally different: she fell genuinely, completely in love. She did not understand—or refused to understand—that the situation called for Mizi's detachment. Her love was not appropriate to the context in which it had been placed. This was the play's central dramatic irony, established in the first act with extraordinary economy.

The second act, set in Christine's lodgings, reversed the spatial logic. Fritz was now in her world, and the effect was revealing. Christine's home was modest but warm—a space of genuine domesticity, of a father who loved his daughter and a life conducted according to real if modest values. Weiring, the theater musician, was drawn with remarkable sympathy: a decent man whose decency had no purchase on the social mechanisms that would destroy his daughter. Fritz's presence in this space had a quality of intrusion. He was kind, tentative, beginning to feel something more substantial than he had bargained for—but visibly uncomfortable, not because the lodgings were unpleasant, but because their emotional reality was more demanding than he could navigate. The second act was the play's pivot: we saw Fritz at his most sympathetic and most limited, and understood the two qualities were inseparable.

The third act was a masterpiece of devastating understatement. Fritz was already dead when it began; the dramatic tension came not from the duel itself—which we never saw—but from the terrible business of informing Christine. The information arrived in layers, each more destructive than the last: the fact of death, the circumstances (a duel), the occasion (the Baroness, the letters, the married woman), and finally the annihilating revelation that Christine understood with full force: she had been a *Liebelei*. Fritz had died for another woman—a woman of his own class, whose claim on him could be publicly acknowledged and honorably defended. Christine, for whom the affair was the most transforming experience of her life, had been for him a distraction, a comfort, a pleasant interlude. The hierarchy of his attachments, which she had perhaps managed to suppress from her imagination, was now publicly and permanently legible.

Schnitzler's decision to leave Christine's probable suicide off-stage was formally and ethically significant. It refused the aestheticization of female death that was a persistent danger in the bourgeois tragedy tradition—the operatic staging that turned suffering into spectacle and death into a kind of beauty. Christine's death was the most private possible act: it took place not on stage but in imagination, in the off-stage space that corresponded to the social invisibility of her suffering throughout. She died, as she had lived, unwitnessed by the institutions that might have protected her.

What made the play more than social critique was Schnitzler's mastery of language. Richard Alewyn would later praise him as one of the few "masters of conversation" in German literature, and the achievement was nowhere more evident than here.[2] The dialogue was colloquial, lightly inflected with Viennese dialect, stripped of the rhetorical elevation German theatrical tradition had associated with serious drama. Characters spoke as people actually spoke—in half-finished sentences, in deflections, in the small social lubricants of polite evasion. Yet every exchange was calibrated for what it revealed about psychology, power relations, and the social codes that both enabled and constrained communication. This was the *Kammerspiel* aesthetic at its finest: an intimate dramatic form where small gestures and casual words carried enormous emotional freight.

The conversation between Fritz and Christine in Act II exemplified this technique. On the surface they were simply talking—about small things, about her life, about his. Beneath the surface, a more consequential drama proceeded: Fritz discovering, to his surprise and discomfort, that Christine was a person with a real inner life; Christine discovering, without fully articulating it, that Fritz's inner life had no room for her as she had imagined. Neither discovery was stated. Both were legible to an audience attending to what was not said, to the pauses, the deflections, the moments when a character changed subject or answered a question with a question.

The play was also deeply, uncomfortably autobiographical. Schnitzler's diary entry about Jeanette Heeger—the woman who most directly inspired the Christine type—was preserved with unsettling directness: "It will be something nice to remember."[3] The sentence was perfectly Fritzan: it aestheticized, it distanced, it converted present experience into anticipated nostalgia. It focused entirely on the speaker's future emotional life, with no imaginative purchase on the woman to whom it implicitly referred. Schnitzler knew this about himself. His diary showed throughout a capacity for self-awareness that did not always translate into different behavior.

What was remarkable was that he chose to make the critique as thorough and unsparing as it was. He did not write a play that acknowledged Fritz's limitations while sympathizing with them, or that allowed the social order's mechanisms to seem merely unfortunate. He wrote a play demonstrating, with theatrical and psychological precision, that the social practice he himself engaged in produced a particular kind of death—not only Christine's probable physical death, but the moral and emotional death of a young woman's trust, her capacity for investment in the world, her sense that her own feelings were real and consequential. The play was an act of imaginative reparation: an effort to make visible the inner lives of women whose inner lives men like Schnitzler—men like Fritz—had failed to adequately imagine.

He submitted the play to the Burgtheater—the most prestigious stage in the German-speaking world, the cultural crown jewel of the Habsburg Empire—in late October 1894.[4] Acceptance by the Burgtheater conferred a legitimacy no other venue could provide. Director Max Burckhard's willingness to take the financial and reputational risk of staging a three-act play by a relatively unknown author—a play whose subject matter, cross-class erotic entanglement and its fatal social consequences, was far from uncontroversial—was itself a cultural event.

The play was accepted within months, and on October 9, 1895, it premiered to an audience that included, in the role of Christine, Adele Sandrock herself.[5] The collision of life and art was almost too perfect: Schnitzler's lover, a woman of formidable talent and ungovernable temperament, playing the part of the innocent girl destroyed by a man who could not love her honestly. Sandrock was not an ingénue but a powerful and technically accomplished actress, and her interpretation of Christine reportedly brought an emotional intensity to the role that subsequent productions struggled to match. Whether Sandrock recognized the irony—whether the irony enhanced or undermined her performance—the biographical entanglement reflected the degree to which Schnitzler's theatrical imagination was fueled by lived experience. He had been, in his own behavior, something very like Fritz Lobheimer—a man who kept a young woman of modest social origins as a source of uncomplicated warmth while maintaining the social life appropriate to his class—and he knew it. *Liebelei* was, among other things, an act of self-examination so rigorous it became self-indictment.

The premiere was a triumph. The result was Schnitzler's first and greatest stage success. *Liebelei* would run for years and establish him, definitively, as a dramatist of the front rank. Friedrich Torberg would later call it "a genuine love tragedy, rooted nowhere but in love"—recognizing that the roots were in the invisible emotional soil of what the characters could not quite say to each other.[6] The play's continuing theatrical vitality would be demonstrated through decades of productions and adaptations. Max Ophüls' 1933 film, with Magda Schneider as Christine, would be recognized as a major cinematic achievement; the 1958 remake with Romy Schneider in her mother's role carried an inescapable biographical pathos. Tom Stoppard's 1986 adaptation, *Dalliance*, produced at the National Theatre in London, would demonstrate the play's capacity to survive not only translation but significant reimagination, confirming that the mechanisms Schnitzler identified were not historically local but structurally perennial.[7]

But in 1895, what mattered was the immediate impact. The play's success proved decisive in two respects. It convinced Schnitzler that writing could be not merely a vocation but a career—that the pen could, after all, sustain a life. And it brought him to the attention of S. Fischer Verlag, one of the most distinguished publishing houses in Germany, which would publish *Liebelei* in 1896 and remain his primary publisher for the rest of his career.[8] Alongside the play, Fischer published the novella *Sterben—Dy-*

ing—a work that drew on the same reservoir of intimate observation and moral complexity.

Liebelei was the work in which Schnitzler discovered the full range of his theatrical voice. What he discovered was not merely dramatic technique but a moral seriousness his earlier work had approached without fully achieving. *Anatol*, for all its psychological intelligence, maintained an ironic distance that allowed the audience aesthetic comfort—one could enjoy Anatol's absurdity even while recognizing its pathos. *Liebelei* refused this comfort. It placed the audience in proximity to Christine's suffering in a way that made ironic detachment impossible. One was made to feel the cost, not merely observe it.

The reluctant doctor had become, by 1895, a professional writer. The transformation was complete, and it was irreversible. But the price of that transformation—the self-knowledge required to write *Liebelei* with such devastating precision—was the permanent recognition that he had been, in his own life, complicit in the very mechanisms the play exposed. The success was genuine. So was the self-indictment. They were inseparable, and they would remain so throughout his career.

CHAPTER EIGHT

The Great Love (1895–1899)

PARACELSUS, DIE GEFÄHRTIN, DER GRÜNE KAKADU

MARIE REINHARD ENTERED SCHNITZLER'S life as a patient. She had come to consult him about voice problems—he was still, intermittently, practicing his father's specialty—and the love affair that developed from the medical consultation carried, from its inception, the imprint of the power dynamics that structured all of Schnitzler's relationships with women.[1] The physician-patient dynamic was not merely a circumstantial detail but a structural feature: it established, from the first encounter, who possessed expertise and who sought it, who diagnosed and who presented symptoms. That this asymmetry should become the foundation of an erotic relationship was, in the context of late nineteenth-century Vienna, entirely unremarkable. That Schnitzler—whose theatrical work was increasingly preoccupied with exposing such asymmetries—should participate in it without apparent hesitation suggests the persistent gap between intellectual recognition and lived behavior that characterized his entire life.

She was a voice teacher and aspiring actress, twenty-three years old when they met in the summer of 1894, from a respectable bourgeois Viennese family; her father was a civil servant who had risen to become deputy general secretary of the Austrian Alpine Mining Company.[2] She could read in English and French, had encountered feminist literature, and had survived a broken engagement, a depressive collapse, and a stay in a psychiatric institution. She was, in the phrase of one biographer, not the sort of woman one could have at a moment's notice.[3] This matters because it distinguishes Marie Reinhard from the "sweet girls" who populated both Schnitzler's work and his life. She was educated, cultivated, from his own social class—precisely the sort of woman with whom marriage would have been socially intelligible and practically viable. The obstacles to marriage were not external but internal: they existed in Schnitzler's psychology, not in the social order.

The relationship that developed between 1894 and 1899 was the most serious of Schnitzler's life to that point. Two hundred and thirty of her letters to him survive in the Marburg literary archive, alongside the diary entries in which he documented the affair with his usual compulsive thoroughness.[4] The letters reveal a woman of considerable intelligence and emotional depth, capable of articulating her own needs and frustrated by Schnitzler's persistent evasions. She was not naive about what she wanted: she wanted marriage, legitimacy, a future that extended beyond the present arrangement. Schnitzler appears to have hoped that the question would not arise. This asymmetry—of desire, of expectation, of willingness to imagine a shared future—structured the relationship from beginning to end.

The affair coincided with the most productive period of Schnitzler's career. Between 1894 and 1899, he was writing steadily, placing work at major theaters, establishing himself as one of Vienna's leading dramatists. The professional success and the personal relationship proceeded in parallel, each feeding the other in ways that were not always comfortable to observe. Marie encouraged his work, read drafts, offered opinions. She was intellectually engaged with what he was doing in a way that previous lovers had not been. Yet this engagement also meant she could see, with uncomfortable clarity, the gap between the psychological insight Schnitzler brought to his female characters and the emotional availability he brought to the woman sharing his life. She could read *Liebelei* and recognize what it said about men like Schnitzler—and recognize, simultaneously, that Schnitzler's ability to write such a play did not translate into his ability to be different from Fritz Lobheimer.

In early 1897, Marie became pregnant.[5] Schnitzler's response was not to propose. The fact deserves to be stated baldly, because it reveals something essential about his character. A pregnancy, in the social context of 1890s Vienna, was not merely a personal matter but a social crisis for an unmarried woman of Marie's class. The scandal would be considerable, the damage to her reputation potentially permanent. For Schnitzler, the social consequences would be comparatively minor—men were not ruined by such things. The pregnancy created an emergency that was asymmetrically distributed: her crisis, his inconvenience. That he did not immediately offer marriage—the conventional and honorable response—suggests the depth of his resistance to the commitment she wanted.

Nobody was to know of the pregnancy in Vienna. Marie left the city and traveled to Mauer, a village outside the capital, where Schnitzler's cousin Ludwig Mandl served as her physician. The labor lasted more than five days. On 24 September 1897, the child—a boy, whom they named Paul—was stillborn.[6] The diary records genuine grief. Schnitzler noted what he called a "deep feeling of a connection between the death of the child and my lack of interest for the child before the birth."[7] It is important to register this, because what happened next would raise questions that genuine grief alone could not answer. The grief was real. So was the relief. The stillbirth resolved, at least temporarily, the crisis that the pregnancy had created. It permitted the relationship to continue without the question of marriage being forced to an immediate resolution. Schnitzler mourned the child he had wanted; he also, one suspects, experienced a complicated gratitude that the social and emotional decision he had been unable to make had been made for him by circumstance.

The relationship continued. Marie's hope for marriage did not diminish with the loss of the child; if anything, it intensified. The stillbirth had been a shared tragedy, and shared tragedy, in the logic of emotional commitment, should deepen bonds rather than dissolve them. For Marie, the loss confirmed that she and Schnitzler belonged together, that they should formalize what was already, in substance, a marriage. For Schnitzler, the calculus was different and considerably less generous. The relationship provided him with emotional stability, intellectual companionship, and regular sexual intimacy—all the benefits of marriage without its legal and social constraints. Why, from his perspective, would he alter an arrangement that served him so well?

Meanwhile, Schnitzler was also writing what would prove among the most consequential works of his career. *Reigen*—the cycle of ten dialogues depicting successive sexual encounters across the full spectrum of Viennese society—was composed in three months during the winter of 1896–97, while Marie's first pregnancy was advancing.[8] The timing was significant. At the very moment Schnitzler was evading marriage to a woman pregnant with his child, he was writing the most systematic theatrical anatomy of sexual hypocrisy and class exploitation in the German language. The work's circular structure—prostitute to soldier, soldier to parlor maid, parlor maid to young gentleman, onward through actress and count until the circle closed with the count visiting the prostitute—enacted a vision of erotic life as mechanical, repetitive, and fundamentally dishonest. Each encounter followed the same pattern: desire, consummation, disillusionment. The gap between what the characters said before and after was the play's devastating subject.

Schnitzler himself considered *Reigen* unprintable and unperformable. He was right that it would cause scandal, though wrong that it could not be staged. He authorized a private printing of two hundred copies in 1900, then a public edition in 1903. The play would not be officially performed until 23 December 1920 in Berlin and 1 February 1921 in Vienna, and when it was, it provoked the most violent theatrical controversy of the young Austrian republic. But all of that lay far in the future. In 1897, *Reigen* existed only in manuscript, a work too dangerous to publish, written by a man who was himself engaged in exactly the kind of erotic compartmentalization the play anatomized.

By January 1899, Marie was pregnant again.[9] She was upset, and the reason was simple: Schnitzler was, in the diary's formulation, "putting things off" regarding marriage—"sie war wieder verstimmt, weil ich das Heir. auf die lange Bank schiebe."[10] The phrase captures both the fact of his evasion and his awareness of it. He was not refusing marriage outright—that would have forced a crisis he did not want. He was deferring it, postponing it, suggesting that circumstances were not yet right. He was busy, he said—three one-act plays were about to premiere at the Burgtheater. The excuse was transparent and insufficient.

The pattern was by now well established: he cultivated long-term relationships with women who hoped for marriage, because such arrangements provided emotional continuity without the legal entanglements and social obligations of marriage. They allowed him to maintain the fiction of being in a serious relationship while preserving the option to leave.

The women's calculations were different, and their leverage was smaller. Marie could hope, she could press the question, she could express her unhappiness—but she could not compel. The power in the relationship was distributed according to the same logic that distributed power in the society at large: the man who could delay indefinitely held more cards than the woman for whom delay meant the erosion of her childbearing years and the progressive compromise of her social position.

The three one-act plays that Schnitzler cited as the reason he was too busy to address the question of marriage—*Paracelsus*, *Die Gefährtin* (The Companion), and *Der grüne Kakadu* (The Green Cockatoo)—premiered at the Burgtheater on 1 March 1899, just fifteen days before Marie Reinhard fell ill.[11] The coincidence of dates is worth noting: Schnitzler was occupied with theatrical triumph during the precise weeks when Marie's second pregnancy was forcing the marriage question to a crisis.

The three plays, presented together as a triple bill, represented different facets of Schnitzler's theatrical range. *Paracelsus*, a verse play set in Basel in 1517, was Schnitzler's most sustained attempt at historical drama—a philosophical meditation on the relationship between knowledge and power, centered on the historical physician and alchemist. The play examined the question of whether love could be manufactured through hypnotic suggestion, and whether a husband could use such power to ensure his wife's fidelity. The thematic connection to "The Question to Fate" from *Anatol* was unmistakable: once again, Schnitzler was exploring the male desire to know and control female desire, and once again, the conclusion was skeptical. Paracelsus discovers that even hypnotic power cannot penetrate the mystery of another person's autonomous will. The

play was intellectually ambitious but dramatically inert—too much philosophy, not enough action—and critics received it with respect but not
enthusiasm.

Die Gefährtin was a more intimate piece, derived from Schnitzler's
1894 novella *Der Witwer* (The Widower). Set on an autumn evening
in a summer resort near Vienna, the play centers on Professor Pilgram,
whose wife Eveline has just died of a heart attack.[12] In the aftermath of her
death, Pilgram's neighbor Olga Merholm arrives to reclaim letters she had
written to the dead woman, and through the ensuing conversation Pilgram
is forced to confront uncomfortable truths about his marriage—about
Eveline's inner life, her friendships, and the degree to which he had been
blind to her reality while she was alive. The play was a distillation of one
of Schnitzler's most persistent themes: the impossibility of truly knowing
the person one lives with, and the husband's belated discovery that his wife
possessed an autonomous inner world he had never troubled to imagine.
Schnitzler himself later acknowledged that the play's problem was only
touched on, not fully developed—"Essentially it's more atmosphere than
real working-out of the problem," he told a Danish interviewer in 1904.
"There's more in it than one can express in a single act."[13]

But it was *Der grüne Kakadu* that proved the most successful and
enduring of the three. Set in a Parisian tavern on the night of 14 July
1789—the night the Bastille fell—the play was Schnitzler's most formally
experimental work to date. The Green Cockatoo was a theatrical establishment where actors performed improvisations for an aristocratic clientele,
blurring the boundary between performance and reality. The play's central
conceit was that the actors, playing criminals and conspirators, begin to
perform their roles with such intensity that the line between acting and
authentic emotion dissolves. When the actor Henri discovers that his wife
Léocadie has genuinely been unfaithful with the Duke, his feigned rage
becomes real rage, and he actually murders the Duke—on stage, in front
of an audience that thinks it is witnessing a performance.

The play was a theatrical tour de force, and it demonstrated Schnitzler's increasing sophistication about the relationship between theater and reality. The aristocratic audience within the play comes to the Green Cockatoo to experience a frisson of danger, to enjoy a staged version of the revolutionary violence that is, unbeknownst to them, about to consume their entire world. They watch criminals perform criminality, unaware that actual criminality is erupting around them. The play's conclusion, in which news of the Bastille's fall reaches the tavern and the actors join the real revolution outside, suggests that the distinction between theatrical performance and political action is more porous than the comfortable aristocrats imagine.

The formal innovation of *Der grüne Kakadu* was considerable, but so was its political audacity. Schnitzler had written a play about revolution that did not condemn the revolutionaries, that presented the aristocratic class's obliviousness to the suffering around them as a form of moral culpability, and that suggested the inevitability—perhaps even the justice—of their downfall. Critics and audiences understood the contemporary resonances. Vienna in 1899 was not revolutionary Paris, but it was a city experiencing profound social tensions: between classes, between nationalities, between the old aristocratic order and the rising bourgeoisie.

The play's success was followed, almost immediately, by its suppression. The Burgtheater removed it from the repertoire after just seven performances—initially merely declaring it "not permitted," and only later formally banning it. Schnitzler recalled the sequence bitterly in a 1903 interview: "What happened with my Kakadu? I can only hint at it. It was taken off after seven performances, at first merely 'not permitted' and only late r—banned."[14] The censorship confirmed what the play itself dramatized: that the powerful preferred the consolations of staged transgression to the discomfort of genuine critique. The Burgtheater, that imperial institution, had staged a play about the blindness of aristocratic institutions—and then enacted exactly the kind of repressive response the play had predicted.

The triple bill's overall reception confirmed Schnitzler's position as one of Vienna's leading playwrights. To have three new works premiered simultaneously at the Burgtheater was an achievement few dramatists of his generation could claim. The cultural capital was considerable. He was now a Burgtheater author, a regular presence on Vienna's most prestigious stage, a writer whose new work would be anticipated and reviewed by the city's leading critics.

Yet the timing remains impossible to ignore. The premiere occurred on 1 March. Marie Reinhard became severely ill on 16 March. She died on 18 March. The theatrical triumph and the personal catastrophe were separated by two weeks.

On 16 March 1899, Marie fell ill. On 17 March, she was, in the diary's terse notation, "extremely sick." A gynecologist was consulted—Ludwig Mandl, the same cousin who had attended the stillbirth in Mauer. So was Schnitzler's brother Julius—a surgeon who was, by this time, one of Vienna's leading experts on appendectomies.[15] Julius examined her. He did not hospitalize her. On 18 March, Marie Reinhard died at home. She was twenty-seven years old. The death certificate, registered at the Augustinerpfarre, listed the cause as peritonitis. She was buried two days later at the Zentralfriedhof. Schnitzler paid for the funeral.

The facts are stark and their sequence is damning in its rapidity. Two days from the onset of illness to death. An expert surgeon consulted but no hospitalization. A young woman dying at home of a condition that, properly treated, was survivable. The official cause—peritonitis—was medically plausible. Appendicitis could, if undiagnosed or untreated, progress rapidly to peritonitis and death. But the timeline was unusually compressed, and the decision not to hospitalize was, for a surgeon of Julius Schnitzler's expertise confronting a case of suspected appendicitis, difficult to explain within the bounds of standard medical practice.

And then Schnitzler's diary went silent. For approximately three weeks—from mid-March until early April—the man who had recorded his life with obsessive regularity wrote nothing.[16] The silence is, in its way, more eloquent than anything he might have set down. It suggests a grief so overwhelming that even his formidable powers of self-observation could not contain it. The diary had been his mechanism for processing experience, for converting the chaos of lived feeling into the ordered prose of documentation. That the mechanism failed—that he could not write—testifies to the magnitude of what he was experiencing.

When he resumed, four days after her death, the entry he managed was a record of devastation. He described a loneliness without comparison, and reflected that he had always tried to depict people who lose what is dearest to them—but that there was something in this experience that could not be expressed, something as resistant to language as eternity or infinity: "loneliness, having been made lonely; being made to be lonely."[17] The formulation was characteristically precise even in its extremity. He was not merely alone; he had been acted upon, made lonely by a force he could not name. The passive construction suggested both grief and guilt—he was the object of something that had been done to him, and yet the circumstances that produced it were partly of his own making.

It may also suggest something else. In 2014, the scholar Rolf-Peter Lacher published an account arguing that Marie Reinhard's death was the result not of appendicitis but of a botched abortion.[18] The theory rests on circumstantial evidence, but the circumstantial evidence is considerable: Marie was pregnant and unmarried; Schnitzler was evading the question of marriage; Julius Schnitzler, an expert in abdominal surgery who would have recognized appendicitis and known that hospitalization offered the best chance of survival, examined her but did not take her to a hospital;

and the timeline of the illness is consistent with complications from a clandestine procedure. In fin-de-siècle Vienna, abortion was illegal, and women who sought it did so through underground networks whose medical competence varied enormously.

The theory is not provable. Academic Schnitzler scholars have received Lacher's argument with skepticism or silence, and the evidence is not conclusive.[19] Against the theory stands Schnitzler's documented desire for fatherhood, his grief at the 1897 stillbirth, and the absence of any direct evidence—a confession, a reference in correspondence, a notation in the diary—of an abortion. The German Wikipedia article on Reinhard notes a further objection: Schnitzler recorded in his diary on multiple occasions his wish to become a father, and the death of the first child had genuinely devastated him. The medical records, if they were detailed, have not survived. The death certificate lists peritonitis, and peritonitis can result from multiple causes.

We do not know what happened in the apartment where Marie Reinhard died. We know that something went terribly wrong, that an expert was present and could not or did not save her, and that the man who documented everything chose, for once, to document nothing. The uncertainty is part of the story, and it would be dishonest to resolve it with more confidence than the evidence permits. What we can say is this: whether Marie died from appendicitis or from an abortion, her death occurred within a situation that Schnitzler had created and sustained—a situation in which a woman pregnant for the second time by a man who would not marry her faced a crisis that ended in her death. If it was appendicitis, the question remains why she was not hospitalized. If it was abortion, the question is whether Schnitzler pressured her toward it, acquiesced to it, or merely failed to prevent it by the simple expedient of offering marriage.

Years later, writing to Marie's sister Karoline Burger on 25 May 1903, Schnitzler described the death as the result of "unforeseen appendicitis."[20] The word "unforeseen" carried a weight he may or may not have intended.

Appendicitis is, by its nature, unforeseen—it is an acute medical emergency that strikes without warning. But if Marie died from a different cause, the word becomes a euphemism whose cynicism is almost unbearable.

In 2014, Vienna designated Marie Reinhard's grave at the Zentralfriedhof a historical site and place of remembrance—an official acknowledgment that her life, and the manner of its ending, belonged not only to Schnitzler's private history but to the history of the city.[21] The designation separated Marie from Schnitzler's biography and recognized her as a person whose life and death had independent historical meaning. Whether she died from appendicitis or abortion, she died from being a woman whose reproductive capacity exceeded the commitment of the man with whom she was involved, and whose options were constrained by laws, social conventions, and medical practices designed to protect male freedom at the expense of female survival.

At the end of March 1899—within days of Marie's funeral—Schnitzler was awarded the Bauernfeld Prize for his novellas and dramatic works.[22] The juxtaposition was almost unbearably Schnitzlerian: public recognition arriving at the precise moment of private catastrophe, the literary career ascending as the personal life collapsed. He accepted the prize. He resumed work. That spring, he had his first encounter with the twenty-year-old drama student Olga Gussmann, who would become his wife—but not before repeating, with eerie precision, the Marie Reinhard pattern: pregnancy, evasion, a small house outside Vienna where the child could be born without scandal.[23]

The grief Schnitzler experienced was genuine. So was the silence. So was the resumption of life, the return to work, the continuation of his career. He would hold the anniversary of Marie Reinhard's death in remembrance until the end of his life—the diary records him marking 18 March year after year, long after he had married Olga, long after the marriage had ended, long after the circumstances of 1899 had become a private grief rather than a public crisis.[24]

The question of whether Schnitzler felt guilt is unanswerable. Guilt does not leave clear traces in someone as psychologically defended as Schnitzler. What we can say is that the man who emerged from the spring of 1899 was different from the man who entered it. The evasiveness remained, the pattern of long-term relationships without marriage continued, the diary's compulsive documentation resumed. But something had changed. Years later, the interviewer Paul Wilhelm would observe that Schnitzler had long outgrown the easy label of "poet of the sweet girl"—that his art had deepened into something darker, more searching, more pitiless in its examination of human self-deception.[25] The plays and prose that followed—the late one-acts, *Frau Bertha Garlan*, the mature fiction—showed a willingness to examine the mechanisms of masculine self-deception and erotic exploitation with a severity that earlier work had approached but not quite achieved.

Reigen, written before Marie's death but still unpublished, would not see print until 1900 and would not be performed for another two decades. When it finally reached the stage in 1920–21, it provoked riots, parliamentary debates, and antisemitic attacks that made the *Kakadu* ban seem quaint by comparison. Schnitzler responded to the scandal with the controlled irony of a man who had survived worse. "The dialogues were written eighteen years ago," he told a reporter in February 1921. "They are a youthful work."[26] To Stefan Großmann he wrote more revealingly: "I have no intention of saying anything more about *Reigen* and the so-called Reigen affair in public. After a few years, nothing will remain of all this noise except the books I have written, and a dim memory of my opponents' embarrassment. In this case it will be no different."[27]

The confidence was earned. By the time the *Reigen* scandal erupted, Schnitzler had written *Professor Bernhardi*, *Der einsame Weg*, *Das weite Land*—works of increasing psychological complexity and moral seriousness. He would go on to write *Fräulein Else* and *Traumnovelle*, his late masterpieces. He would become one of the defining literary voices of his generation. But the unanswered questions about March 1899 would remain unanswered, preserved in the archive not as evidence but as absence. The silence that followed Marie Reinhard's death was Schnitzler's most revealing utterance, and its meaning—whether it expressed unspeakable grief, unbearable guilt, or some more complicated admixture of both—remains, like so much in his life, subject to interpretation but resistant to certainty.

Scandal (1896–1900)

REIGEN

IN THE WINTER OF 1896–1897, while Marie Reinhard was carrying the child who would be stillborn, Schnitzler wrote the play that would haunt him for the rest of his life. His diary records the beginning of the project on 23 November 1896, when he first conceived the plan for a cycle of ten dialogues exploring sexual encounters across the full spectrum of Viennese society. He worked with unusual speed and concentration, completing a draft he titled "Liebesreigen" by 24 February 1897—a span of barely three months.[1] The finished work, eventually titled simply Reigen—later known in French as La Ronde—was a cycle of ten scenes, each depicting a sexual encounter between two characters drawn from different social strata, arranged in a circular chain so that each figure appeared in two consecutive scenes and the last encounter returned to the first.

A prostitute and a soldier; the soldier and a parlor maid; the maid and a young gentleman; the young gentleman and a young wife; the wife and her husband—the only licit coupling, positioned at the center of the structure like a hinge—the husband and a sweet girl; the sweet girl and a poet; the poet and an actress; the actress and a count; and the count, finally, with the prostitute who had opened the circle. The structure was mathematical and merciless.

What Schnitzler had achieved was not merely a sequence of scenes but a formal argument about the nature of desire and the fiction of social hierarchy. The circular structure—the Reigen, a traditional round dance—made visible what the social order worked to conceal: that desire operated identically across all social classes, that the supposedly respectable figures in the chain were, in their sexual behavior, structurally equivalent to the prostitute at its base. The Count and the Prostitute were mirror images of each other. The rigid demarcations between respectable and disreputable, virtuous and fallen, were effects of social power rather than reflections of any natural moral reality. The democracy of desire was not a celebration. It was an accusation.

The formal elegance of the structure expressed a devastating social critique. Fin-de-siècle Viennese society depended, for its self-legitimation, on the idea that its upper echelons were not merely more powerful than the lower but morally superior. A woman's social standing was inseparable from her sexual reputation; a man's honor was partly constituted by his ability to control the sexual behavior of women associated with him. The rigid demarcation between respectable women—wives, daughters of good family—and disreputable women—prostitutes, actresses, women of the working class—was a structural feature of the social order rather than a reflection of natural moral difference. Liebelei had examined this logic from within, through tragic narrative. Reigen exposed it systematically, through structure. By showing the Count and the Prostitute as equivalent in the domain of physical desire, Schnitzler was attacking the ideological foundations of the social order itself.

Each scene was calibrated with clinical precision. The ten figures represented not merely individuals but social types, and the encounters between them revealed the specific asymmetries of power—social, economic, gendered—that shaped each interaction. The Soldier's scene with the Parlor

Maid was different from the Husband's scene with the Sweet Girl not because different acts were performed but because the social positions of the participants determined the terms on which the encounters proceeded, the language available to describe them, and the consequences that followed. Schnitzler was not suggesting that class made no difference to sexual experience; he was demonstrating that class made the same difference to everyone—that the universal fact of desire cut across all social distinctions without erasing them.

The Young Gentleman's encounter with the Parlor Maid established, with almost clinical economy, how class power shaped the erotic encounter. The maid could not refuse; her social position made refusal practically impossible. The Young Gentleman did not experience this as coercion because his social world had not equipped him with the conceptual vocabulary to recognize it as such. His behavior was not unusual—it was the ordinary exercise of social power his class position conferred. The scene's dramatic irony—the gap between the Young Gentleman's blithe self-presentation and the Parlor Maid's knowing awareness of the actual terms—made the power differential legible to the audience even when invisible to the Young Gentleman himself.

The figure of the Young Wife was constructed with equal precision. She entered the cycle at its social center—the figure the social order was most invested in protecting and regulating, the wife whose sexual fidelity secured the legitimacy of family lines and the stability of property inheritance. Her scene with the Young Gentleman was an extended study in the process by which a woman socialized to identify her own sexual desire as a moral threat managed the cognitive dissonance of acting on it. Her elaborate performance of reluctance was not simple hypocrisy. It was the authentic voice of a social formation that had taught her to experience her own desire as alien to her respectable self, as something that happened to her rather than something she chose. Schnitzler did not mock her; he rendered the psychological reality of her situation with a precision closer to compassion.

But the scene also made legible the social mechanisms that produced this particular form of self-division.

The play's most radical formal innovation was the device that marked each sexual act: the typographical ellipsis. In each scene, the dialogue proceeded to a point of physical culmination, and then the text provided only a row of dots before resuming with the post-coital conversation. The act was not shown, not described, not narrated—it was marked by an absence. This was not, as censors and scandalized readers would assume, a thin veil over pornographic content the audience was invited to fill in with imagination. It was a precise formal argument about the relationship between sex and language, between physical and communicative intimacy, between what happened between people and what could be said about it.

The structure of each scene—pre-sex dialogue, ellipsis, post-sex dialogue—systematically highlighted the gap between the two halves of every encounter. The pre-sex dialogues were performances: characters deployed charm, flattery, seduction, occasionally coercion to achieve their desired end. They spoke with apparent feeling; they made implicit or explicit claims about love, tenderness, the special nature of this particular connection. The post-sex dialogues were revisions or retractions. The warmth evaporated; promised feelings failed to materialize or were hastily qualified; characters who were expansive became monosyllabic; intimacies that seemed genuine were revealed as tactical. The ellipsis stood between these two registers as a marker not of the act itself but of the transformation the act did not produce. The characters arrived at the ellipsis hoping the physical encounter would deliver what their emotional lives lacked; they emerged from it to discover it had not. The dots were the formal expression of disappointment.

What the ellipsis withheld was not the erotic experience but the revelation that it had not been transformative, had not produced the intimacy the pre-sex performance implied was being sought. This structure repeated ten times, with variations in social register and comic tone, and the repetition was the argument: desire did not, in the world this work depicted, connect people to each other. It isolated them more completely. The post-coital conversations had a quality of emotional aftermath that was, cumulatively, deeply affecting. Characters became awkward, monosyllabic, brusque; they found sudden reasons to leave; they responded to questions with non-sequiturs revealing they were no longer really present to their partner.

The cumulative effect of the ten scenes was not comedy but something closer to desolation. There was abundant irony, genuine comedy in the gap between characters' self-presentations and their behavior, but the total experience was tragicomic rather than celebratory. What the circle revealed, by the time it closed, was not the gayness of universal desire but its vacuity—the degree to which sexual encounter, as Schnitzler depicted it, failed to produce lasting connection, genuine knowledge of another person, any relief from the fundamental solitude each character inhabited. The circle turned, connected everyone to everyone, and left everyone alone.

Reigen was also a work about the systematic misuse of communicative capacity in service of erotic strategy. Every character in every scene was performing rather than speaking: using language not to establish genuine contact with another person but to manage that person's behavior toward the speaker's own ends. The pre-sex language was language as instrument, as technique, as the verbal component of seduction. The post-sex language was, in its deflation and withdrawal, a kind of negative truth-telling: the characters, having achieved their object, no longer had motive to maintain the performance, and the resulting conversational collapse revealed more about their actual emotional states than anything said before the ellipsis.

Schnitzler would later describe the play's central observation to the Danish journalist Julius Bangert in March 1921 as rooted not in the celebration of desire but in its social conditioning. In that interview, conducted during the height of the Reigen scandal, he insisted that the play could not be understood apart from Austrian political and social history. Everything in Austrian life was, in the last instance, politics, he told Bangert, and the outrage over Reigen was inseparable from the antisemitism that had grown steadily since the work's composition. The attack on the play was a convenient instrument for those who wished to target a Jewish author.[2]

This observation was not defensive posturing but a precise diagnosis of how cultural reception functioned in the late Habsburg and early republican periods. Schnitzler returned to it in virtually every interview where Reigen was discussed. Speaking to the Swedish press during his Scandinavian tour in May 1923, he was more explicit still: the play had been used as a weapon of political agitation, with clerical and nationalist factions seizing on it to mount antisemitic offensives. In Stockholm, he told the journalist for Nya Dagligt Allehanda that the Munich premiere had been stormed by two hundred schoolboys who threw stink bombs into the audience and onto the stage, driving the public from the theater.[3] In every account, Schnitzler drew the same distinction: one could legitimately debate, on aesthetic and dramaturgical grounds, whether Reigen belonged on the stage, but the claim that it violated public morality was a pretext for political violence.

The relationship between Reigen and Schnitzler's medical and psychoanalytic milieu was direct. He had trained as a physician, practiced as a laryngologist and neurologist, and his engagement with the Freudian intellectual atmosphere of Vienna in the 1890s was collegial rather than discipleship—a mutual recognition between two minds working on related problems from different angles. In a 1929 interview with the American journalist Edward Loving, Schnitzler himself described the play in clinical terms. Reigen, he said, had been conceived as a series of case histories. The question he had posed himself was: clinically speaking, how do certain people, drawn from all classes, act under the stress of sexual passion?[4] This was not retrospective rationalization. The ten scenes of Reigen were, among other things, case studies—precisely observed instances of a social pathology whose symptoms he was documenting. The pathology was the impossibility of genuine intimacy within a social system that had organized sexuality primarily as a mechanism of social reproduction and class maintenance, leaving individuals with sexual desires the system simultaneously inflamed and frustrated.

Reigen thus performed, in theatrical terms, something analogous to what psychoanalysis performed in the consulting room: it created a structure in which the socially unconscious—the mechanisms of desire and social performance that normally operated below the threshold of explicit awareness—became visible, legible, available for critical examination. Freud's later description of Schnitzler as his "double" reflected this parallel.

In his famous birthday letter of 14 May 1922, Freud confessed that he had long avoided meeting Schnitzler out of a kind of reluctance to encounter his Doppelgänger—a man who had arrived through intuition and self-observation at the same insights Freud believed he had uncovered through laborious clinical investigation.[5] The letter was a remarkable document: a confession of competitive anxiety dressed as a compliment. But it also testified to the degree to which both men were engaged in the same fundamental project—bringing to consciousness the unconscious social and psychological mechanisms that governed sexual life.

Schnitzler's own view of the relationship was characteristically more skeptical. He was wary of psychoanalysis as a system even while acknowledging its insights. In a 1930 conversation recorded by the journalist Franz Goldstein during a walk near his villa, Schnitzler remarked that literature had always been engaged in the exploration of the soul through intuition, and was in that sense psychoanalytic in a broader meaning of the term, long before Freud had codified the practice.[6] He found it amusing when foreign critics cast him as a disciple of psychoanalysis. The influence, insofar as it existed, ran in both directions.

The scene between the Poet and the Actress deserves particular attention, for it was modeled, with transparent audacity, on Schnitzler's own tempestuous affair with Adele Sandrock. Hermann Menkes, writing in

1922 about the early days of Jung Wien, recalled seeing the Reigen scenes when they first circulated in private printings among friends, and noted that Schnitzler had harbored a reluctance to release them to a wider public, knowing they could easily be consigned to the category of pornography. Menkes observed that these "boldly witty sketches of an ironic eroticist" sat uneasily alongside the brooding, almost melancholic temperament Schnitzler displayed in person, and speculated that the work may have been inspired by Balzac's Contes drôlatiques.[7] The suggestion was plausible as a literary genealogy, but the emotional material of the Poet-Actress scene was unmistakably autobiographical. Schnitzler had used, as scholars have since documented, near-verbatim transcriptions of his own dialogues with Sandrock, transforming private theatrical combat into public literary form.

He knew immediately that the play was unpublishable, or at least un-performable, in the Vienna of his time. The sexual act itself occurred offstage, marked not by a curtain drop at the end of each scene but at its midpoint—a structural choice that emphasized the before and after, the rhetoric and the reckoning, over the act itself. The language was not explic-it; the stage directions were not lurid; the treatment of sexuality was clini-cal, even melancholic, in ways that were the opposite of erotic incitement. But the candor was still too much. More fundamentally, the crime was not pornography but democracy: the play showed desire operating identically across all social classes, undermining the hierarchical distinctions on which the social order depended. A work that placed a prostitute and a count in structurally equivalent positions—both equally predatory, both equally lonely, both equally incapable of genuine intimacy—was not a celebration of sexuality. It was a devastating critique of the social arrangements that made genuine intimacy impossible for everyone, regardless of class.

Schnitzler himself acknowledged in his preface to the 1900 private printing that the work's value lay elsewhere than in the content that seemed to prohibit its publication. That preface—a single paragraph of extraordinary compression—stated that he had had two hundred copies printed as a manuscript edition because he believed the work's significance resided in something other than its apparent unsuitability for public consumption.[8] The private printing was itself a strategic choice: it allowed the work to circulate among the literary and intellectual circles whose judgment mattered to him while avoiding the censorship apparatus that commercial publication would inevitably trigger.

In 1903, he allowed a commercial edition to appear through the Wiener Verlag. The censors in Germany promptly banned the book in 1904.[9] The work's commercial suppression was, however, incomplete: it continued to circulate and to acquire the aura of a forbidden text, which only intensified public curiosity and distorted the terms on which the work was received.

In a letter of 13 September 1912, responding to a request from the impresario Giampietro for permission to stage the work, Schnitzler laid out his reasoning for withholding performance rights with characteristic precision. A public performance of the ten scenes in their true form was, he wrote, an absolute impossibility, and any softening of the material would destroy the meaning of the whole.[10] He recounted the only previous attempts at staging: in 1903, an academic dramatic society in Munich had performed three scenes despite his advice against it, and was promptly dissolved; some time later, the cabaret group Die Elf Scharfrichter had staged a single scene without his knowledge or consent. These experiences confirmed his judgment that the work was not suited to theatrical production under existing social conditions.

The letter is remarkable for what it reveals about Schnitzler's understanding of the relationship between form and social context. He was not arguing that the play was too scandalous for the stage—he was arguing that its meaning depended on conditions that could not be achieved in a theatrical performance as the institution then existed. The work's power resided in its totality, in the accumulating weight of the ten repetitions, in the circular structure that only became legible when the final scene returned to the first. Any abbreviation or softening would reduce the work to a series of bedroom comedies, stripping it of the analytical force that was its reason for being. The letter, published in 1921 by Max Epstein in the B. Z. am Mittag, became an important document in the subsequent debate over the play's performance history, because Schnitzler himself had later changed his position.[11]

The change came in the aftermath of the war. In November 1918, Max Reinhardt telegraphed Schnitzler requesting performance rights for his Kammerspiele in Berlin. Schnitzler did not immediately consent but offered Reinhardt priority. Over the following two years, as unauthorized performances proliferated—returning prisoners of war brought reports of Reigen productions in several Russian cities—Schnitzler gradually concluded that controlled, artistically serious performances were preferable to unauthorized stagings over which he had no influence. In a letter of 19 April 1919, Reinhardt assured Schnitzler of his commitment to bringing the work to the stage with full artistic seriousness and discretion. Schnitzler later published this correspondence in his "Berichtigung" of January 1921, a detailed public statement correcting Maximilian Harden's account of the performance history.[12]

The Berlin premiere took place on 23 December 1920 at the Kleines Schauspielhaus, directed by Hubert Reusch. The Vienna premiere followed on 1 February 1921 at the Kammerspiele. What happened next became one of the defining cultural events of the early Austrian Republic. On 16 February 1921, approximately one hundred and fifty demonstrators—organized, as contemporary reports documented, at an afternoon meeting of the Antisemitenbund and a Frontkämpfer organization—stormed the theater during a performance. They threw the heavy armchairs from the gallery boxes down onto the fleeing audience below, acts that could easily have been fatal. Schnitzler, who happened to be backstage conferring with the director Bernau, described the scene in a statement to the press: the hydrants had been turned on by the stagehands to repel the invaders, flooding the dressing rooms and the stage; the iron curtain held against the demonstrators who hammered against it from the auditorium side.[13]

The identities of those arrested told a story of their own. The Neues Wiener Journal reported them as a cobbler's apprentice, an upholsterer's apprentice, a clerk, a commercial academy student, and a dental technician's apprentice—none of whom, the paper pointedly observed, were likely to have drawn their moral outrage from deep literary learning.[14] Schnitzler's own comment on the matter, in a letter to Stefan Großmann published in Das Tage-Buch on 26 February 1921, was characteristically precise. He would find it unspeakably ridiculous, he wrote, to polemicize with the parliamentary deputies Kunschak or Seipel, or with the cobbler's apprentice who stormed the theater shouting "Down with the Reigen! They are defiling our women! Down with the Social Democrats!" After a few years, he predicted, nothing would remain of the uproar except the books he had written and a dim memory of his opponents' embarrassment.[15]

The prediction proved both right and wrong. The books survived; the embarrassment was not remembered, because the forces that had produced the riots—the convergence of antisemitism, political Catholicism, and nationalist agitation—did not retreat but intensified over the following decade. The Reigen affair was, in retrospect, a dress rehearsal for the cultural politics of the 1930s.

The parliamentary dimension of the scandal was extraordinary. On the same day that the Austrian parliament learned its deficit exceeded forty-two billion crowns—a disclosure of national insolvency—members received the news with bored indifference. The following day, when the Interior Minister's ban on Reigen was announced, the chamber erupted. Members pounded benches, exchanged blows, and issued threats of armed class conflict. The Social Democrat Karl Seitz, a former president of the Republic, declared that if the clericals were determined to employ violence, the Socialists would respond with forcible resistance. As the British Daily Herald correspondent reported with undisguised astonishment, the admission of the state's insolvency had left the government intact, but a play about adultery on a darkened stage had nearly brought it down.[16]

Schnitzler's response to the scandal was a study in controlled fury. In an interview with the Illustrirtes Wiener Extrablatt on 12 February 1921, he made the argument that would become his consistent position: whether Reigen belonged on the stage was a legitimate question that could be debated on aesthetic and dramaturgical grounds, but the claim that his work violated public morality was a position about which serious discussion was impossible. He noted that the same supposedly offended moral sensibility had never manifested itself on other occasions where equal or greater provocations had been offered.[17]

In the unpublished draft of a letter to the Neue Freie Presse, written in February 1922 but never sent, Schnitzler developed this argument at greater length. If works that by their nature might excite sensual interest in the general public were to be excluded from performance, he observed, then a considerable number of other plays would have to vanish from the repertoire along with Reigen—and most art galleries would need to close their doors. No one had yet, to his knowledge, thrown stink bombs in a museum because a painting offended their moral sensibilities. The comparison between theater and gallery was pointed: the objection to Reigen was not about its content but about its audience, about who was permitted to encounter representations of sexuality and under what institutional conditions.[18]

Despite—or because of—the intensity of the scandal, Schnitzler chose not to withdraw the work during the initial crisis. In an interview with the Copenhagen press during his Danish visit in May 1923, he explained his reasoning with the directness that characterized his Scandinavian conversations: the play was not immoral, and there was in art, properly speaking, neither morality nor immorality.[19] But his position hardened over the following years. He refused new performance requests, telling interviewers that he would not release the rights so quickly, that he did not want the work performed with speculative intent.[20] By the late 1920s, he had effectively withdrawn it from the stage. In his 1929 conversation with Loving, he described Reigen as among the least important of his efforts—a judgment that was clearly a defensive understatement, but one that reflected his exhaustion with the decades of scandal that had attached themselves to the work.[21]

The formal innovation of Reigen extended Anatol's episodic structure into something more systematic and explicitly circular. It was more politically direct than Liebelei, whose social critique operated through tragic narrative rather than systematic exposition. In writing it, Schnitzler was working at the outer edge of what the dramatic form could do: using the conventions of theatrical dialogue not to represent a social world but to analyze it, not to tell a story but to demonstrate a mechanism. When the Count and the Prostitute concluded the final scene, completing the circle and returning the chain to its point of origin, the work achieved a formal closure that was also a kind of philosophical openness. The circle closed, but the dance continued: desire would go on, the chain would extend itself indefinitely, new figures would rotate into and out of the positions the ten figures of this particular cycle had occupied. Nothing was resolved; no character had achieved genuine connection; no social mechanism had been reformed or even named. What had changed was the audience's awareness—their ability, having watched the circle complete itself, to see the mechanism for what it was.

But in 1897, those consequences were unforeseeable. Reigen existed only as a manuscript and a private conviction. Schnitzler had written something that said what could not be said about the way Viennese society organized its erotic life, and the fact that it could not be said publicly was itself part of the diagnosis. The work was a structural perspective, a view from outside the circle that allowed the circle to be seen as a circle. The individual scenes, taken alone, might yield only irony or pathos. Assembled in their circular sequence, they yielded analysis. The form was the argument.

He had also written, whether he fully understood this in 1897 or came to understand it only through the decades of scandal that followed, a work that made a social mechanism visible to the people it operated on—and a work that was, potentially, empowering precisely because of that visibility. This was why the censors would ban it, why the riots would follow, why the antisemitic demonstrations would target him personally, why he would eventually withdraw the work himself in disgust. But in 1897, those consequences were unforeseeable. The play would wait. Its author, in the meantime, had more immediate concerns: a dead child, a grieving lover, and a literary career that was accelerating toward a reckoning with the very institutions whose hypocrisies he had just anatomized.

CHAPTER TEN

Innovation (1896–1900)

LEUTNANT GUSTL

ON CHRISTMAS DAY, 1900, the *Neue Freie Presse* published a novella by Arthur Schnitzler that did something no work of German-language fiction had done before. *Leutnant Gustl* was written entirely in interior monologue—the unbroken stream of a single consciousness, rendered without narration, without external description, without any voice but the character's own.[1] Schnitzler had first sketched the idea during a mountain excursion near Puchberg on 27 May 1900, jotting the word "Lieutenantgesch" in his diary.[2] The story itself was composed with extraordinary speed that July at the Kurhaus in Reichenau: the diary records work on 17 July, and on the 19th, Schnitzler noted that he had completed it that afternoon, "in der Empfindung, dass es ein Meisterwerk"—with the feeling that it was a masterpiece. The speed of composition suggests that the technique had been gestating for years, waiting for the right subject. The story was based partly on a real incident involving a Herr Lasky, an acquaintance of Felix Salten, who had an altercation in the foyer of the Musikvereinssaal.[3]

Lieutenant Gustl was that subject: a young Viennese officer, vain and shallow, attending an oratorio concert he found boring—Schnitzler dated the fictional action to 4 April, corresponding to an actual performance of Mendelssohn's *Paulus* at the Wiener Musikverein on that date in 1900[4]—who is insulted by the baker Habetswallner at the coat-check and spends the night wandering the city, contemplating suicide, because the rigid code of military honor offers no other remedy for an affront he cannot avenge through a duel—the baker being too far beneath him in social rank to qualify as an opponent. The incident itself was trivial to the point of absurdity: in the jostle and confusion of the coat check, the baker pressed against him, grabbed Gustl's sword hilt, called him a "dummer Bub" (stupid boy), and briefly held the sword in a way Gustl could not prevent. The encounter was witnessed by, at most, a few bystanders. The baker did not pursue the confrontation; it ended as quickly as it began. By any rational calculation, the incident was nothing—an accidental collision, a rude exchange, the kind of minor social friction that occurred constantly in crowded public spaces.

By the calculation of the Austro-Hungarian military honor code, it was catastrophic. The code held that an officer's honor was his most essential possession—more essential than his physical safety, more essential than his relationships, more essential than his happiness or his life. An insult to an officer's honor must be addressed through the formal mechanisms the code provided, which for a challenge between social equals meant a duel, and which for a challenge from a social inferior meant—in the code's own terms—nothing, because a social inferior could not in principle insult an officer's honor. But this formal logic, which seemed to provide an escape from the crisis, was precisely what created it: the baker had grabbed Gustl's sword and called him a stupid boy, and Gustl was unable to prevent it or respond immediately. The code held that an officer who suffered a public humiliation without immediate appropriate response had, by that failure to respond, confirmed the humiliation. The possibility of a formal duel was unavailable because the baker was a civilian; the possibility of ignoring the insult was unavailable because Gustl was visibly helpless. By the code's own internal logic, there was only one available response: suicide before the humiliation became known.

The technical achievement was extraordinary. Schnitzler was not the absolute inventor of the interior monologue—he acknowledged Édouard Dujardin's *Les lauriers sont coupés* (1888) as a precursor, and Hermann Bahr had anticipated the technique theoretically in *Die Überwindung des Naturalismus* (1891)—but he was the first to use it in German-language fiction, and the first to deploy it with such sustained psychological precision.[5] His method predated James Joyce's *Ulysses* by more than two decades, and while his approach was more coherent than Joyce's—the sentences more ordered, the consciousness more accessible—the innovation was no less radical. He had found a way to render the inside of a mind on the page, complete with its evasions, its self-deceptions, its failure to achieve the self-knowledge that classical drama had always promised. But this was not simply a technical experiment in search of a subject. Schnitzler had invented a technique precisely fitted to what he needed to examine: what a rigid social code does to the psychology of a person who has thoroughly internalized it. The stream of consciousness was the only form adequate to his specific purpose, which was to show, from the inside and in real time, what the honor code did to the mind of a man who had absorbed it completely.

The dominant tradition of German-language narrative prose in 1900 was organized around the figure of an omniscient or semi-omniscient narrator who mediated between reader and represented world—who described, explained, contextualized, interpreted. Even when novelists represented characters' inner thoughts and feelings, they typically did so through a layer of narratorial framing: the character "thought that," "felt as if," "reflected that." The boundary between narrator's voice and character's inner voice was maintained, and the narrator's superior perspective was implicit in the structure of every sentence.

Schnitzler's innovation was the complete elimination of this narratorial layer. There was no narrator. There was no external description, no contextualizing frame, no interpretive perspective outside Gustl's own consciousness. The text began in the middle of Gustl's thoughts—he was at the concert, bored, noticing the people around him, thinking about music he didn't particularly understand or enjoy—and it ended with his thoughts, and in between there was only the continuous, associative, colloquial, neurotic flow of one man's consciousness across a single night. No quotation marks signaled the transition to direct speech; there were no "he thought" tags; there was no distinction between what Gustl observed and what he felt about what he observed, between his immediate perceptions and the memories, anxieties, and social calculations those perceptions triggered. The reader was placed inside Gustl's head without any means of exiting it, and the experience of reading was the experience of inhabiting a consciousness that had no outside.

What made the technique devastating rather than merely innovative was what it revealed about its subject. Gustl's thoughts moved by association rather than logical sequence: one thought triggered another through sonic or semantic resemblance, through the intrusion of anxiety into a moment of apparent calm, through the involuntary return of the central obsession beneath every apparently unrelated surface. His language was colloquial Viennese—the speech patterns of a young man of limited education and strong social formation, not the elevated diction of literary introspection. The repetitiveness was deliberate and precise: the same phrases, the same obsessive returns to the central crisis, the same formulaic self-reassurances that failed to reassure.

Gustl's stream of consciousness was not the stream of a rich inner life. It was the stream of a consciousness that was, in its fundamental architecture, remarkably impoverished—stocked primarily with social anxieties, professional calculations, sexual fantasies, and the rigid categories of the honor code. This was the innovation's deepest irony: the technique that would subsequently be used to render the richness of modern subjectivity—by Joyce, Woolf, Faulkner—was here deployed to reveal its subject's inner life as essentially empty. Gustl's monologue was a comedy of failed recognition: the character who could not see himself clearly, presented in a form that let the reader see everything.

The structural feature of Gustl's consciousness that emerged most forcefully from the sustained stream-of-consciousness narration was the degree to which it was organized entirely around the perceptions and judgments of others. Gustl did not think about himself in terms of his own desires, values, or experiences except insofar as those desires and experiences were already socially defined and socially ratified. He thought about himself primarily in terms of how he appeared—to his fellow officers, to his girlfriend Steffi, to his family, to the anonymous social world whose gaze he incessantly imagined. The question "What will they think?" was not one question among many in Gustl's consciousness; it was the fundamental organizing principle around which all other thoughts arranged themselves.

The people who populated Gustl's thoughts during his night of wandering were not encountered as full persons with their own inner lives and independent existences; they were encountered as audiences and judges whose verdicts on Gustl's situation constituted, collectively, the social reality that mattered to him. His girlfriend Steffi was imagined primarily in terms of whether she would mourn him adequately and what she would do after his death. His fellow officers were imagined in terms of what they would make of his absence from morning roll call. His family was imagined in terms of the shame his suicide would bring them, and—almost immediately—the ways in which they might manage that shame. The quality of engagement in each case was notable for its superficiality, its instrumentalism, its radical absence of genuine feeling. Gustl did not love Steffi, or if he did, love did not figure in his consciousness as a reason to live; she figured as a social accessory whose behavior after his death would reflect on him.

What was remarkable in the stream-of-consciousness narrative was not that Gustl contemplated suicide but that he contemplated it with so little of what an outside observer would call genuine existential anguish. He was frightened of death, certainly; he rehearsed the various scenarios of its approach with the anxious specificity of someone who had never genuinely confronted mortality. But he was not, at any point in the long night's wandering, engaged in a genuine contest between the will to live and the obligation to die. The obligation was simply there, as given and as irresistible as a mathematical axiom, and what Gustl's consciousness circled around was not whether to die but how—the logistics of suicide, the anticipated reactions of various people who mattered to him, the small social calculations of who would be informed and how. The absence of genuine existential depth in the face of the decision to die was the most devastating thing the stream of consciousness revealed.

Gustl's night walk through Vienna—from the concert hall, through the streets, to the Prater, and eventually to the café where he would learn of the baker's death—was experienced not as a place with its own reality but as a succession of surfaces that triggered associations in his consciousness. Streets, parks, cafés, the Danube Canal: each location was a prompt for a new associative chain, a new set of social calculations, a new return to the central anxiety. The novella covers approximately eight hours, from ten in the evening to six in the morning, with a brief sleep on a park bench in the Prater. The sustained intimacy of the interior monologue created a sense of temporal saturation that the text's brevity did not prepare for. As dawn approached, the associative chains became more fragmented, the returns to the central crisis more frequent, the small social calculations more desperate.

By morning, Gustl learned that the baker had died of a stroke during the night. The only witness capable of confirming what happened at the coat check was dead. No one else who was present remembered the incident with sufficient clarity to report it. Gustl's honor was, therefore, intact—not because it was never genuinely compromised, not because his conduct in the face of the baker's challenge was adequate, but because the one person who could destroy him had been conveniently removed from the situation by the arbitrary intervention of biological chance. He would not have to die.

The resolution was one of the great instances of narrative irony in German-language fiction. Gustl was relieved—genuinely, viscerally relieved—and his relief was entirely comprehensible and entirely human. He did not want to die. Whatever the honor code demanded, the biological organism that was Gustl wanted to continue existing, and the news of the baker's death produced a rush of released tension that was among the text's most vivid moments. But almost immediately, with a comic timing that was simultaneously funny and appalling, his consciousness moved on to planning a duel with a doctor who had offended him in some earlier minor social dispute. The existential crisis of the preceding night had changed nothing. He was already back in the ordinary social calculations of the honor code, already organizing his next act of ritualized aggression, already preparing to place someone else—possibly himself—at risk of death for a trivial matter of social precedence.

This ending was the most devastating piece of social analysis in the text. Gustl had been given, by the arbitrary gift of the baker's stroke, something his social formation had entirely prevented him from using: the opportunity to reconsider. A man who had spent a night contemplating his own death, reviewing his life, confronting the emptiness of the social performances that constituted his existence, might be expected to emerge from that confrontation with some altered perspective—some question about whether the code he had lived by was worth what it cost. Gustl emerged from it wanting to challenge someone to a duel. The stream-of-consciousness technique had made fully legible what was most horrifying: there was nothing in Gustl's consciousness to be altered, because the consciousness itself was nothing but the code's operation. There was no person beneath the performance of the officer. The circle was complete.

In the same year that Schnitzler completed *Leutnant Gustl*, Freud published *Die Traumdeutung*—the book appeared in November 1899, though it bore the imprint date 1900.[6] The parallel was not coincidental. Both men were Viennese, both were Jewish, both were interested in what lay beneath the surface of consciousness, and both arrived at their insights through methods that owed as much to intuition as to system. What Schnitzler achieved in the stream of consciousness was something very close to what the free association of the psychoanalytic session was designed to produce: an unmediated flow of associative thought in which the contents and movements of an individual consciousness became available for examination. The techniques were different—literary representation versus therapeutic practice—but the epistemological ambition was the same: to make the invisible interior available to scrutiny, to show the workings of a mind from the inside rather than inferring them from external behavior.

Freud would later acknowledge the kinship in a famous letter dated 14 May 1922, written for Schnitzler's sixtieth birthday. He confessed that he had avoided direct personal contact with Schnitzler despite their mutual admiration, explaining that he feared encountering his own Doppelgänger—a figure who had arrived, by the routes of literary and psychological intuition, at the same territory that Freud was mapping through clinical practice and theoretical construction. Schnitzler had learned through intuition, Freud wrote—"though actually as a result of sensitive introspection"—everything that Freud had had to unearth through laborious work on other persons.[7] The encounter with *Leutnant Gustl* made Freud's self-description of the relationship comprehensible: the novella was, in its formal method, a literary enactment of free association, and in its analytical result, a case study of a consciousness organized entirely by social convention.

Among all his works, Schnitzler named *Leutnant Gustl*, along with *Reigen* and *Professor Bernhardi*, as the socially critical works that had provoked the most opposition and were most dear to him—"besonders ans Herz gewachsen."[14] In a 1904 interview, he pushed back against the charge that he had attacked the entire army in *Freiwild* and *Lieutenant Gustl*, calling such claims either hypocrisy or a simple-minded misunderstanding of solidarity. The best members of any profession, he argued, were those who rose above its prejudices, not those who most perfectly embodied them.[12] In a letter to Theodor Sosnosky in May 1901, he defended the character of Gustl himself, describing him as fundamentally a decent young man confused by the prejudices of his class, who would in time become a capable and respectable officer. But he insisted on his right as a writer to invent any character he pleased—even one who habitually murdered his grand-cousins—without being accused of hostility toward any class.[17]

In a 1923 Swedish interview, Schnitzler recalled the affair with sardonic brevity. When *Leutnant Gustl* appeared, he said, he had clashed with the Austrian military; a kind of honor court had convened and concluded that the honor of the Austrian army had been violated by the work. "Aber was soll man tun? Schließlich ist man auf die Welt gekommen, um einen anderen zu beleidigen"—but what can one do? After all, one was born into this world to offend others. He then pressed his monocle into the corner of his eye and changed the subject.[13] Years later, during the *Reigen* scandal of 1921, he drew the parallel explicitly: "Erinnern Sie sich nur an den 'Leutnant Gustl' und den 'Professor Bernhardi.' Nach einigen Jahren bleibt von all dem Lärm nichts weiter übrig als die Bücher, die ich geschrieben, und eine dunkle Erinnerung an die Blamage meiner Gegner"—after a few years, nothing remains of all the noise but the books he had written, and a dim memory of the embarrassment of his opponents.[15]

The military did not appreciate the novella. On 28 December 1900, only three days after publication, the conservative military newspaper *Reichswehr* published a fierce attack, written by the officer Gustav David.[8] The expectation in certain quarters was that Schnitzler, as a reserve officer, would defend his honor by challenging the attacker to a duel. He refused. The refusal was deliberate—the entire point of *Leutnant Gustl* was the mindlessness of the dueling code—but it gave the authorities the pretext they needed.

An *ehrenrätliches Verfahren*—a military honor-court proceeding—was initiated in January 1901.[10] Schnitzler, advised by the jurist Max Burckhard, a former director of the Burgtheater, adopted the strategy of not appearing before the tribunal, declining to engage with a proceeding whose premises he rejected.[9] The non-public trial concluded on 26 April 1901. The formal charge cited the novella's alleged violation of the army's honor, and part of the basis for the verdict was Schnitzler's failure to take any steps against the personal attacks in the *Reichswehr* article—as though the code demanded that a writer challenge his critic to a duel.[11] On 14 June 1901, the formal announcement was made: Schnitzler was stripped of his reserve officer's commission as Oberarzt der Reserve (medical officer) and demoted to the rank of Sanitätssoldat—medical private. The title was never restored.

The military's response confirmed the accuracy of the text's analysis. If the honor code was not a sensitive and absurd institution whose authority rested on nothing more substantial than social convention and the threat of violence, there would have been no reason to punish a writer who said as much. The military had found Schnitzler guilty of having violated the honor of the army—he had not actually violated anyone's honor; he had written a story that made the concept of honor look ridiculous, which within the code's own framework was precisely equivalent to a violation, because the code's authority depended on not being looked at directly. By stripping Schnitzler of his commission, the military placed him definitively outside the institution whose culture he had examined—precisely the position from which the most clear-eyed examination of that culture was possible.

The editor of the *Neue Freie Presse*, Moriz Benedikt, published a leading article on 21 June 1901 defending Schnitzler on grounds of artistic freedom—a defense that, however well-intentioned, only sharpened the antisemitic dimension of the affair, since both Schnitzler and Benedikt were Jewish.[22]

The affair—the "Gustl-Affäre," as it became known—was shot through with antisemitism. As a Jew, Schnitzler found little support among either conservative or liberal commentators, and the novella was widely perceived as a thinly veiled Jewish attack on the military establishment. Schnitzler was a Jewish reserve officer in an army whose upper echelons were increasingly hostile to Jewish participation in military life. The antisemitic press—which had already attacked *Reigen* and would continue to attack Schnitzler throughout his career—framed the charges against him in specifically antisemitic terms: a Jewish writer had used his literary talents to undermine the institution of the Austrian military, confirming the conventional antisemitic narrative about Jewish disloyalty and cultural subversion. The *Deutsche Zeitung* of 22 June 1901 declared bluntly that what "der Jude Schnitzler" attributed to Lieutenant Gustl was not how any officer thinks, speaks, or acts.[18] The punishment served two institutional functions simultaneously: it disciplined a specific individual who had embarrassed the military, and it demonstrated, to the satisfaction of the antisemitic political culture, that Jewish cultural production was properly understood as a threat to Austrian values rather than a contribution to Austrian literature.

The antisemitic reading was not confined to Schnitzler's enemies. An English-language interviewer in the Müller collection described *Lieutenant Gustl* as being "full of" the Jewish question—a characterization that the editor's note gently corrects, observing that while the title character does express antisemitic views, the claim that the novella is primarily about antisemitism reveals the interviewer's unfamiliarity with the text rather than a feature of the text itself.[16] The distinction is important: Gustl's antisemitism is one feature among many in a consciousness organized entirely by received prejudices. The novella examines the honor code's colonization of the mind, and antisemitism is part of the furniture of that colonized mind—present, unreflected, symptomatic—rather than the novella's central subject.

The charge was absurd on its face—the story was a critique of a code of honor, not of an ethnic group—but in the Vienna of Karl Lueger, who had been mayor since 1897 on a platform of populist antisemitism, the distinction scarcely mattered.[19] This was not the first time Schnitzler's Jewishness had been weaponized against his work, and it would not be the last. The punishment carried a message that went beyond the literary: there were limits to what a Jewish writer could say about Austrian institutions, and those limits would be enforced.

Schnitzler had written a masterpiece and been punished for it. The significance of what he had achieved extended far beyond the immediate scandal. He had not invented the stream-of-consciousness technique and then looked for a subject to apply it to. He had invented the technique because his subject demanded it. The question he was asking—what does a rigid social code do to the psychology of a person who has thoroughly internalized it?—could not be answered by any narrative form that maintained an external, omniscient perspective on its subject. It required a form that could show the inside of the colonized consciousness, could render the texture and movement of a mind that had no resources outside the social categories it had been given.

The honor code that organized Gustl's consciousness was not presented as an obviously absurd or evil institution. It was presented as a fully coherent social system with its own internal logic, its own hierarchy of values, its own mechanisms for maintaining and enforcing compliance. The code was, in structural terms, a total social institution—one that defined the terms of existence so comprehensively for its adherents that life outside its framework was not merely difficult but unimaginable. Gustl did not think about whether to follow the code because the code was not experienced by him as an external set of rules but as the basic structure of reality. Its demands were not felt as impositions but as necessities—like the laws of physics, they were simply the conditions under which existence proceeded. This was why the stream-of-consciousness technique was not merely appropriate but necessary for the text's purposes: only from inside Gustl's consciousness, without any external narrative perspective that might provide critical distance, could the reader experience the code as Gustl experienced it—as simply the way things are, not as one possible arrangement among others.

That the text cost Schnitzler his military commission was, in retrospect, a measure of its accuracy. Social institutions do not punish literary works for being inaccurate; they punish them for being accurate in ways that are inconvenient. The Austro-Hungarian military found *Leutnant Gustl* inconvenient because it showed, from the inside, what the honor code actually did to the minds of the officers who maintained it—showed not heroism and martial virtue but anxiety, narcissism, social calculation, and a nearly complete absence of any inner life not already constituted by the code's categories. This was not a flattering portrait, and the military's response confirmed it was a recognizable one.

Not all of Schnitzler's contemporaries recognized the achievement. Writing decades later, the Hebrew literary figure Reuben Brainin dismissed the early works—*Anatol, Liebelei, Sterben, Leutnant Gustl*—as "a light sort of writing, in form and in content," the work of an elegant senti mentalist.[21] The judgment missed entirely what the interior monologue had made possible: a form of social analysis that no amount of elegant sentimentalism could have produced.

The technical innovation that Schnitzler deployed to make his analysis possible would become, in the hands of Joyce, Woolf, and Faulkner, the dominant form through which the twentieth century attempted to understand the experience of being a self in a social world. That Schnitzler arrived there first—and arrived there not through abstract formal experimentation but through the specific demands of a specific social critique—was one of the more quietly remarkable facts in the history of modern literature. The text survived the punishment. The institution it analyzed did not survive the century.

CHAPTER ELEVEN

A Younger Woman (1899–1902)

IN THE SPRING OF 1899, weeks after Marie Reinhard's death, Schnitzler met Olga Gussmann.[1] She was seventeen. He was thirty-seven, still grieving, and embarking on a relationship that would follow, with depressing fidelity, the pattern of every relationship that had preceded it: attraction, intimacy, pregnancy, evasion, and—eventually, reluctantly, under pressure—commitment.

The age gap was not merely a number but a chasm of experience. Schnitzler was an established writer, a man who had buried lovers and published plays at the Burgtheater. His novella *Leutnant Gustl* had not yet cost him his military commission—that would come in June 1901—but he had already accumulated enough romantic entanglements to stock a small library of psychological case studies.[2] Olga was a teenager at the beginning of her adult life, talented and ambitious but not yet formed, not yet aware of what it would cost to love a man whose capacity for self-examination exceeded his capacity for change. That Schnitzler, of all people, could not see the asymmetry for what it was—or could see it and proceed anyway—suggests the limits of psychological insight when applied to one's own behavior. He had written *Anatol*. He had written *Liebelei*. He had anatomized, with devastating precision, the mechanisms by which men of his class and temperament constructed romantic relationships that served their needs at the expense of women's hopes. And then he did exactly what his characters did, with the same rationalizations and the same outcome.

Olga was not a *süßes Mädel*. She came from a Jewish middle-class family—respectable, educated, culturally engaged. Her father, Wilhelm Gussmann, was a businessman; her mother had artistic inclinations and supported Olga's theatrical ambitions.[3] She was training as an actress and singer, studying at the Vienna Conservatory, and she had ambitions of her own that did not reduce to the desire for a husband.[4] She wanted a career. She wanted recognition as an artist in her own right. She was not entering the relationship as a starstruck girl grateful for the great man's attention; she was entering it as someone who believed she had her own claim to artistic seriousness and who expected that claim to be respected.

The twenty-year age difference was conspicuous but not, by the standards of the era, scandalous. Older men routinely married much younger women, and the social world that Schnitzler moved in would have found nothing particularly unusual about the pairing. What was less conventional was Olga's insistence on maintaining a career identity separate from Schnitzler's. She was not content to be the great man's wife, the domestic support system for a literary career, the woman who managed the household and raised the children while he wrote. She wanted to be Olga Gussmann, performer. She wanted to sing, to act, to appear on stages under her own name. This combination of youth, ambition, and independence attracted Schnitzler, who had spent years in the company of women who were either socially beneath him—and therefore could not make demands he had to take seriously—or emotionally unattainable, like Adele Sandrock, whose tempestuousness had made sustained partnership impossible. Olga was neither. She was available, she was his intellectual and social equal in aspiration if not yet in achievement, and she was difficult in ways that interested him.

The relationship developed quickly. By early 1901, less than two years after they met, Olga was pregnant. The pregnancy was terminated. The circumstances are not fully documented—whether Olga sought the abortion herself, whether Schnitzler pressured her toward it, whether they arrived at the decision jointly, the diary does not definitively say.[5] What is documented is that Schnitzler was, once again, evasive about marriage. The pattern was so established by now that it had the quality of compulsion, a psychological script he could not deviate from even when he could see exactly what he was doing. He wanted women, he wanted intimacy, he wanted the domestic comforts of a sustained relationship and the regular sexual access that came with it, but he could not bring himself to formalize what he felt. Marriage, for Schnitzler, was a concession rather than a fulfillment—a surrender of the independence he prized, a closing of possibilities he preferred to keep open, a commitment that felt like a trap even when made to someone he genuinely cared for.

That this independence came at a cost to the women who loved him was a fact he was capable of recognizing in his fiction and incapable of acting on in his life. He could write Christine Weiring's tragedy in *Liebelei* with exquisite empathy; he could anatomize the mechanisms by which men like Fritz Lobheimer constructed relationships that served their convenience while destroying the women involved; he could see, with clinical precision, how the social arrangements of his world distributed suffering asymmetrically along lines of gender and class. And then he could enact those same arrangements in his own life, with the same evasions and the same consequences, as if the insight conferred no obligation to behave differently. This was not hypocrisy in the simple sense—hypocrisy implies a gap between professed values and actual behavior. This was something more troubling: a form of self-knowledge so thorough that it exhausted the will to change.

In early 1902, Olga was pregnant again. She had just turned twenty.[6] She wanted marriage—not as an abstract preference but as a practical necessity.

She was pregnant, unmarried, and a woman whose career prospects depended on maintaining a respectable public image. An illegitimate child would be a scandal that could destroy her professional ambitions before they had properly begun. Schnitzler's response was to search for a small house outside Vienna where Olga could give birth away from the public eye—a gesture that combined practical concern with a furtiveness that spoke for itself.[7] He was solving the immediate problem—where and how the child would be born—while evading the larger question of legitimacy, marriage, and public acknowledgment of his relationship and impending fatherhood.

On August 9, 1902, in Hinterbrühl, a small village outside Vienna, their son Heinrich was born. He was born out of wedlock. Schnitzler was present for the birth, a fact that was itself somewhat unusual for fathers of that era, and he recorded the event in his diary with a terseness that has become one of the most quoted passages in the entire span of his journals. The entry for that day notes simply that the boy arrived at four in the afternoon, and that by five Schnitzler had begun work on a new piece of writing.[8]

The entry has been read, by critics and biographers, as evidence of monstrous detachment—the writer who cannot stop working even at the birth of his child, who experiences the moment of becoming a father and immediately returns to his desk as if nothing consequential had occurred. It has also been read as evidence of a mind so thoroughly shaped by its vocation that the boundary between living and writing had effectively dissolved, that every experience, even the most intimate and supposedly transformative, was for him simultaneously lived and converted into material for observation and eventual literary use. Both readings are probably correct, and neither quite captures the full complexity of what the diary entry reveals.

Schnitzler was not a cold man. The diary shows, across thousands of pages, a capacity for feeling that was deep even if it was compartmentalized.

He grieved Marie Reinhard's death. He felt genuine tenderness for the women he was involved with. He would, in the years to come, prove to be a devoted if complicated father to Heinrich. But he was a man for whom observation was a form of existence, for whom every experience, including the most intimate, was simultaneously lived and noted, felt and documented, inhabited and analyzed. The cost of the gift was the gift itself: he could not fully inhabit a moment because he was always, at some level, recording it. The birth of his son was not exempt from this pattern. Even as he witnessed it, even as he felt whatever complex mixture of emotions the moment produced, he was also watching himself feel those emotions, noting them for future reference, and when the immediate crisis had passed—when the child was born and Olga was recovering—he returned to the activity that had always been his primary relationship to the world: writing.

The work depended on the same quality of character that made him an impossible partner: the inability to surrender completely to any experience without maintaining an observational distance from it. He was, in this sense, always alone—not because he lacked relationships but because even within those relationships he remained the observer, the analyst, the diagnostician of his own emotional states and those of the people around him.

The question of marriage, which Schnitzler had evaded for years, was finally resolved in August 1903. A false report in the *Neues Wiener Journal* in April 1903 claimed the couple had already wed, prompting Schnitzler to tell Hermann Bahr it was "untrue, at least very considerably premature."[9] The actual wedding took place on August 26, 1903—a few weeks after Heinrich's first birthday.[10] That the marriage came only after the child had survived infancy is telling; as the Müller edition notes, what proved decisive was not Olga's wishes but the fact that this pregnancy, unlike earlier ones, had resulted in a living child.[11] The family moved into a new apartment at Spöttelgasse 7 (renamed Edmund-Weiß-Gasse after 1918), and with the birth of a daughter, Lili, in September 1909, they eventually purchased a villa at Sternwartestraße 71.[12]

Olga's artistic ambitions did not subside with marriage. She had given up the idea of an acting career but pursued singing with increasing determination, giving her first public concert in February 1911. The successes she hoped for never materialized.[13] Her partnership with the composer and pianist Wilhelm Grosz became one of the central conflicts preceding the divorce, which was finalized on June 26, 1921.[14] The marriage had lasted eighteen years. The artistic ambitions that had originally attracted Schnitzler to Olga became, in the end, one of the forces that drove them apart.

Heinrich Schnitzler would grow up in a household marked by literary celebrity, domestic tension, and the complex dynamics of parents who were temperamentally mismatched. He studied philosophy, art history, and literary history at the University of Vienna and took acting lessons from Franz Herterich.[15] He debuted on stage in 1921 at the Raimundtheater, then worked in Berlin from the early 1920s through 1932, before returning to the Deutsches Volkstheater in Vienna as both actor and director.[16] He would live through the collapse of the Austria his father had anatomized, would witness the rise of the very antisemitism that had shadowed Schnitzler's career, and would flee Austria in 1938 when the Anschluss made remaining impossible. He would emigrate to the United States, where he taught theater, directing, and theater history at the University of California in Berkeley and in Seattle, eventually becoming a professor.[17]

In the late 1950s, Heinrich returned to Vienna and became affiliated with the Theater in der Josefstadt, serving as its deputy director from 1959.[18] Under prodding from the actress Vilma Thimig-Degischer, he began regularly staging his father's plays, and these productions—featuring performers such as Degischer, Leopold Rudolf, and Michael Heltau—became genuine theatrical successes that reignited interest in Schnitzler on

German-speaking stages.[19] As sole heir, Heinrich also managed his father's literary estate: he oversaw the four-volume collected works published by S. Fischer in 1961–1962, and co-edited important volumes of correspondence and the fragment of autobiography that was given the title *Jugend in Wien*.[20]

On January 1, 1982, Heinrich allowed a circle to close that his father had been forced to leave open. Arthur Schnitzler had imposed a performance ban on *Reigen* in 1922, after the Berlin scandal and the antisemitic riots that accompanied the play's first productions in 1920–1921.[21] Heinrich had maintained the ban after his father's death. Now, by letting it lapse, he released the play for performance on German-speaking stages, ending six decades of enforced silence.[22] The gesture was both practical—copyright law allowed it—and symbolic. The son completed what the father could not: he gave *Reigen* back to the public, freeing it from the censorship and scandal that had pursued it since its earliest performances. That it took two generations and the near-total destruction of European Jewry to achieve this completion is a measure of how deeply the forces that had opposed Schnitzler's work were embedded in the culture he inhabited.

Heinrich Schnitzler died on July 12, 1982, in Vienna, six months after *Reigen* returned to the stage.[23] He was buried in his father's honorary grave. The play survived. So did the son, long enough to see his father's work reclaimed. Both were legacies, and both carried the weight of everything that had been lost in the interval.

Part III: The Domestic Years (1903–1921)

Chapter Twelve

Early Marriage (1903–1909)

Der einsame Weg, Zwischenspiel, Der Ruf des Lebens

Just over a year after Heinrich's birth, on August 26, 1903, Arthur Schnitzler and Olga Gussmann were married in the synagogue on Schopenhauerstraße in the eighteenth district of Vienna.[1] Richard Beer-Hofmann and Gustav Schwarzkopf stood as witnesses.[2] Heinrich, their son, was one year old. The groom was forty-one; the bride was twenty-one. The twenty-year difference in their ages was conspicuous even by the tolerant standards of Viennese bourgeois society, and the fact that the child had preceded the ceremony by a full year was conspicuous by any standard at all.

The timing was not accidental. As Karl Müller has observed, what appears to have been decisive for the marriage was that the child—unlike earlier pregnancies by Schnitzler's partners—survived.[3] Schnitzler had waited until Heinrich celebrated his first birthday before committing to the ceremony, as though the child's survival were a precondition rather than an occasion. He had resisted until resistance was no longer sustainable, and then he had conceded, but the concession came grudgingly, as if the decision had been extracted from him rather than made by him. Olga had, in the end, gotten what she wanted: legitimacy for her child, social respectability, the legal status of wife. But she had gotten it through persistence and pressure rather than through Schnitzler's willing embrace of marriage as a desired state. The terms on which the marriage began—reluctance on one side, determination on the other—would shape its entire trajectory.

The Viennese press had, characteristically, gotten the story wrong before the story happened. In early April 1903, the Neues Wiener Journal reported that Schnitzler had already quietly married a young woman who had recently left the conservatory.[4] Schnitzler's friend Ludwig Basch visited him and published a denial. The diary entry for April 3, 1903, records the incident with characteristic dryness, noting the newspaper report and the denial. The following day's entry adds a telling detail: Olga was upset.[5] Schnitzler's letter to Hermann Bahr on April 6 acknowledged the report was untrue—or, as he put it with careful precision, "at the very least considerably premature."[6]

The marriage certificate made Heinrich legitimate, retroactively correcting the circumstances of his birth. This was important not merely for social respectability but for practical questions of inheritance and legal status. But the legitimation was also, in a sense, a formality that could not undo the year of illegitimacy, could not erase the fact that Schnitzler had needed to be compelled toward marriage rather than moving toward it freely. Olga knew this. She was young but not naive, and she understood that she had won a battle that had required winning—which meant she had not, in the deeper sense, won at all.

The family settled into a newly built apartment at Spöttelgasse 7, in the same eighteenth district, Währing, where the synagogue stood.[7] The apartment was adequate for a couple and would become too small for a family, but for the early years it served. Schnitzler's literary career was accelerating: the Bauernfeld Prize, awarded on March 16 by the Bauernfeld-Stiftung for his one-act cycle Lebendige Stunden, had come with a purse of 2,000 Kronen, and the award provoked a characteristically Viennese scandal when antisemitic members of parliament filed a formal interpellation protesting the prize's bestowal on a Jewish writer.[8] Anatol and Liebelei were in regular performance across German-speaking theaters, and S. Fischer was publishing his work to a growing readership.

The plays kept coming—Der einsame Weg (The Lonely Way), which premiered at the Deutsches Theater in Berlin on February 13, 1904, Zwischenspiel (Intermezzo) in 1905, Der Ruf des Lebens (The Call of Life) in 1906—and with them came a financial stability that allowed the young family to live, if not lavishly, then comfortably enough that Schnitzler's decision to abandon medicine no longer looked like a gamble.[9] The titles were suggestive of a shift in preoccupation: The Lonely Way, Intermezzo. Schnitzler was writing, as he always wrote, from the material of his own experience, and the material was changing. He was no longer the young man cataloguing his seductions in Anatol; he was a middle-aged husband charting the distance between what marriage promised and what it delivered. Der einsame Weg, which Schnitzler had worked through multiple drafts under revealing earlier titles—Der Junggeselle, Egoisten, Einsame Wege—explored precisely this territory: the consequences of evading emotional commitment, the solitude that follows from choosing freedom over responsibility.[10]

Olga, for her part, had not married in order to be comfortable. She was intelligent, cultured, and trained as an actress and singer, and she had married a famous writer not as a retirement from ambition but as what she imagined would be a partnership between two artistic temperaments. The reality was different. Schnitzler's work demanded solitude and routine; domestic life, with its interruptions and obligations, was the medium in which his writing occurred but also the thing from which his writing required protection. He needed a household; he also needed to be left alone in it.

Olga, twenty years younger, energetic, and unwilling to reduce herself to the role of the great man's wife, found the arrangement confining almost from the start. She would pursue a singing career from within the marriage—her first public concert would not come until February 1911—and the success she had hoped for would elude her for the rest of her life.[11] The frustration this generated was slow, cumulative, and corrosive, and it would prove, in the end, more destructive to the marriage than any single betrayal.

On September 13, 1909, Olga gave birth to a daughter, Lili.[12] Schnitzler was forty-seven. Around the same time, he engaged Frieda Pollak as his secretary, a position she would hold for the rest of his life; the diary first mentions her in connection with this role on September 23, 1909.[13] The young Lili, in one of those childhood distortions of language that become permanent, would later twist Pollak's surname into "Kolap," and it was under this name that the family and Schnitzler's wider circle knew her for decades.[14] The juxtaposition was characteristic: the birth of a child and the hiring of a literary assistant, the domestic and the professional, side by side, each essential, each demanding its own kind of attention.

Lili's birth also made the apartment on Spöttelgasse too small for the growing household. After some searching, the Schnitzlers purchased a villa at Sternwartestraße 71, roughly four hundred meters away.[15] The house, which already contained a Bauernstube from the previous owners, was furnished in what Müller describes as an "old Viennese style"—a notable choice for a writer whose literary circle was otherwise drawn to modernist architecture. Beer-Hofmann and Bahr had commissioned modern villas; Hofmannsthal rented the centuries-old Fuchs-Schlössl in Rodaun. Schnitzler's purchase placed him outside both camps, neither ostentatiously modern nor self-consciously historical.[16]

The family was now complete—Arthur, Olga, Heinrich at seven, Lili newborn—and the shape of Schnitzler's daily existence was fixed. He would write in the mornings, dictate to Frieda Pollak in the afternoons, attend the theater in the evenings, and return to a household in which his wife's ambitions were quietly, steadily, failing to find their outlet. Lili would become, in the years ahead, the center of her father's emotional life in a way that neither his wife nor his son ever quite managed to be. The bond between them was immediate and deep, and it carried, though no one could have known it then, the weight of everything that was to come.

The marriage would last eighteen years, slowly disintegrating under the weight of temperamental incompatibility, professional rivalry, mutual resentment, and the basic structural problem that Schnitzler had married someone he had never genuinely wanted to marry.[17] Both partners would accumulate grievances with foundation in reality. Neither would be sufficient to make the marriage work. But in 1903, at the moment of marriage, and in 1909, with the birth of Lili, the future's disappointments were not yet fully visible. What was visible was that Schnitzler had entered into precisely the domestic arrangement that his entire emotional history suggested he was constitutionally unsuited for. Whether this represented growth, capitulation, or simply the exhaustion of alternatives was a question that would be answered only in the decades to come.

CHAPTER THIRTEEN

The Road into the Open

DER WEG INS FREIE

THE MOST AMBITIOUS WORK of these early married years was Der Weg ins Freie—The Road into the Open—begun as early as 1902 and published in 1908 by S. Fischer Verlag, after first appearing as a serial in the Neue Rundschau from January through June of that year.[1] It was Schnitzler's first major novel, running to nearly five hundred pages in its first edition, and it was unlike anything else he had written: more panoramic than his dramatic works, less tightly focused on a single consciousness or a single crisis, more explicitly engaged with the social and political landscape of Vienna at the turn of the century than any other work in his oeuvre. It was also, by common critical assessment, the most Jewish of his works—the work in which the question of what it meant to be Jewish in Austria in 1900 received its most comprehensive and most direct examination. In an interview at the time of its publication, Schnitzler described his intention as an attempt to depict the relationships between various Viennese social strata and groups.[2]

On its surface, the novel told the story of Baron Georg von Wergenthin, a young Christian aristocratic composer of talent and charm but weak professional discipline, who conducted an affair with Anna Rosner, a

Catholic girl from the lower middle class. Georg drifted through Vienna's intellectual and social life with the ease of someone who had never had to fight for the right to drift. He was talented enough to be taken seriously as a composer, but too comfortable, too easily satisfied, too fundamentally undriven to develop the discipline that serious artistic achievement required. His relationship with Anna was conducted with the same amiable inadequacy as his artistic career: he intended to commit, he delayed, he drifted, and when the crisis came—Anna's pregnancy, the stillbirth of their child, the deterioration of the relationship—he was found to be, as he had always been, insufficiently present.[3] He returned to Vienna alone at the novel's end, still drifting, the road into the open still elusive.

The autobiographical dimension was unmistakable. Georg's evasiveness with Anna—his inability to commit, his habit of deferring decisions until circumstances made them for him—reproduced exactly the pattern Schnitzler had enacted with Jeanette Heeger, with Marie Reinhard, with Olga Gussmann. Even the motif of a lost child drew on painful personal experience.[4] That he could see the pattern clearly enough to write it, and still enact it in his own life, suggested the limits of self-knowledge as an agent of change. Years later, Schnitzler himself would identify with the character of Heinrich Bermann, acknowledging in conversation that his relationship to the novel's cast was intimate: he was Bermann, and the figure of Leo Golowski was drawn from a Russian Zionist friend he had loved deeply.[5]

But the novel's reputation rested not on this love story but on the world that surrounded it. Georg moved among the assimilationist, artistically sensitive Jewish bourgeoisie of Vienna, and their conversations—about identity, belonging, the proper response to rising antisemitism—constituted the novel's true subject. The central formal decision was audacious: the novel that explored the Jewish Question in its fullest form was organized around the consciousness of a young Christian aristocrat who was not Jewish and whose relationship to the Jewish Question was that of the comfortable outsider—sympathetic, curious, but fundamentally untouched. Georg's comfortable incomprehension—his ability to move through the Jewish Question as through a weather system that affected others without touching him—was itself a social fact of the first importance. It was the social fact that the novel's Jewish characters had to navigate in every interaction with the Christian world: the fact that their defining existential crisis was, for the Georgs of their social world, simply an interesting topic of conversation.

The intellectual achievement that gave the novel its historical significance was the systematic exposition of the full range of positions available to Austrian Jews of the period in response to the Jewish Question. Schnitzler deployed his large cast of Jewish characters not as representatives of simple types but as embodiments of genuinely held and internally coherent positions, each of which had its own logic, its own appeal, its own costs, and its own ultimate inadequacy to the situation it was attempting to address.

Heinrich Bermann, the writer, embodied the assimilationist position in its most intellectually sophisticated form. He wanted to be understood as a writer who happened to be Jewish—not a Jewish writer, not a representative of a community, not a figure whose ethnic identity was the primary lens through which his work should be read. He had internalized the Enlightenment's promise: that universal human values transcended particular identities, that the quality of an individual's mind and work was the only relevant measure of contribution to culture. His position was not naive; he understood that antisemitism was real and powerful, that the assimilationist project met resistance at every turn. But he persisted because the alternative—accepting the tribal definition of identity that both antisemites and Jewish nationalists imposed—seemed to him a capitulation to the logic he was contesting. The cost of his position was a permanent form of social insecurity: the awareness that his status as a writer rather than a Jewish writer was always provisional, always vulnerable to the withdrawal of the social tolerance on which it depended.

Leo Golowski, the young mathematician and pianist, offered the most direct counter to Bermann's assimilationism: the Zionist position, arguing that only a Jewish homeland could solve the Jewish Question, because only in a Jewish state could Jews live as a majority rather than a tolerated or intolerated minority, free from the structural vulnerability that minority status inevitably produced.[6] His position had a clarity and a historical logic that Bermann's lacked: rather than contesting the terms on which Jewish identity was defined by the surrounding society, Leo accepted the definition and drew from it the conclusion that Jews must have their own political community. This was Theodor Herzl's vision, articulated with increasing urgency in the years leading up to his death in 1904. The novel gave Leo's Zionism a personal cost as well as a political one: arrested and imprisoned for assaulting the officer who had tormented him during his year of military service, he was ultimately pardoned by imperial grace—a resolution that was itself an illustration of the precariousness of Jewish existence under a regime whose benevolence was always discretionary.[7]

Therese Golowski—Leo's sister, a socialist activist—represented the position that the Jewish Question was ultimately a class question: that the antisemitism directed at Jews was a symptom of broader structures of economic exploitation and social hierarchy that the socialist movement was organized to overcome, and that the solution was not specifically Jewish or individually assimilationist but collectivist and class-based. Her figure was drawn in part from a real woman—Lotte Glas, who appeared in Schnitzler's diary and from whom he borrowed traits for the character.[8] Therese's position had its own compelling logic—the overlap between antisemitic rhetoric and anti-capitalist scapegoating was a real feature of the period—but it required the prior solution of a different, equally large problem, and it asked Jewish people to subordinate their specific vulnerability to a broader political project whose success was uncertain and whose relationship to the specifically Jewish experience of persecution was indirect.

Oskar Ehrenberg represented a different kind of attempted escape: the social assimilation of a wealthy Jewish industrialist's son into aristocratic circles, through the cultivation of connections with the Christian elite. The novel's treatment of Oskar's trajectory was among its most devastating: his efforts at social climbing—befriending a prince, adopting the manners and attitudes of the gentile aristocracy—placed him in an untenable position between the Jewish community he was leaving and the Christian world that would never fully accept him. His attempted suicide near the novel's end was a pointed demonstration that the Jewish Question could not be solved through individual social reidentification, because the social definition of Jewish identity that produced antisemitism was not primarily theological but ethnic and cultural, and it did not yield to social aspiration.[9]

Around these central figures, the novel assembled a broader ensemble: the proud and blunt-spoken patriarch Salomon Ehrenberg, a millionaire munitions manufacturer who traveled to Palestine and represented the dignity of unapologetic Jewish identity; the cautious, resigned Dr. Stauber senior and his politically engaged son Berthold; the self-consciously isolated intellectual Edmund Nürnberger; the non-Jewish cavalry officer Demeter Stanzides, whose easy social confidence served as a mirror for the precariousness that the novel's Jewish characters could never escape.[10] The characters represented a spectrum of positions available to Austrian Jews in the years before the catastrophe: assimilation into Viennese culture, social climbing through conversion and aristocratic connection, Zionism as Herzl had articulated it, socialism as a class-based solution, and the stance Schnitzler himself favored, which scholars have described as an "enlightened apolitical individualism"—a refusal to join movements or adopt programs, combined with a stubborn insistence on the dignity of the individual conscience.[11] It was a position that required intelligence, integrity, and a certain blindness to the fact that the forces gathering against Jewish life in Austria would not be deterred by the scruples of individuals, however enlightened.

The title—Der Weg ins Freie, the road into the open, the path to freedom—was among the most ironic in Schnitzler's work. Every character in the novel was seeking some version of the road into the open: Georg through artistic fulfillment and romantic happiness; Heinrich Bermann through assimilation and literary achievement; Leo Golowski through Zionism; Therese through socialism; Oskar Ehrenberg through social reinvention. Anna Rosner sought it through the love of a man who could not give it to her. Each road was pursued with genuine conviction and genuine effort; each closed. The title named what everyone wanted and no one found.

For Georg, freedom meant the open space of artistic achievement unencumbered by domestic and professional obligation—a kind of perpetual potentiality that never had to commit to the limitations of actual accomplishment. His version of the road into the open was, from the beginning, a fantasy of infinite possibility rather than a genuine goal, and his inability to find it was less a social tragedy than a psychological one: he was not prevented from achieving his artistic ambitions by antisemitism or class prejudice; he was prevented by his own constitutive unwillingness to submit to the discipline that achievement required. His road closed from the inside.

For the novel's Jewish characters, the road closed from the outside. Heinrich Bermann's assimilationist freedom—the freedom to be judged as an individual rather than as a representative of a community—was perpetually denied by a social world that insisted on reading him as a Jew first and a writer second. Leo Golowski's road into the open required the creation of a political entity that did not yet exist. Therese's road required the prior transformation of an economic and social order that was not on the verge of transformation. Oskar Ehrenberg's road had been closed by both sides simultaneously. The contrast between Georg's internally produced failure and the externally produced failures of the Jewish characters was the novel's most important structural observation: what looked, from the outside, like a general human failure to find freedom was in fact two quite different kinds of failure, distributed according to social position and ethnic identity in ways that were neither accidental nor symmetrical.

One of the novel's most significant formal achievements was its rendering of antisemitism not as a series of dramatic incidents but as an atmosphere—a persistent, pervasive background condition that shaped every social interaction and every individual calculation without necessarily erupting into specific violence or confrontation. The action of the novel was set in 1898, a Vienna under the antisemitic Mayor Karl Lueger and the Christian Social Party whose political success depended substantially on the exploitation of anti-Jewish sentiment.[12] It was a city in which this atmospheric antisemitism was simply a feature of daily life: present in social slights and professional obstacles, in the casual assumptions embedded in ordinary conversation, in the political language of the newspapers and the pulpit, in the legal structures that limited Jewish access to certain positions and institutions.

The conversations between the novel's Jewish characters were marked by an awareness of this atmosphere that was always present even when not explicitly named. When Heinrich Bermann discussed his literary ambitions, the question of how his Jewishness would be read by the critical and social world was always a background pressure, even when the discussion was nominally about aesthetics. When the Golowskis discussed their family's declining circumstances, the precariousness of that situation—its dependence on a social tolerance that could be withdrawn at any moment—was palpable beneath the surface of ordinary family conversation.

The novel was overshadowed by deaths: during the year it charts, Heinrich's father dies, the actress with whom Heinrich is involved drowns herself, and Oskar Ehrenberg attempts to end his own life.[13] Georg's own father and his friend Labinski, who had taken his own life for mysterious reasons shortly before the novel opens, haunt Georg's consciousness throughout. The stillbirth of Anna and Georg's child extends the atmosphere of loss into the novel's central love story. These deaths and near-deaths were not incidental to the social analysis; they were its consequences, the human cost of the social pressures the novel mapped.

No response was endorsed; no position was exempted from irony; the novel demonstrated, with the cumulative force of its nearly five hundred pages, that every road its characters attempted to take led not into the open but back into the impasse of a society organized around the irreducible fact of Jewish difference. The ensemble was the argument: by presenting each position as compelling within its own terms while allowing each to be implicitly undermined by the others and by the social reality surrounding all of them, Schnitzler made the case that the Jewish Question did not have a solution that any individual could adopt—that it was a structural feature of the social world rather than a personal problem with a personal answer.

The Grillparzer Prize, awarded on January 15, 1908, for Zwischenspiel, confirmed Schnitzler's standing in the literary establishment.[14] In interviews marking the occasion, Schnitzler was characteristically measured: he told reporters he had considered himself an outsider for the prize and was pleasantly surprised by the award, and he took care to note that he valued Der einsame Weg even more highly than the work that had won the prize.[15] Der Weg ins Freie, published that same year, confirmed something larger: that his ambitions now extended beyond the theater and into the terrain of the novel, and that the Jewish question—which he had spent his career approaching obliquely, through characters and situations that refracted rather than confronted—had become a subject he could no longer avoid.

Late in life, Schnitzler would single out Der Weg ins Freie as the work of which he was most proud. In a 1923 interview, he declared that the novel was the one work to which he could commit himself without reservation, adding that he was almost proud to have written it and that he intended to place it on his desk among the books he wanted to re-read when he had time.[16] The remark was revealing: among all his dramatic and narrative works, it was the panoramic social novel—the work that had taken the longest to write, the work in which the Jewish question received its fullest treatment—that he valued most.

The novel's prophetic quality would become undeniable in the decades after its publication, as the world it depicted was systematically destroyed by the political forces whose early operations Schnitzler had identified. Schnitzler did not foresee the Holocaust; no one in 1908 could have imagined the specific form that European antisemitism's logical conclusion would take. What he foresaw, with the clarity of a social analyst working from carefully observed evidence, was the structural impossibility of the situation he depicted: the impossibility of Jewish assimilation in a society organized around Jewish exclusion, the impossibility of conversion as a solution in a context where Jewish identity was defined ethnically rather than theologically, the impossibility of Zionism as an immediate practical answer to an immediate political problem, the impossibility of socialism as a specific solution to a specifically ethnic persecution. He foresaw that every road was closed—that the roads his characters attempted were not roads into the open but roads that curved back, in different ways and at different speeds, into the impasse.

In 1933, when Joseph Goebbels organized book burnings across Germany, Schnitzler's works were thrown into the flames along with those of other Jewish writers, including Einstein, Kafka, Freud, and Stefan Zweig.[17] His works were called "Jewish filth" by Adolf Hitler and were banned in Austria and Germany. The archive itself—over forty thousand pages of manuscripts, diaries, and correspondence—survived only through the intervention of Olga Schnitzler, who in March 1938, days after the German invasion of Austria, arranged for a Cambridge student named Eric Blackall to smuggle the papers out of Vienna under a diplomatic seal.[18] The archive was preserved; the world the novel had described was not.

What the novel's Jewish characters had navigated in fiction—the daily calculations, the impossible choices, the structural impossibility of finding a road into the open within a society organized against them—would be visited upon their real-world counterparts with a thoroughness that no literary imagination had foreseen. The Heinrich Bermanns and Leo Golowskis and Therese Golowskis of the novel were not real people, but the community they represented was, and the spectrum of responses they embodied to the inescapable pressure of their social position was the spectrum of responses actually available to Austrian Jews in the years before the catastrophe. The novel preserved that spectrum intact.

Schnitzler was writing, in the early years of his marriage, from a position of relative security: married, a father, financially stable, professionally established. He was also writing as a Jewish man who had spent his entire career negotiating the social and professional consequences of his Jewishness, who had been attacked by antisemitic critics, who had seen his work banned and his military commission stripped, who understood from lived experience what it meant to be judged not as an individual but as a representative of a suspect community. Der Weg ins Freie was the work in which that lived experience found its fullest literary expression—not in autobiography but in a panoramic social portrait that took the individual experiences of marginalization, the daily accommodations and calculations that Jewish existence in Vienna required, and elevated them into a systematic analysis of a society that was, in Schnitzler's careful rendering, already approaching its dissolution.

CHAPTER FOURTEEN

The Villa on the Sternwartestraße: The Years Before the War (1910–1912)

DAS WEITE LAND

Arthur Schnitzler 1912 (chapter note 26)

On April 14, 1910, Schnitzler signed the purchase contract for a villa at Sternwartestraße 71 in Währing, paying 95,000 Kronen to the seller, Hedwig Bleibtreu.[1] Bleibtreu was herself a celebrated Burgtheater actress; the villa had belonged to her and her first husband, the court actor Alexander Römpler, who had died in December 1909.[2] After renovations supervised by the architect Hermann Müller—who had designed the villa in the first place, back in 1895—Schnitzler spent his first night in the house on July 16, 1910.[3] The family of four—Arthur, Olga, seven-year-old Heinrich, and baby Lili, not yet a year old—had outgrown the apartment on the Spöttelgasse. The villa was large enough for the family, Schnitzler's secretary Frieda Pollak, and whatever domestic staff the household required. It was quiet, set in a residential neighborhood near the observatory that gave the street its name, and it would remain Schnitzler's home for the rest of his life. He would write there, quarrel there, grow old there, and die there, on October 21, 1931, at the age of sixty-nine. For two decades, the villa on Sternwartestraße was the fixed point around which everything else—the plays, the scandals, the war, the marriage's slow collapse—revolved.

A journalist who visited soon after the purchase described the view from Schnitzler's first-floor study: the autumn Viennese landscape, veiled in mist, the gentle hills and fields that Schnitzler loved and had rendered in his fiction with such lyrical precision.[4] Another visitor, writing in the 1920s, recorded the daily routine the villa's spaces had come to support: a morning walk around the Türkenschanzpark, reading, then after lunch a brief rest followed immediately by work. Schnitzler owned a fine broad desk and a comfortable leather chair, but they stood apart when the poet wrote. He preferred his tall standing desk, and from there the verses and prose flowed easily. Seldom did an afternoon pass without Schnitzler advancing some work in progress, whether a novella or a drama. When finished, the piece went into a drawer for at least three weeks before he took it out again and read it as a stranger, with a critic's eye.[5]

From the outside, the years between the villa's purchase and the outbreak of the war were the most settled and productive of Schnitzler's career. He was in his late forties, established, financially secure, working with a discipline that the villa's ordered spaces encouraged. He was writing with a range and ambition that surpassed anything he had attempted before, and the works of this period—a historical drama, a play about marriage, a play about institutional antisemitism—represent the summit of his achievement as a dramatist who could move between subjects with equal authority.

If *Der Weg ins Freie* had examined the Jewish question through the oblique lens of fiction, *Professor Bernhardi*, completed in 1912, confronted it head-on. But between these two major statements on Jewish identity in Austria came a work of different preoccupations: *Das weite Land—The Vast Domain*—which received its German-language premiere on October 14, 1911, simultaneously at nine theaters across the German-speaking world, including the Burgtheater in Vienna, the Lessingtheater in Berlin, and theaters in Breslau, Munich, Prague, Leipzig, Hamburg, Hannover, and Bochum.[6] A Russian-language premiere had already taken place at the Novyj dramatičeskij teatr in St. Petersburg on November 2, 1910.[7] The simultaneous German opening across nine stages was a mark of the extraordinary reputation Schnitzler had achieved—and a measure of the theatrical event the play's completion represented. At the Viennese premiere, Schnitzler was called before the curtain twenty-four times.[8]

The play was a five-act tragicomedy of exceptional scope and psychological depth. Its title carried a weight of meaning that Schnitzler himself was careful to delineate. In an interview, asked where this "vast domain" was to be found, he replied concisely: "Das weite Land ist das Land der menschlichen Seelen!"—the vast domain is the domain of human souls.[9] The phrase originated with a character in the play, Dr. von Aigner, who declares: "Die Seele ist ein weites Land"—the soul is a vast domain. Schnitzler was emphatic that the line should not be mistaken for his own philosophical credo: he pointed out that Aigner was "ein affektierter Herr"—an affected gentleman—who expressed himself "ziemlich aphoristisch," and that he did not identify himself with any of his characters.[10] When Tom Stoppard adapted the play for the National Theatre in London in 1979, he chose the title *Undiscovered Country*, drawing on the Hamlet soliloquy's "undiscovered country from whose bourn no traveler returns." Stoppard's title, directed by Peter Wood and starring John Wood as Hofreiter, restored a Shakespearean resonance for English-speaking audiences—but the connection was Stoppard's, not Schnitzler's.[11]

The play told the story of Friedrich Hofreiter, a Viennese lightbulb manufacturer in his forties who had been married to Genia for years. They summered at a resort in Baden bei Wien with their son Percy. Friedrich openly philandered; Genia had maintained her fidelity—a fidelity that, in the play's devastating opening, had already proven fatal. The Russian pianist Alexei Korsakow, a regular visitor to the Hofreiter villa, had shot himself before the play's action began, leaving a farewell letter to Genia that confirmed her virtue: he had killed himself because she had refused his advances.[12] Korsakow's death was one of the shadows that fell across the play's holiday setting, a reminder that desire had already proven lethal in Genia's immediate social world. Friedrich's response to the suicide was characteristically perverse: rather than admiring his wife's fidelity, he reproached her for it, finding something threatening—something almost hostile—in a virtue so resolute that it had driven a man to his death.

Meanwhile, Friedrich pursued a new affair with the young Erna Wahl while still disentangling himself from the previous one with Adele Natter, the wife of his banker. During a trip to the Dolomites, Friedrich began a relationship with Erna and even proposed marriage; she, though she had loved him since childhood, declined to commit. Back at the resort, a naval ensign named Otto von Aigner—the son of the philosopher Dr. von Aigner who had coined the play's central aphorism—pursued Genia with a directness that the social codes of the period made both forward and reco gnizable.[13] Genia, worn down by years of tolerating Friedrich's infidelities, reciprocated Otto's feelings, and they consummated their relationship.

Friedrich, confronted with evidence of his wife's affair, experienced a reaction the play dissected with merciless precision. His first response was paradoxically one of relief: if Genia had also transgressed, then his own serial infidelities were in some sense normalized. But this relief proved unsustainable. What he could not tolerate was the implication that his wife was a person with her own desires, her own capacity for action, her own interior life—that she had been, all along, the vast domain he had presumed to have fully mapped. He challenged Otto to a duel and killed him.[14] The duel was not an act of injured love but an act of injured self-image. Friedrich did not, at the deepest level, believe that Genia's infidelity had destroyed something he genuinely valued; if he believed that, the preceding decade of his own infidelities would require a moral reckoning he had never undertaken.

Friedrich Hofreiter was the most fully developed version of a character type Schnitzler had been refining throughout his career—the charming, intelligent, self-regarding man whose relationships with others were ultimately organized around his own emotional needs and his own self-image. He was recognizably in the lineage of Anatol, but older, richer, more powerful, and more consequential. Where Anatol's narcissism expressed itself in a series of inconsequential romantic episodes, Friedrich's narcissism was embedded in the institution of marriage, in the ownership of property, in the exercise of social power, and in the possession of a son. His self-deceptions cost an actual human life: Otto von Aigner was dead because Friedrich could not tolerate the possibility that his wife had exercised the same sexual freedom that he had exercised habitually and without guilt for the entirety of their marriage.

What distinguished Schnitzler's treatment of Friedrich from simple moral indictment was the care with which he made Friedrich's self-deceptions internally coherent. Friedrich did not experience himself as a hypocrite. His affairs had, in his self-understanding, been meaningless—pleasures of the moment, without emotional consequence, without claims on his deeper attachments. He had convinced himself, and could articulate with apparent sincerity, the distinction between physical appetite and genuine feeling; he had arranged his inner life so that his infidelities did not register as violations of anything he truly valued. This was not cynicism—or rather, it was cynicism so thoroughly internalized that it had ceased to feel like cynicism and had come to feel like sophistication.

When he confronted the possibility of Genia's infidelity, the architecture of this self-deception collapsed. The distinction he had maintained between appetite and feeling, between the body and the heart, suddenly could not be applied to his wife's case, because to apply it would be to accept her on the same terms on which he had always accepted himself, and that acceptance was the one thing his narcissism could not accommodate.

Genia Hofreiter was among the most carefully constructed female protagonists in Schnitzler's dramatic work. She had tolerated—with a patience that was simultaneously admirable and troubling—Friedrich's serial infidelities, accepting them as the terms of the social arrangement she had entered and could not easily exit. That Genia had rejected Korsakow's advances—maintaining her fidelity at the cost of a man's life—was evidence of her genuine moral seriousness, her capacity to navigate desire with a responsibility her husband had never found necessary. Her eventual affair with Otto was therefore not a lapse but an assertion: a refusal, however belated, to continue occupying the position Friedrich had assigned her.

The five-act structure allowed for the systematic accumulation of dramatic irony over a sufficiently extended time that the audience could watch Friedrich's self-understanding and the play's evidence about his actual situation diverge with slow inevitability. The play's subplot involving Dr. Franz Mauer, Friedrich's closest friend, served a specific ironic function: Mauer was the moral center of the play, the character who could see most clearly what Friedrich could not see in himself. Mauer's unsuccessful proposal to the young Erna Wahl provided a counterpoint—a man who, unlike Friedrich, could offer genuine feeling and was refused, while Friedrich, who offered only appetite disguised as sophistication, was accepted. The duel was not inevitable; Friedrich chose it, and the presence of Mauer made that choice legible as a choice.

Schnitzler himself judged the play with a severity he rarely turned on his other works—and with an equally rare confidence. After reading it to Olga and to the Berlin theater director Otto Brahm, he noted in his diary: "Exposition matt, noch manches schnarrende im Dialog – als ganzes mein bestgebautes Stück, eine glänzende und so gut wie neue Hauptgestalt, inhaltlich viel zukunftsweisendes; in Nebendingen manches conventionell und billig."[15] —the exposition weak, some dialogue still grating, but on the whole his best-constructed play, with a brilliant and virtually new central character, and much in its substance that pointed toward the future. In April 1910, rereading the finished work, he was blunter still: "Finde das Stück gut – ja möglicherweise zu gut für einen Theatererfolg."[16] And four years after the premiere, in a diary entry of June 14, 1915, he recorded a judgment he rarely permitted himself: this was one of the very few works to which he could commit himself without reservation. "Ich bin – etwas mehr," he wrote—here, he was something more than what he usually considered himself as an artist.[17]

The play drew on Schnitzler's immediate social world with a directness unusual even for him. The Hofreiters were modeled in part on the alpinist couple Louis Friedmann and Rose von Rosthorn-Friedmann, who kept a salon in their villa in Baden bei Wien.[18] The boy Percy took his name from Percy Eckstein, the son of the philosopher Friedrich Eckstein, who also lived in Baden. In his diary, Schnitzler identified the mountain-climbing hotelier Dr. von Aigner as based on Theodor Christomannos.[19] These were not disguised portraits—Schnitzler was too careful a craftsman for simple transposition—but the social milieu of the play was inseparable from the milieu in which he lived, and the accuracy of observation that reviewers praised was the accuracy of first-hand knowledge.

The critical consensus that *Das weite Land* marked a significant development beyond the "decadent" label that had clung to Schnitzler since

Anatol was correct. This was not a departure from the concerns of the earlier work but their extension into richer and more complex terrain. The epistemological anxiety that drove the *Anatol* cycle—the impossibility of truly knowing another person—was here not the property of a narcissistic bachelor projecting fantasies onto a succession of lower-class women, but a condition of marriage itself. Friedrich Hofreiter was not Anatol grown older, though the family resemblance was visible. He was what Anatol might have become if the consequences of his narcissism had been allowed to accumulate to the point of destroying not only individual women but an entire domestic structure and, ultimately, a human life.

The play's setting in Vienna at the turn of the century, a decade before the assassination at Sarajevo and the beginning of the war that would destroy the world it depicted, gave it a quality of valediction—of a society being recorded in a spirit of preservationist urgency. Otto Brahm, writing to Schnitzler in June 1910, called the play's style "durchaus neuartig"—entirely novel—and described it as "pointilistisch."[20] Georg Brandes, after the premiere, observed that in the play's rich and shimmering world, trust had become impossible; everyone was working free of their attachments and bonds.[21] Alfred Polgar called it "ein wohlorganisiertes Konzert der Würmer im Holz"—a well-organized concert of worms in the wood.[22] In the weeks following the premiere, Schnitzler traveled to Prague, Berlin, Hamburg, and Munich to attend productions of the play, and was celebrated at each.[23]

Schnitzler's own marriage to Olga, which had begun in 1903, was by 1911 already strained by complications that would eventually lead to their separation. His growing understanding of marital complexity from the inside—of the forms of distance, mutual deception, and frustrated communication that accrued within even a relationship entered with genuine feeling—gave *Das weite Land* its particular texture of lived authority. He was writing not from clinical detachment but from the more complicated position of someone who was himself implicated in the patterns he was describing.

In February 1911, shortly before *Das weite Land* premiered, Olga gave her first public concert as a singer.[24] The event was the culmination of years of preparation—she had trained throughout the marriage, practiced at the villa, sustained her ambition through the demands of motherhood and the overshadowing presence of her husband's fame. The success she had hoped for did not materialize, and it would elude her for the rest of her life. The failure was not dramatic; it was the quieter, more corrosive kind that consisted of a career that never quite arrived, of talent that was real but insufficient, of ambition that had no adequate object.

Olga was not without ability. She was simply not exceptional, and in a household dominated by a man whose exceptionality was recognized across Europe, the distinction was felt with particular sharpness. Her frustration, which had been building for years, entered a new phase after 1911: no longer the impatience of a young woman waiting for her chance, but the bitterness of a woman approaching thirty who was beginning to understand that the chance, when it came, had not been enough. She had married not to be comfortable but to be a partner of two artistic temperaments. The reality was that Schnitzler's work demanded solitude and routine; domestic life was the medium in which his writing occurred but also the thing from which his writing required protection. She had become what she had not wanted to be: the great man's wife, the manager of the household, the woman whose own artistic aspirations were perpetually deferred to his established career. After the war, she would attempt to revive her singing career in partnership with the composer and pianist

Wilhelm Grosz—an effort that became one of the central conflicts leading to the divorce in 1921.[25]

The marriage would continue for another decade, but the terms were increasingly unsustainable. Schnitzler could write Genia Hofreiter's trajectory with such precision because he understood, from the inside, what it meant when one partner's patience with hypocrisy reached its limit. That understanding did not translate into different behavior in his own marriage—it rarely does. But it deepened the psychological complexity of the work.

CHAPTER FIFTEEN

Professor Bernhardi and the Jewish Question (1912–1913)

PROFESSOR BERNHARDI, FRAU BEATE UND IHR SOHN

BETWEEN *DAS WEITE LAND* and the work that would follow, Schnitzler completed the play that would prove to be his most directly political, his most explicitly Jewish, and his most stubbornly prophetic: *Professor Bernhardi.*

The play—billed, with characteristic Viennese irony, as a "comedy in five acts"—told the story of a Jewish physician who was destroyed by the institutions of Catholic Austria for doing what his conscience and his medical training demanded. The situation Schnitzler devised was precise and unresolvable. Professor Bernhardi, the director of a private clinic called the Elizabethinum, was attending a young unmarried woman who was dying of septicemia following a botched illegal abortion. She did not know she was dying; she was, in fact, euphoric, convinced she was recovering. A Catholic priest, Father Reder, arrived to administer the last rites. Bernhardi, reasoning that the priest's presence would reveal to the patient that she was about to die and destroy her last hours of peace, refused him entry to the room.

The decision was humane, medically defensible, and politically cata-strophic. A press campaign erupted. False testimony was given that Bern-hardi had struck the priest—he had not. The fabrication inflamed the antisemitism that was endemic in Viennese public life. Bernhardi was tried, convicted, sentenced to two months in prison, and stripped of his medical license. A colleague, Professor Ebenwald—modeled, as Schnitzler later acknowledged, on the German-nationalist surgeon Julius Hocheneg-g[1]—offered to arrange a bribe that would make the charges disappear, on the condition that Bernhardi appoint a Christian physician to a post for which a Jewish doctor was better qualified. Bernhardi refused. Father Reder, in a private meeting after the trial, admitted that Bernhardi had acted properly—but explained that he could not say so publicly, because to do so would acknowledge that a physician's authority could legitimately override a priest's access to a dying Catholic, an acknowledgment the in-stitutional hierarchy of the Church could not permit. The play ended not with vindication but with a philosophical conversation between Bernhardi and a friend, in which the impossibility of justice in a society organized around prejudice was acknowledged without being resolved.

The ethical dimensions of Bernhardi's original decision were genuine-ly complex, and Schnitzler was careful to establish them as such. The Catholic Church's position was not simply irrational: the administration of last rites was, within Catholic theology, a matter of genuine spiritual consequence, and Father Reder's insistence that the woman had a right to the sacrament was grounded in a coherent moral framework. Bernhardi's position was equally grounded: his medical judgment was that the woman was better served by dying in peace, and his broader philosophical stance was that human dignity and the minimization of suffering were values that overrode institutional obligation. Neither position was self-evidently correct; the play was not a tract arguing for the superiority of secular medicine over religious ritual.

What the play did argue—with mounting irony—was that the actual question of who was right in this specific encounter was entirely irrelevant to what followed from it. The moment Bernhardi's decision became politically useful to forces that had nothing to do with the welfare of the dying woman, the ethical substance of the original incident ceased to matter. What mattered, from that point forward, was the symbolic utility of a Jewish doctor who had allegedly struck a Catholic priest. The fabrication was crucial: Bernhardi had not struck Father Reder; this was clear from the dramatic action and was acknowledged privately by Reder himself. The antisemitic press campaign that transformed the incident into a cause célèbre depended entirely on an invented detail—the physical assault—that converted a complex medical-ethical judgment into a simple narrative of Jewish violence against Christian authority.

The ease with which this fabrication was generated and sustained, the speed with which it circulated and became the accepted version of events in the political world, was itself one of the play's most important observations about the mechanics of antisemitic propaganda. The lie did not need to be plausible or carefully constructed; it needed only to be useful, and the existing social infrastructure of anti-Jewish sentiment provided the distribution network through which it traveled.

The play was the most directly political work Schnitzler had ever written, and also his only major dramatic work without a sexual theme. A persistent misreading presented it as a play about the conflict between scientific rationalism and religious authority—a Viennese entry in the ongoing nineteenth-century drama of secular modernity versus institutional faith. This reading missed the point, as the scholar Max Haberich has argued.[2] The real conflict was not between science and religion but between the critically-minded individual—the person who insisted on evaluating situations on their actual merits rather than their political utility—and the various institutional forces, religious and secular alike, that required the subordination of individual judgment to collective interest.

Haberich has described Bernhardi as embodying what he terms "enlightened apolitical individualism"—a stance that was, simultaneously, the play's moral center and one of its most searching objects of scrutiny.[3] Bernhardi did not think of himself as a Jewish physician; he thought of himself as a physician who happened to be Jewish. He did not experience the political world in terms of collective identities and group interests; he experienced it in terms of individual cases, individual judgments, and individual responsibilities. When his colleagues advised him to engage politically—to organize resistance, to build alliances, to fight antisemitism on its own collective terms—he refused. He did not believe in collective action; he believed in individual integrity. He would not compromise on his own case, but he would not generalize his case into a political program.

The play's treatment of this stance was more complicated than simple endorsement. Bernhardi maintained his integrity throughout: he refused the bribe, accepted the unjust conviction, declined to appeal on pragmatic grounds, and emerged from prison with his self-respect intact. The play did not punish him in the melodramatic sense. But the conversation that concluded the play raised questions about what his integrity had actually achieved. The clinic continued; the institutional corruption continued; the antisemitism that powered the campaign against him continued. Bernhardi's personal dignity was intact. The world was unchanged. Whether the first fact was sufficient in the face of the second was the question the play left open, and its openness was not evasion but honesty.

The question of the play's relationship to Schnitzler's father became, almost immediately, a matter requiring correction. The elder Johann Schnitzler had indeed cofounded a clinic—the Allgemeine Poliklinik—and had experienced professional difficulties there, including ingratitude and personal slights, particularly toward the end of his life. But when Georg Brandes published an account suggesting that *Professor Bernhardi* dramatized "ein Lebensschicksal, wie es mein Vater erfahren hat"—a fate his father had experienced—Schnitzler wrote a public letter of correction, published in *Der Merker* in February 1913. The content of the play, he insisted, was "frei erfunden"—freely invented. Bernhardi had borrowed "nur wenige Züge"—only a few traits—from his father. His father had served as director until his death on May 2, 1893, and had not been intrigued out of his position. The other characters, too, were freely created, "with the admittedly indispensable use of details from reality," and only those "kunstfremde"—strangers to art—could call it a roman à clef. The play's only truth, Schnitzler concluded, was that its events could have taken place exactly as depicted—"at least in Vienna at the end of the last century."[4]

Professor Bernhardi was inseparable from the question of what it meant to be Jewish in Austria at the turn of the twentieth century—the same question that animated *Der Weg ins Freie*. Both works addressed the impossible position of the assimilated Austrian Jew who had internalized the values of the liberal Enlightenment—rationality, individual merit, the universality of human dignity—only to discover that the social world in which those values were supposed to be operative was organized, in practice, by the tribal logic of ethnic and religious identity that the Enlightenment was supposed to have superseded. Bernhardi was not merely a physician who happened to be Jewish; he was a physician whose specifically Jewish intellectual formation—the tradition of rational inquiry, the commitment to evidence over authority, the valuing of individual conscience over institutional compliance—placed him in irresolvable tension with the Catholic-nationalist political culture surrounding him.

One of the most striking and, for contemporary audiences, most disturbing features of *Professor Bernhardi* was the density and specificity of the antisemitic utterances that populated its dialogue. The play was riddled with remarks that ranged from the casually dismissive to the openly vicious: comments about Jewish honor, about Jewish subhumanity, about the supposedly special relationship between Jewish professional success and Jewish moral corruption.[5] These utterances were placed in the mouths of characters who were not cartoonish bigots but recognizable professional and social types—colleagues, politicians, church officials, opportunists. They spoke as people spoke when antisemitism was the ambient language of the political culture: not with the intensity of conviction but with the casual ease of shared assumption.

Schnitzler was documenting, not endorsing. The play was set in 1900, during the mayoralty of Vienna's openly antisemitic Karl Lueger, whose Christian Social Party had made political exploitation of anti-Jewish sentiment a governing strategy.[6] The language its characters spoke was the language of that specific historical moment reproduced with clinical accuracy. The effect of this reproduction was not to normalize the language but to make it strange—to expose the mechanisms through which casual prejudice became institutional persecution, to show how the ambient antisemitism of the social world provided the political raw material from which the campaign against Bernhardi was constructed.

Between *Der Weg ins Freie* and *Professor Bernhardi*, Schnitzler's engagement with Jewish identity had shifted from the observational to the confrontational. The novel had examined; the play accused. Together they constituted what might reasonably be described as a diptych: two works that approached the Jewish Question from complementary angles and that together constituted Schnitzler's fullest and most sustained statement on Austrian-Jewish identity in the early twentieth century. The novel's approach was panoramic and sociological: it surveyed the full landscape of Jewish Vienna, depicted the range of positions available within it, and rendered the Jewish Question as a social fact experienced collectively. The play's approach was focused and dramatic: it took a single incident involving a single Jewish professional and traced, with forensic precision, the institutional mechanisms through which that individual's Jewishness was converted into a liability by the political forces that found it convenient to do so.

The play was completed in 1912 and published by S. Fischer Verlag the same year. Austrian censors answered the question the play posed—whether a Jew could be right when every institution in his society insisted he was wrong—by banning it. The world premiere took place on November 28, 1912, at the Kleines Theater in Berlin, where Prussian censorship operated under different rules.[7] That same evening, in the same city, Schnitzler's longtime friend and theatrical champion Otto Brahm died.[8] Brahm—the great naturalist director who had premiered *Der einsame Weg* and championed Schnitzler's work for two decades—died on the night his friend's most political play first reached the stage. The coincidence was one of those biographical ironies that Schnitzler, who spent his career exploring the gap between what people intended and what actually happened, might have used in his fiction but would have hesitated to believe in his life.

It would not be performed in Austria until December 21, 1918, at the Deutsches Volkstheater in Vienna, after the empire whose hypocrisies it anatomized had ceased to exist.[9] The ban confirmed, with an irony that Schnitzler would have appreciated had it not been directed at his own work, exactly the thesis the play advanced: that Austrian institutions could not tolerate honest scrutiny of their own prejudices. In a later interview, Schnitzler said he could write an entire book about the play's censorship history. He noted that even after the revolution, when theater censorship was declared abolished—"was aber nicht stimmt," he added wryly, which is not true—the play had been staged to great success, but that the current antisemitic atmosphere in Vienna would make a revival impossible.[10]

Responding to his own diary's record of the critical reception, Schnitzler observed: "Die Tendenz der Kritik heißt missverstehn – wenigstens dem Lebenden gegenüber." The tendency of criticism is to misunderstand—at least where the living are concerned.[11] It was one of those compressed, weary aphorisms that carried the authority of long experience. Schnitzler had watched, across a career spanning two decades, as critics reduced his work to categories it was designed to resist. *Professor Bernhardi* was no exception: critics who saw a simple plea for secularism missed the play's ambivalence about Bernhardi's individualism; critics who saw a Schlüssel-stück—a roman à clef—missed the freedom of its invention.

Schnitzler himself drew an unexpected connection between *Professor Bernhardi* and his earlier play *Der einsame Weg*, noting that the latter had originally been set in medical circles, and that the idea for the hospital comedy *Letzte Masken* had been sketched on the same afternoon, during a boat trip on an Italian lake at Le Prese.[12] The seeds of *Professor Bernhardi* lay buried in the earlier work's discarded medical milieu; the play about institutional antisemitism had grown out of a play about solitude.

The novella *Frau Beate und ihr Sohn* (*Beate and Her Son*), serialized in *Die Neue Rundschau* between February and April 1913 and published as a book by S. Fischer the same year, belonged to a different register.[13] It told the story of Beate Heinold, a widow living with her seventeen-year-old son Hugo at a lake resort in the Salzkammergut. After five years of sexual abstinence following her husband's death, Beate yielded to the advances of Fritz, a young schoolmate of Hugo's, and began an affair. The story traced, with Schnitzler's characteristic attention to interior states, the conflict between Beate's reawakened desire and the social and moral norms that made her situation untenable. When she overheard Fritz boasting crudely about their nights together, and when Hugo learned of his mother's affair, the resulting shame drove both mother and son to a shared suicide—rowing out onto the lake at night and drowning together.[14]

The work explored territory Schnitzler had not previously mapped with such directness: the possessiveness of maternal attachment, the ways in which family structures reproduced the same patterns of desire and ex-clusion that governed romantic relationships, and the impossible position of the woman whose identity had been subsumed entirely into her role as mother. Peter Sprengel, analyzing the novella, identified its true subject as the power of sexuality—the same force that had animated *Frau Berta Garlan* over a decade earlier—and the normative crises it generated when women experienced it on their own terms.[15] The novella was less celebrated than his major theatrical works, but it demonstrated the range of psychological terrain he was willing to examine and the increasing complexity of his engagement with female subjectivity.

The war that would destroy the world Schnitzler had anatomized was coming. The plays and novels of the period between the villa's purchase and 1914 were written in the shadow of that approaching catastrophe, though Schnitzler could not have known its specific form. What he did know, with the clarity of a social analyst working from carefully observed evidence, was that the social arrangements he had spent his career examining—the sexual double standards, the institutional antisemitism, the honor codes that killed young men for nothing, the marriages that isolated people more completely than solitude ever could—were unsustainable. The literary work of this period was increasingly preoccupied with endings: the end of relationships, the end of illusions, the end of the social world that had made those illusions possible.

CHAPTER SIXTEEN

The War Years and Jugend in Wien (1914–1918)

JUGEND IN WIEN, DOCTOR GRÄSLER, BADEARZT, CASANOVAS HEIMFAHRT

"WORLD WAR. WORLD RUIN. / *Der Weltkrieg. Der Weltruin.*"
—Arthur Schnitzler, Tagebuch, August 5, 1914

In August 1914, Schnitzler was vacationing in Switzerland when the news arrived. His diary entry for August 5 recorded the declaration of war by England on Germany, and then erupted into a passage of stunned comprehension: "Der Weltkrieg. Der Weltruin. Ungeheuere und ungeheuerliche Nachrichten." World war. World ruin. Monstrous and monstrous news. He continued: "Wir erleben einen ungeheuern Moment der Weltgeschichte. In wenig Tagen hat sich das Bild der Welt völlig verändert. Man glaubt zu träumen! Alle Menschen sind rathlos." We are living through a monstrous moment in world history. In a few days the image of the world has completely changed. One believes oneself dreaming! Everyone is at a loss.[1] He was fifty-two years old, too old for military service, and the posture he adopted toward the catastrophe that would destroy the world he had spent his career describing was one of principled detachment—a refusal to lend his name or his pen to the public enthusiasms of the moment, combined with a private anguish that found its outlet in the diary rather than in manifestos.

The detachment was principled, and it was also intolerable to those who expected more from him. Olga diagnosed her husband with what she called "unzeitgemäße Selbstbewahrung"—untimely self-preservation—and criticized his "reservirte kühle Haltung," his reserved cool attitude, regarding the war.[2] She expected him to use his symbolic capital, to publish his thoughts, to engage. He refused.

The refusal was consistent with everything he had ever been—the man who had left Café Griensteidl to become what he called a "Virtuose der Einsamkeit," who had never joined a literary movement or a political party, whose deepest conviction was that the individual conscience was the only authority worth respecting. But what had been a temperamental preference in peacetime became, in wartime, a political statement, and it was a statement that satisfied nobody: not the patriots who wanted his endorsement, not the critics who wanted his dissent, and not his wife, who saw in his silence a confirmation of the emotional distance that had been widening between them for years.

Many of his contemporaries made different choices. Hugo von Hofmannsthal, Schnitzler's friend and the author of the prologue to *Anatol*, worked in the Austrian War Archive and contributed to propaganda efforts, lending his literary gifts to the cultural dimension of the war effort.[3] Hermann Bahr, another member of the Jung Wien circle, wrote enthusiastically in support of the war. Stefan Zweig initially embraced the war's outbreak with patriotic fervor before revulsion set in.[4] Schnitzler's silence was conspicuous, and it was noted. He received letters—some pleading, some accusatory—asking why he would not speak. He did not answer them, or he answered them privately, and the private answers made clear that he would not be moved.

On his fifty-fifth birthday, May 15, 1917, a private catastrophe under-scored the atmosphere of the war years. Stephi Bachrach, a young nurse and friend of the family, poisoned herself. Schnitzler was deeply shaken; certain details of this tragic event would later find their way, transformed, into the novella *Fräulein Else*.[5]

What he did, instead of engaging with the war, was begin his autobiography. In May 1915, less than a year after the war's outbreak, he started writing what he initially planned to call *Leben und Nachklang – Werk und Widerhall* (Life and Echo – Work and Resonance)—the project that would eventually be published posthumously in 1968, edited by his son Heinrich and Therese Nickl, under the title *Jugend in Wien*.[6] The turn away from the disintegrating present and toward the lost world of his childhood and early manhood was a characteristic response: when the present became unbearable, he looked backward, not in nostalgia but in the conviction that understanding where one had come from was the only reliable way of understanding where one was.

Jugend in Wien would become one of the essential documents of nine-teenth-century Viennese cultural life—a memoir of extraordinary psychological honesty, written with the same clinical precision Schnitzler brought to his fiction but applied to the material of his own formation. He began with his earliest memories of the 1860s and 1870s, reconstructing the Vienna of his childhood: the apartment on Praterstraße where his father had established his medical practice, the theaters his father loved, the social world of the assimilated Jewish bourgeoisie climbing steadily into cultural prominence. The Vienna he described was not the glittering imperial cap-ital of tourist imagination but a city of social anxieties, class distinctions, and carefully calibrated performances of belonging.

The autobiography was most valuable—and most painful—in its treat-ment of Schnitzler's early romantic and sexual life. He wrote with un-flinching directness about the patterns of behavior that would define his entire adult life: the pursuit of "süße Mädel," the affairs with married women, the emotional arrangements that preserved his freedom at others' expense. The memoir also examined his relationship with his father, Johann Schnitzler, with a complexity that fiction would have struggled to achieve. Johann was a man of formidable intelligence and professional success who had climbed from modest origins to become one of Vienna's leading laryngologists. Arthur's decision to abandon medicine for literature was experienced by Johann not merely as a professional choice but as a betrayal of the family's hard-won respectability. The relationship between father and son was marked by genuine affection and mutual incomprehension.

What made *Jugend in Wien* extraordinary was its refusal of apologetics. Schnitzler did not present himself as a hero or a victim; he presented himself as a case study—a young man formed by specific historical and social circumstances, shaped by the contradictions of assimilated Jewish identity in Vienna, driven by desires he could analyze but not fully control. The autobiography was an act of self-examination as rigorous as anything in *Leutnant Gustl* or *Professor Bernhardi*, and its rigor extended to the acknowledgment of his own moral failures. He had hurt women. He had evaded commitments. He had constructed his emotional life around the preservation of his own freedom at others' expense. The memoir did not excuse these things; it documented them.

The act of writing *Jugend in Wien* during the war—of reconstructing the Vienna of the 1870s and 1880s while the Vienna of 1915–1918 was sending its young men to die in Galicia and the Dolomites—was itself a form of testimony. It was also a way of inhabiting time differently: when the future had become unimaginable and the present unbearable, the past offered a space in which meaning could still be constructed and examined. Schnitzler completed the autobiography in the summer of 1918.[7] It would not be published in his lifetime—it appeared posthumously in 1968—but the act of writing it sustained him through the war years in ways that engagement with the war itself could not have.

The literary work Schnitzler produced during the war years was marked by a turn toward isolation, aging, and the humiliations of the body. *Doktor Gräsler, Badearzt* (*Doctor Gräsler, Spa Physician*), written in 1914 and published in the *Berliner Tageblatt* between February and March 1917, was a novella about a middle-aged physician practicing in a provincial spa town.[8] Dr. Emil Gräsler, forty-eight years old, a former ship's doctor now working as a seasonal physician at a thermal resort, finds himself alone after his sister Friederike's suicide. His carefully ordered but emotionally vacant life is disrupted by a belated and ill-fated attempt at romantic connection.

The plot turned on Gräsler's courtship of Sabine Schleheim, a twenty-seven-year-old woman, the daughter of a failed opera singer, who represented the possibility of a different life—marriage, domesticity, emotional presence. Sabine was practical and forward: she proposed to Gräsler in writing, suggested he purchase and renovate a local sanatorium, and offered her father's financial support. But Gräsler, paralyzed by indecision, fled from her proposal to his home city, where he drifted into a liaison with Katharina Rebner, a much younger shop clerk. When he finally tried to return to Sabine, the sanatorium was no longer for sale and Sabine wanted nothing to do with him. Katharina, meanwhile, had contracted scarlet fever—possibly through Gräsler's own contact with a sick child—and died. Gräsler, having lost every woman for whom he had felt anything, married within weeks a widow he barely knew.[9]

The novella was a portrait of emotional paralysis, and its autobiographical resonance was unmistakable. Schnitzler was writing about a provincial doctor's loneliness during a period when his own marriage was collapsing, when his own patterns of emotional reserve were costing him the domestic

life he had ambivalently entered. An interviewer in 1922 observed that
Schnitzler had been preoccupied for some years with the problem of the
aging man, and that from this preoccupation he had created the figures of
both Doktor Gräsler and Casanova.[10]

Casanovas Heimfahrt—Casanova's Homecoming—completed on August
20, 1917, serialized in *Die Neue Rundschau* in mid-1918, and published
as a book by S. Fischer the same year, became Schnitzler's most celebrated
work of prose fiction from the war period and remains one of his finest
achievements in the novella form.[11] It was a masterful examination of
aging, desire, and the humiliations that time inflicted on men who had
built their identities around sexual conquest. The subject could hardly
have been more personal. Schnitzler was fifty-five when he completed it,
his marriage had deteriorated past the point of repair, and the social world
that had sustained the erotic adventures of his youth had been destroyed
by four years of mechanized slaughter.

The novella took as its protagonist the historical Giacomo Casanova,
but at a moment in his life far removed from the legendary exploits of
his youth. This was Casanova at fifty-three, impoverished and diminished,
living in exile from his beloved Venice and desperate to return. He has been
offered the possibility of return if he will agree to work as a spy for the
Venetian state—a humiliating condition for a man who has prided himself
on his independence. The novella follows Casanova as he travels toward
Venice, stopping at the estate of Olivo, an old acquaintance, where he encounters Marcolina, a beautiful and intellectually serious young woman,
and a group of Italian officers.

What Schnitzler anatomized with clinical precision was the gap between Casanova's self-image and his actual capacities. Casanova still experienced himself as the great lover, the irresistible seducer. But his body had aged; his face had coarsened; his legendary virility was no longer reliable. The officers were younger, handsomer, more physically vital. Marcolina—who represented a new generation of women, educated and unimpressed by the sexual braggadocio of an earlier era—was politely but firmly uninterested in Casanova's advances.

The novella's central sequence—Casanova's desperate attempt to possess Marcolina through an arrangement with Lorenzi, one of the young officers—was among the most psychologically acute and most painful passages in Schnitzler's work. Casanova arranged for Lorenzi, who was Marcolina's lover, to gamble away money he did not have, then offered to forgive the debt on one condition: that Lorenzi allow Casanova to take his place, in darkness, in Marcolina's bed. The encounter occurred as planned. Casanova, impersonating Lorenzi, had sex with Marcolina, who believed she was with her young lover. The experience was, for Casanova, both a triumph and a devastating confirmation of his irrelevance: he had achieved sexual conquest, but only through deception, only by pretending to be someone else.

The duel that followed—Casanova challenged Lorenzi after the deception was discovered, and killed him—was not a triumph but a murder. Casanova had killed a younger version of himself, a man whose vitality and social position he had been attempting to inhabit and could only destroy. The duel was Schnitzler's final statement on the honor code he had been examining since *Liebelei*: it was not a mechanism for resolving genuine conflicts but a ritual through which aging men attempted to assert dominance they no longer possessed through means other than violence.

Casanovas Heimfahrt was also a meditation on exile and the impossibility of return. Casanova wanted to go back to Venice, the city of his youth and his triumphs, but the Venice he remembered no longer existed—and even if it did, he was no longer the man who had inhabited it. The home-coming of the title was revealed to be impossible: you cannot go home because home is not a place but a conjunction of time, circumstance, and identity, and all three have changed irrevocably. This theme resonated with particular force in 1918, when the Austria-Hungary that Schnitzler had known was collapsing.

The prose style of *Casanovas Heimfahrt* was among Schnitzler's finest achievements: precise, psychologically penetrating, capable of rendering both the external social surface and the interior psychological reality with equal authority. The free indirect discourse that Schnitzler had pioneered in *Leutnant Gustl* was here deployed with greater subtlety: the narrative voice moved seamlessly between Casanova's self-justifying interior mono-logue and a more objective rendering of the situation, allowing the reader to see both what Casanova believed about himself and what the evidence suggested about him.

At the villa on Sternwartestraße, life continued in a diminished register. Heinrich was twelve when the war began, sixteen when it ended—passing through adolescence during years of privation and anxiety.[12] Lili was five when the war started, nine when it ended, a child absorbing the atmos-phere of parental discord and historical catastrophe without the capacity to understand either. Schnitzler continued to write: the autobiography, *Doktor Gräsler*, *Casanovas Heimfahrt*, the comedy *Fink und Fliederbusch* (1917), stories and sketches and the relentless diary. The routine held. But the routine was now a fortress, not a habit, and the world outside the fortress was becoming unrecognizable.

The war years accelerated the deterioration of the marriage. Olga's criticism of Schnitzler's detachment was not merely political; it was personal. She saw in his refusal to engage with the war a version of the same reserve that characterized his behavior as a husband—the same coolness, the same self-protective distance, the same unwillingness to be fully present in a shared experience. She was not wrong. The qualities that made Schnitzler a great observer of human behavior—the clinical eye, the instinct for pattern, the capacity to stand outside a situation even while inhabiting it—were the same qualities that made him a difficult partner. In early 1917, Olga fell into a deep personal crisis and blamed her failed career on her husband, the children, and the name "Schnitzler."[13]

On November 12, 1918, the empire ended. The Republic of German-Austria was proclaimed. Schnitzler recorded the event in his diary with the measured understatement that was, by now, his signature register: "Ein bedeutsamer Tag der Weltgeschichte ist vorbei. Aus der Nähe sieht er nicht so großartig aus." An important day in the history of the world is over. From close up it does not look that wonderful.[14] The remark captured something essential about his temperament and his position. He was a man of the old world—born under Franz Joseph in 1862, educated in its institutions, shaped by its contradictions—and the new world that was emerging from the wreckage of the war was not one he had wished for or could easily inhabit.

The small, uncertain Austrian republic that replaced the multinational empire was poorer, angrier, more polarized, and more openly antisemitic than the society Schnitzler had known. The liberal assumptions on which his career had been built—that talent and intelligence could transcend the accidents of birth, that art could speak to a common humanity, that the individual conscience was sovereign—were not abolished by the empire's collapse, but they were no longer supported by the institutional structures that had made them plausible.

Professor Bernhardi had been banned because a Jewish writer had written honestly about antisemitism. The play had finally received its Austrian premiere in December 1918, after the empire's collapse removed the censorship apparatus that had suppressed it.[15] But the freedom to perform it came at a moment when the mechanisms it anatomized were operating with renewed vigor. What came next would be worse. The world that had produced *Anatol* and *Liebelei* and *Reigen* and *Das weite Land* was gone. The world that was replacing it had no use for the nuanced psychological observation and the ironized social critique that had been Schnitzler's signature. It wanted certainties, and Schnitzler had none to offer.

CHAPTER SEVENTEEN

Divorce & The Reigen Scandal (1920 & 1921)

REIGEN

IN THE WINTER OF 1920, Olga confessed to an affair. The marriage had been deteriorating for years—the war, the frustration, the emotional distance that had widened into an unbridgeable gulf—but the confession brought the crisis to what the diary called a "new climax."[1] Schnitzler claimed that he had maintained the principle of fidelity throughout the marriage, a claim that would have been unthinkable from the man who had conducted his youth as a serial seduction campaign but that he now advanced with apparent sincerity. Olga countered by accusing him of affairs with Hedy Kempny and Vilma Lichtenstern, women with whom Schnitzler had maintained close friendships during the marriage years.[2]

The symmetry was bitter and almost novelistic: the man who had spent his youth as a serial seducer, who had tallied orgasms in his diary and maintained simultaneous liaisons with working-class girls and society women, now stood accused by his wife while professing his own constancy. Whether his claim of fidelity was literally true—and the evidence is inconclusive, the diary entries ambiguous, the testimony of the accused parties unavailable—the irony was inescapable, and it was the kind of irony that Schnitzler, in his fiction, would have rendered with precision and without mercy. He had written Friedrich Hofreiter, the philandering husband of *Das weite Land* who could not tolerate his wife's single possible infidelity. He had anatomized, with clinical detachment, the mechanisms of masculine self-deception and sexual double standards. And now he was living the situation from the inside, experiencing the wounded vanity and the collapse of domestic certainty that he had depicted so many times on the page and the stage.

The arguments escalated through the late autumn and winter of 1920. The villa on Sternwartestraße, which had been a refuge and a workspace, became a battleground. Heinrich was eighteen, old enough to understand what was happening but not old enough to be anything other than a witness to his parents' mutual destruction. Lili was eleven, absorbing the atmosphere of recrimination and rage with the helpless sensitivity of a child who understands that something essential is breaking but cannot name what it is or prevent it from happening.

Olga left Vienna and went to stay with a friend in Munich. The separation was presented as temporary—a cooling-off period, a chance for perspective—but both parties understood that it was a rehearsal for something more permanent. Schnitzler continued to work, continued the diary, continued the routines that had sustained him through every previous crisis. But the routines were now mechanical rather than sustaining. He was fifty-eight years old, his marriage was collapsing, the world he had known had been destroyed by the war, and the new world that was replacing it was increasingly hostile to everything he represented.

Olga returned to spend the Christmas holidays with the family. She had decided upon a divorce and planned to leave Vienna.[3] It was not a threat or a negotiating position; it was a declaration. The marriage that had begun reluctantly in 1903, that had produced two children and seventeen years of accumulating resentments, was ending. The formalities would take time—divorce in post-war Austria was complicated, expensive, and socially consequential—but the psychological fact was accomplished. They would remain married in law until the summer of 1921, but they were already finished.

On December 23, 1920—the same day the family was navigating its private collapse—*Reigen* premiered in Berlin.[4] The coincidence of dates carried a weight that Schnitzler, in his exhaustion and private anguish, may not have fully registered at the time but that retrospective analysis makes impossible to ignore. As his marriage was ending, the play that would define his public notoriety was beginning its journey toward scandal.

The play had waited twenty-three years for this moment. Written in the winter of 1896–1897, while Marie Reinhard was carrying the child who would be stillborn, privately printed in 1900, commercially published in 1903 and promptly banned by German censors in 1904,[5] it had existed for more than two decades as a reputation rather than an experience—a work everyone knew about and almost no one had seen performed. Max Reinhardt, the most celebrated theatrical director in the German-speaking world, had planned to stage the first full production himself. He prepared a detailed promptbook—annotating all 264 pages, with extensive stage directions covering the first 48—and had scheduled the premiere at the Großes Schauspielhaus for January 1920.[6] But Reinhardt left his position as theater director in June 1920 before the production could be mounted. His successor, Felix Hollaender, transferred the rights to Gertrud Eysoldt, who ran the Kleines Schauspielhaus. The premiere ultimately took place under the direction of Hubert Reusch.[7]

The premiere itself was dramatic before a single line had been spoken. On the afternoon of December 23, a court injunction arrived at the theater banning the performance on grounds of indecency, apparently instigated by the Akademische Hochschule für Musik, whose building housed the theater.[8] Eysoldt stepped before the curtain, informed the audience of the ban and the threat of six weeks' imprisonment for the theater directors, and declared that she would not be deterred from defending artistic freedom. The performance went ahead in defiance of the injunction.

The initial critical reception was favorable. Alfred Kerr, one of the most influential critics of the period, praised the work and defended it in the pages of *Der Tag* the following day.[9] Other reviewers recognized the work's serious engagement with the social and sexual hypocrisies of Viennese society. For a moment—a brief, deceptive moment—it seemed possible that *Reigen* might take its place in the repertoire as the serious work of dramatic art its author had always insisted it was. The moment did not last.

By February 1921, the Berlin production had provoked a backlash from conservative, nationalist, and Catholic groups who recognized the play not as an artistic achievement but as a political provocation. The campaign against it was organized, deliberate, and explicitly antisemitic from its inception. Right-wing newspapers published denunciations. Catholic organizations mobilized their members. The attacks were not framed in aesthetic terms—the critics who opposed the play did not argue that it was poorly written or dramatically weak—but in explicitly racial and religious ones. A Jewish writer had written a play about sex, and the play's frankness about the universality of desire across social classes was interpreted, by those who needed such an interpretation, as evidence of Jewish degeneracy and Jewish hostility to Christian civilization.

When the play opened in Vienna on February 1, 1921, at the Kammerspiele on Rotenturmstraße—then a subsidiary of the Deutsches Volkstheater, under the direction of Heinz Schulbaur—the result was one of the era's most notorious theatrical scandals.[10] The opening night audience included both supporters of the production and organized opponents. Right-wing groups, some affiliated with Catholic organizations like the Katholischer Gesellenverein, arrived with the explicit intention of disrupting the performance. Fistfights broke out in the auditorium. Chairs were thrown. Stink bombs were hurled by young agitators. Police intervened. The antisemitic slogans shouted in the theater were not spontaneous expressions of outrage but coordinated talking points from a campaign that had been planned in advance.

On February 16, approximately two hundred people stormed the theater during a performance, throwing stink bombs, attacking audience members, and attempting to destroy the furnishings. Schnitzler himself, who was present, barely escaped to safety.[11] The Interior Ministry banned further performances. In Berlin, where the play continued for several more weeks, there were riots on February 22, thirty-four arrests, and a series of court proceedings in which the theater directors and performers were charged with immoral acts—the notorious *Reigen-Prozess*.[12]

Schnitzler responded to the Vienna riots with characteristic composure in a letter to the journalist Stefan Großmann, published in *Das Tage-Buch* on February 26, 1921. He wrote that he had no intention of engaging publicly with the affair, observing that he would feel "unspeakably ridiculous" trying to argue with politicians like Kunschak and Seipel, or with the apprentice who stormed the theater shouting slogans against the *Reigen* and the Social Democrats in the same breath. He had weathered similar storms before, he noted, recalling the controversies over *Leutnant Gustl* and *Professor Bernhardi*: "After a few years, nothing remains of all the noise except the books I have written, and a dim memory of the disgrace of my opponents."[13]

The courts eventually dismissed the Berlin charges. A panel of experts concluded that *Reigen* was not pornographic. The legal vindication was meaningless. The damage was done, and the damage was not primarily to the play's reputation but to Schnitzler's safety and standing. He was now, in the public discourse of right-wing Austria and Germany, "the Jewish pornographer," the man whose name appeared on lists of cultural degenerates compiled by organizations that would, within a decade, form the base of the Nazi movement.

The *Reigen* scandal—the name by which it became known, as if the play itself were the scandal rather than the violence directed against it—was the culmination of a process that had been gathering force throughout Schnitzler's career: the transformation of his work from literature into a weapon to be used against him. The play had been written by a man in his mid-thirties as an anatomy of Viennese hypocrisy—a demonstration that desire operated identically across all social classes and that the conversations surrounding sex revealed the same self-deceptions at every level of society. It was a work of formal brilliance, psychological precision, and moral seriousness. None of this mattered to the people breaking chairs in the Vienna theater or shouting antisemitic slurs at the stage.

The violence was not spontaneous; it was organized. The right-wing groups that disrupted the performance were the same groups that were, throughout the early 1920s, building the paramilitary infrastructure that would eventually deliver Austria to authoritarianism in 1934 and to annexation by Nazi Germany in 1938. The theater was, for them, a front in a larger war—a war against modernity, against liberalism, against secularism, against the Jewish presence in Austrian cultural life that they regarded as an alien contamination of Germanic purity. *Reigen* was a convenient provocation: sexually explicit, written by a Jew, performed in a city where the old certainties had been swept away and the new ones had not yet solidified, and already famous enough that attacking it would generate publicity for the attackers.

That the play was also a work of art—that it said something true and important about the society it depicted, that it belonged to the tradition of serious European drama, that critics and scholars recognized its value—was irrelevant to the people who organized the campaign against it. They were not arguing in good faith about the play's merits; they were using the play as an occasion to advance a political program, and the program was the elimination of Jewish influence from German cultural life. Schnitzler understood this. The diary entries from this period register not merely frustration or anger but a dawning recognition that the terms of engagement had changed fundamentally. He was not being criticized; he was being targeted. The distinction mattered.

Schnitzler's response was to withdraw the play himself. In 1922, he asked the S. Fischer Verlag, which held the performance rights, to grant no further licenses for German-language productions of *Reigen*.[14] The self-imposed ban would remain in effect until January 1, 1982, when his son Heinrich—the boy born in Hinterbrühl in 1902, by then an elderly theater director who had survived the war and the Holocaust by fleeing to America—authorized its re-release, more than fifty years after his father's death.[15] The self-imposed ban was an act of self-censorship born of exhaustion, disgust, and a pragmatic recognition that the play's continued performance would make him a target for violence he had no means of defending against.

The decision meant that one of the most important plays of the twentieth century was effectively silenced in the language for which it had been written for six decades. Films and radio adaptations circumvented the ban in various ways—Max Ophüls' 1950 French film *La Ronde* became the version by which international audiences knew the work—and the play remained popular in France, Russia, and Czechoslovakia, where it was performed in translation. But in the German-speaking world, *Reigen* became a ghost—present in reputation, absent from the stage, a reminder of what could not be said and what would not be tolerated.

The withdrawal was not a capitulation in the sense of admitting wrongdoing; it was a refusal to continue participating in a spectacle that had ceased to be about the play and had become entirely about the mob's right to shut down what it found offensive. Schnitzler would not give them the satisfaction of repeated opportunities to riot. He would not allow his work to be the occasion for the kind of violence that the emerging fascist movements wanted to normalize. The cost of this refusal was that the play disappeared from the stages where it belonged.

The personal and professional crises of 1920–1921 were inseparable. The collapse of his marriage and the *Reigen* scandal were not causally related—Olga's affair and decision to divorce had nothing to do with right-wing riots in Berlin—but they coincided in ways that compounded each other's effects. Schnitzler was losing his domestic life and his public standing simultaneously. The villa on Sternwartestraße, which had been his refuge, was now a site of emotional wreckage. The theaters, which had been his primary professional venue, were now battlegrounds where his work was used as a pretext for antisemitic violence.

The divorce proceeded in parallel with the scandal. In the spring of 1921, while *Reigen* was still generating riots and court proceedings in Berlin, legal proceedings went forward in accordance with Olga's wishes—she had initiated the separation; he complied. Alterations were made to his will. Custody arrangements were negotiated for Lili, who was twelve and had developed problems at school that were serious enough to require extra tutoring. The stress of her parents' separation, the atmosphere of recrimination that had pervaded the household for months, had manifested in academic difficulties that concerned Schnitzler deeply.

It was during this period that Schnitzler had one of his rare personal encounters with Sigmund Freud. He accompanied Lili to the Freud apartment at Berggasse 19, where he spoke briefly with Freud and his wife.[16] It was one of very few personal meetings between the two men who had spent their careers exploring the same territory from opposite sides: Freud through the systematic investigation of other minds, Schnitzler through the intuitive investigation of his own.

They had maintained, for decades, a relationship of mutual respect and mutual avoidance—a recognition of kinship combined with a reluctance to make that kinship explicit through personal contact. The meeting at Berggasse 19 was brief, formal, and focused on practical matters. The two men did not discuss their work or their parallel preoccupations. They exchanged the courtesies appropriate to a social call and parted without any suggestion that they should meet again.

On May 14, 1922—the eve of Schnitzler's sixtieth birthday—Freud wrote him a letter that became one of the most celebrated documents in the intellectual history of fin-de-siècle Vienna.[17] It was an extraordinary confession: an acknowledgment of the reasons for his long avoidance, an explanation of what Freud called his *Doppelgängerscheu*—his fear of encountering his double. "I have gained the impression that you know through intuition—really from a delicate self-observation—everything that I have discovered in other people by laborious work," Freud wrote.[18] He enumerated the parallels: Schnitzler's determinism, his skepticism, his engagement with the truths of the unconscious, his understanding of the instinctual nature of human beings, and the way his thoughts gravitated toward the polarity of love and death.

The compliment was generous, and it acknowledged a truth that both men understood: that literature and psychoanalysis were parallel methods of approaching the same problem, which was the problem of what human beings concealed from themselves. Schnitzler's *Leutnant Gustl* had done in fiction what Freud's free association technique did in the consulting room: it made the unconscious available for examination. *Reigen* had exposed the mechanisms of erotic self-deception that Freud was systematically categorizing in his theories of sexuality. *Professor Bernhardi* had dramatized the institutional antisemitism that both men, as Jewish professionals in Vienna, experienced as a condition of their professional lives.

But recognition from Freud, however gratifying intellectually, could not alter the political reality. The forces that had attacked *Reigen* were not interested in the play's psychological insight or its formal innovation. They were interested in using it as a weapon in a larger campaign, and that campaign was gathering strength. The 1920s would prove to be not a period of recovery from the war's catastrophe but a rehearsal for something worse.

On June 26, 1921, the divorce was finalized.[19] The marriage had lasted eighteen years. Arthur was fifty-nine; Olga was thirty-nine. Lili, at twelve, would remain with her father—a decision that reflected the depth of the bond between them and the practical reality that Olga, who planned to leave Vienna, could not easily take the child with her. Heinrich, at nineteen, was no longer a minor and went his own way. He had studied acting under Franz Herterich and made his stage debut that same year at the Raimundtheater in Vienna; he also enrolled at the University of Vienna to study philosophy, art history, and literary history.[20] His path would lead him from 1923 to Berlin, where he would build a career as an actor, dramatist, and director—a trajectory that echoed his father's own movement from medicine to the arts, the thwarted first vocation yielding to a different calling.

The separation from Olga became permanent. She moved out of the villa, taking an apartment elsewhere in Vienna before eventually relocating to Berlin to continue pursuing her singing career. The children divided their time between the two households, an arrangement that satisfied no one and that imposed on Heinrich and Lili the burden of navigating their parents' mutual hostility.

The divorce was described as amicable, and in certain practical respects it was: Olga remained involved with the children, maintained contact with Schnitzler, and would later be recognized, despite the legal dissolution, as his widow. When the Nazis came to power, it was Olga who would save his archive from destruction, acting as his heir and protector of his literary estate. She would eventually emigrate to the United States during the Nazi years and outlive her former husband by thirty-nine years, dying in 1970 at the age of eighty-eight. In the long perspective of her life, the marriage to Schnitzler was one chapter among many; in the long perspective of his, it was the central domestic fact of his middle years, the experiment in ordinary life that a man of extraordinary observation had attempted and failed.

But the word "amicable" conceals more than it reveals. The marriage had failed because its foundations were unsound—the age gap, the reluctance, the child who preceded the ceremony, the incompatibility of two people who wanted different things and lacked the flexibility to accommodate each other's needs. Schnitzler's emotional reserve, the quality that made him a penetrating observer and a difficult husband, had been a constant from the beginning; Olga's frustrated ambitions, her desire for a career that the marriage could not support and her talent could not sustain, had been equally constant. The war had accelerated the deterioration by imposing pressures that the marriage's fragile structure could not bear, and Olga's affair—an act of rebellion, desperation, independence, or all three—was the proximate cause of the break but not its explanation. The explanation was simpler and sadder: they had never been well matched, and eighteen years of trying had not made them so.

By the summer of 1921, the world in which Arthur Schnitzler had come of age was gone. The empire had dissolved into successor states. The liberal assumptions that had governed Viennese intellectual life—the belief in progress, in reason, in the possibility of a cosmopolitan culture that transcended ethnic and religious boundaries—had been shattered by the war and its aftermath.

The new Austrian republic was smaller, poorer, and meaner than the society it replaced, and the antisemitism that Schnitzler had examined in *Der Weg ins Freie* and confronted in *Professor Bernhardi* was now not a subject for drama but a condition of daily life. He had been called a Jewish pornographer in the newspapers. His play had been silenced by mob violence. His marriage had ended. He was fifty-nine years old, living alone in the villa on Sternwartestraße with his twelve-year-old daughter, and the work that lay ahead of him—the late novellas, the unfinished autobiography, the diary that would eventually run to thousands of pages—would be produced in a solitude that was no longer chosen but imposed.

He had entered the marriage as a reluctant bridegroom, a forty-one-year-old man whose son was already a year old, and he left it as a reluctant divorcee, a fifty-nine-year-old man whose daughter would stay by his side for the years that remained before her own catastrophe. He had written, during these eighteen years, some of the finest work in the German language: a novel about Jewish identity that mapped every response to antisemitism his generation could devise, a play about institutional prejudice that was banned by the institutions it described, a play about marriage that drew its authority from a marriage that was failing, and a cycle of sexual encounters so honest that it could not be performed for a quarter of a century and, when it finally was, provoked riots. He had also failed as a husband, in ways that his fiction diagnosed with greater honesty than his life could enact.

An interviewer once asked Schnitzler what he thought about the critical view that his works all seemed to treat the same subjects. He replied: "I write of love and death. What other subjects are there?"[21] The remark, which had sounded like a witticism when he made it, had acquired, by 1921, the weight of a confession. Love had failed him, or he had failed it, and death—the death of an empire, the death of a marriage, the death of the assumptions on which his world had been built—was everywhere.

He would not remarry. He would take lovers—Clara Katharina Pollaczek, Suzanne Clauser—but the domestic experiment was over. What remained was the work, the diary, the villa, and the daughter whose presence in the house on Sternwartestraße was both his greatest consolation and, though he could not yet know it, the source of the grief that would break him.

Part IV: Eyes Wide Open (1921–1931)

"*At 10.15 in the evening death. — (While I was in my room holding her picture in my hands and kissing it.)*"
—Arthur Schnitzler, diary, July 26, 1928

CHAPTER EIGHTEEN

Alone on Sternwartestraße, 1921–1923

HE WAS FIFTY-NINE, DIVORCED, and alone in a house that was too large for a man and a girl of twelve. The villa on Sternwartestraße still held its shape—the writing room, the secretary's desk, the domestic routines that Frieda Pollak maintained with the efficiency of someone who understood that her employer's survival depended on structure—but the life it contained had contracted. Olga was gone. Heinrich, at nineteen, was making his own way in the theater.

What remained was the work, the diary, the slow accretion of physical complaints, and Lili: his daughter, his companion, the center of an emotional life that had never found adequate expression in marriage and now concentrated itself, with an intensity that was both tender and perilous, on a child.

The paradox of Schnitzler's final decade was that it combined increasing isolation with increasing fame. Translations of his work into numerous languages were winning him international recognition on a scale he had never enjoyed before, but the man receiving the recognition was growing steadily more alone. His hearing was deteriorating—a loss that would worsen year by year, cutting him off from the conversations and the theater that had been the medium of his life.[1]

In April 1920, he had fallen while walking and injured his shoulder, and the pain from this injury would plague him until his death, a constant low-grade companion that joined the hearing loss and the ordinary depredations of age to make the body an increasingly unreliable instrument.[2] He was not old—fifty-nine is not old—but he was aging in the way that people age who have lived intensely and are now living alone: rapidly, visibly, with diminishing reserves of resilience.

Into this diminished life returned a woman he had met a quarter of a century earlier. Clara Katharina Pollaczek—born Clara Loeb, the daughter of a Viennese banker whose grandfather had made his fortune as a textile magnate clothing Habsburg armies during the Napoleonic Wars—had first encountered Schnitzler at a New Year's Eve party in her parents' house on December 31, 1895.[3] She was twenty; he was thirty-three. On the following morning, January 1, 1896, he recorded in his diary that the young woman had delighted him, noting that she had promised to send him things she had written and had been "sehr zutraulich"—very confiding.[4] Two months later, visiting the Loeb household again, he noted her more fully: "Clara, dieses liebe kleine Mädel mit grossen Augen"—Clara, this dear little girl with big eyes—who had sent him a novelette of remarkable quality, full of longing for freedom and unmistakable talent.[5]

She had literary ambitions of her own: in April 1897, writing under the male pseudonym "Bob," she published *Mimi: Schattenbilder aus einem Mädchenleben*—a sequence of scenes with a prologue by Hofmannsthal—in the *Neue Deutsche Rundschau*.[6] Critics received it as a female counterpart to Schnitzler's own *Anatol*, depicting a young woman's journey from shyness to erotic self-assurance. The work caused a family scandal when an anonymous letter—probably from Minnie Benedikt, the younger daughter of the newspaper magnate Moriz Benedikt—revealed to the Loeb parents that "Bob" was their daughter.[7] Schnitzler, writing from Paris at Hofmannsthal's urging, intervened with S. Fischer Verlag to halt the planned book publication. Clara's parents, alarmed by her friendship with literary men and by the erotically charged content of her work, hastened to arrange a marriage.

Before the engagement was settled, Schnitzler himself had registered as a possible match. He noted in his diary in late November 1897: "Es wird immer deutlicher, dass sie am liebsten mich heiraten möchte"—it becomes ever clearer that she would most like to marry me.[8] There are also traces in both sets of diaries of a brief romantic connection between Clara and Hofmannsthal—she complained, Schnitzler recorded, of "Hugo's staying away," and he wrote to Hofmannsthal that Clara felt "very forsaken" by him.[9] Nothing came of either possibility. In May 1898, Clara married Otto Pollaczek, the heir to the largest wholesale leather-hide business in the Habsburg monarchy, at the Seitenstettengasse synagogue in Vienna's first district.[10] She gave up writing and submitted to the life her parents had chosen.

When her husband took his own life in 1908—apparently because of financial difficulties, at the age of only thirty-five—she felt, according to her son's memoir, liberated.[11] She returned to writing, now as a financial necessity as well as a vocation. Contact with Schnitzler had resumed around 1915—letters, encounters, even a telephone conversation documented in his diary.[12] After the divorce from Olga in 1921, they met far more frequently: theater visits, museum visits, walks in the parks of Vienna. By February 1923, they were, for most purposes, a couple. She was forty-eight; he was sixty-one. Both had been formed by the conventions of their class and both had spent their lives negotiating the distance between those conventions and their desires.

Clara's decision to enter a sexual relationship outside marriage would have been taboo for a woman of her generation and background—a convention she chose to disregard. For eight years, from 1923 until his death, she was his companion, his audience, his most attentive reader, and his witness. He read almost everything she wrote; she became a critic of his work whose judgment he valued.[13] In 1924 he gave her a typewriter for

Christmas. Her own literary output during these years—stories, novellas, a play called *Redoute* in 1926, another called *Dame* in 1930, and contributions to the *Neue Freie Presse*—was steady if never celebrated.[14] They did not live together, and there is no evidence that either contemplated marriage. The relationship was punctuated by jealousies and tensions: Schnitzler maintained other attachments, including his continued contact with Olga and his relationship with Hedy Kempny, a young journalist and aspiring writer thirty-three years his junior, which caused Pollaczek frequent anguish.[15]

Their most characteristic shared activity was the cinema. They went together over five hundred times between 1923 and 1931—both kept careful records in their diaries—and the films they saw ranged, with cheerful indiscrimination, from sentimental melodramas to recognized classics.[16] The evenings followed a reliable pattern: the film, then dinner at a nearby restaurant, then the walk or ride home. Pollaczek's diaries suggest that the cinema served a distractive function—a way of being together without the pressure of conversation, a shared darkness in which the difficulties of the relationship could be temporarily suspended. She recorded his behavior with a diarist's eye, noting in one characteristic entry that "A. ist manchmal wie ein kleines Kind"—A. is sometimes like a little child.[17]

In his final year, when the cinema became too difficult, they discovered listening to the radio together as an alternative. The companionship was not always easy—there were jealousies, tensions, recriminations, and other women—but it was sustained, and it was present. Pollaczek noted in her diary that Schnitzler insisted he could not let her go, that no one meant as much to him as she did, and yet that he wanted his freedom too—a pattern she recognized and endured.[18] When he died on October 21, 1931, she was at his side. She later wrote that she held his head in her hands until his last breath.[19]

A memorial service took place at the Burgtheater on November 15, 1931. Clara Katharina Pollaczek delivered the address in the form of a five-stanza poem she had written for him, published that same day in the *Neue Freie Presse*.[20] In subsequent years she continued to publish poems in the *Neue Freie Presse* on each anniversary of his birthday and death. She also composed, on the basis of her diary notebooks and their correspondence, a memoir of approximately nine hundred typescript pages—*Arthur Schnitzler und ich*—which she bequeathed to the Vienna City Library with instructions that it be published only after her death.[21] She died in Vienna on July 22, 1951, at the age of seventy-six, having survived the Nazi period under the protection of a Czechoslovak passport acquired through her marriage to Otto Pollaczek.[22]

CHAPTER NINETEEN

Late Masterpieces: Fräulein Else (1924)

FRÄULEIN ELSE

THE WORKS SCHNITZLER PRODUCED in his sixties are among the finest things he wrote, and they are shadowed, in retrospect, by a prescience that their author could not have intended and that his daughter's death would render unbearable. *Fräulein Else*, published on October 1, 1924, by Paul Zsolnay in Vienna, is a novella written entirely in interior monologue—the technique Schnitzler had pioneered in *Leutnant Gustl* a quarter of a century earlier, now brought to a perfection that surpassed the earlier work in psychological depth and formal control.[1] Its subject is a nineteen-year-old woman's destruction.

Schnitzler had begun work on the novella in 1921, and on December 14, 1922, he noted in his diary that he was conceiving it in "Gustl Technik"—the interior monologue form he had invented two decades earlier.[2] His original conception, sketched that same year, had been simpler and stranger: a young girl walks naked into the dining room of a mountain hotel to test the men who are courting her.[3] Over the following months he would transform this scenario into something far more psychologically complex, grounding the act of public exposure in financial coercion and familial betrayal. The most intensive writing occurred between December 1922 and April 1923, when he declared a first draft complete; he revised through the autumn and into 1924 before judging it ready for publication.[4]

The twenty-four years separating *Leutnant Gustl* from *Fräulein Else* had given Schnitzler time to refine the stream-of-consciousness technique into something that transcended its origins. The technique in *Gustl*—groundbreaking as it was—bore the marks of a first full experiment: the associative chains were somewhat mechanical in their repetitiveness, the returns to the central anxiety somewhat predictable in their timing, the colloquial language rendered with accuracy but not with the full musical range of which the technique was capable.

Fräulein Else deployed the same fundamental form but with a command that transformed it. The associations were richer, more surprising, more genuinely responsive to the specific qualities of Else's consciousness rather than to a generic model of anxious interiority. The fragmentation was more artfully varied—not simply the compulsive return of a single obsession but the complex polyphony of a mind that was simultaneously processing immediate social reality, remembering the past, fantasizing the future, and conducting an internal argument with itself about what it was, what it owed, and what it was worth. Hugo von Hofmannsthal, reading the finished novella, wrote to Schnitzler that although *Leutnant Gustl* was admirably told, *Fräulein Else* surpassed it decisively: within German literature, he declared, Schnitzler had created a genre entirely his own.[5]

The Italian publisher and essayist Roberto Calasso observed, in his afterword to the Adelphi edition, that perhaps no modern narrator had succeeded in fusing interior monologue, fantasy, action, and dialogue with such intimacy.[6] The text did not maintain clean distinctions between what Else thought and what she said, between what she imagined and what she observed, between the internal drama of her consciousness and the external social drama proceeding around her. These registers bled into each other with a fluidity that mimicked the actual operation of consciousness under stress—the way an anxious mind, rather than processing events in an orderly linear sequence, experienced them as simultaneous layers of perception, memory, anticipation, and self-narration.

Else is young, aristocratic, Jewish, and vacationing at a luxury resort in the Italian Alps when a telegram arrives from her mother in Vienna: her father, a lawyer, is facing financial ruin and possible imprisonment for embezzlement. The family needs thirty thousand gulden immediately. There is, her mother believes, one possible source of rapid help: Herr von Dorsday, a wealthy art dealer of middle age who is also staying at the resort and who has a social acquaintance with the family. Else must ask him for the money.

The request was already laden with implications that the text, through Else's stream of consciousness, explored with mounting horror: a mother asking her daughter to solicit a wealthy older man on behalf of a father who had spent his life borrowing money and failing to repay it was already a transaction in which Else's social capital—her youth, her attractiveness, her presumed capacity to charm—was being deployed as a family resource. The familial coercion operated through the language of daughterly duty. The financial coercion was stark: her father faced prison, her family faced ruin, and she was in a position to prevent this.

Dorsday agrees—on a condition. He wants to see Else naked. Not to touch her; merely to look. Fifteen minutes, just looking, nothing more. The proposition was framed as a request and experienced as an assault, and the novella's power lay in the unbroken stream of Else's consciousness as she circled the dilemma: family duty against personal dignity, survival against self-destruction, the demands of others against the sovereignty of the self.

Dorsday's counter-proposal was constructed with the precision of a philosopher's thought experiment about power, consent, and the conditions under which genuine choice was possible. He was careful about the terms: just looking, nothing more, no touching, no further demands. The qualification was deliberate and, in its way, the most disturbing aspect of the proposal. By specifying that he wanted only to look—that his demand was entirely visual, entirely non-contact—Dorsday placed Else's situation in a legal and social no-man's-land where the mechanisms that might otherwise provide her with recourse or protection became unavailable. He could not be prosecuted for what he proposed; it fell below the threshold of any recognized violation. He was not offering rape or assault; he was offering a transaction in which Else's body served as the medium of exchange. The precision of his limitation—the insistence on the minimal version of his demand that still constituted a complete degradation—revealed a sophisticated understanding of power: he wanted the maximum that could be taken with the minimum that could be prosecuted.

The structure of the trap was what made the novella so devastating. The coercion operated on multiple levels simultaneously. There was the financial coercion: her father faced prison. There was the familial coercion: the request came from her mother, who framed it in the language of daughterly duty. There was the social coercion: Else had been raised in a world that defined female value substantially in terms of attractive appearance and the capacity to please men of means, and Dorsday's proposal was, in a grotesque way, simply an explicit version of the implicit transaction that the social world had always been conducting around her body. And there was the coercion of the proposal's own apparent reasonableness: it was only looking, it was only fifteen minutes, it would save her father. Each of these pressures was, taken alone, potentially manageable; taken together, they constituted a situation in which genuine free choice—choice unconstrained by threats to values the chooser could not abandon—was structurally impossible.

Dorsday's demand made explicit a mechanism that the social world of the resort—the same social world that Schnitzler had been examining since the *Anatol* cycle—ordinarily kept implicit: the asymmetric distribution of the power to look along gendered lines, the constitution of women as objects of visual appraisal rather than subjects of autonomous experience. In the ordinary course of resort life, this mechanism operated through social codes and expectations that remained unnamed. Dorsday's proposal stripped away the coding and named it directly: he was offering to pay for the right to look, and the price he was willing to pay was the resolution of a crisis that would otherwise destroy Else's family. He was not departing from the logic of the social world; he was simply articulating it.

Else's thoughts looped and spiraled—obsessive, repetitive, interrupted by flashes of fantasy and desire—and the reader was given access to a mind in the process of confronting an impossible situation. She had Veronal capsules in her room, the sedative that had become, in the pharmacology of the 1920s, a common means of suicide. Thoughts of death circled even before the crisis fully materialized. Her consciousness engaged with the proposal in ways that were, by turns, horrified, calculating, fantastical, and self-aware in a manner that went beyond the capacity of any straightforwardly resistant response. She knew she was being exploited; she could analyze the structure of the exploitation with considerable precision; and yet her analysis did not free her from the situation it identified. This was one of the text's most psychologically acute observations: knowing that you were trapped did not, in itself, provide the means of escape.

Else was explicitly Jewish—unusual for a Schnitzler protagonist, whose Jewish identity was typically present through implication rather than direct statement.[7] She thought about being Jewish: she was aware of it as an aspect of her social position, aware of the specific double exposure that being both a woman and a Jew created in the social world she inhabited, aware of the ways in which her family's financial precariousness intersected with the social vulnerabilities of Jewish identity in the declining years of the Habsburg liberal era. She belonged to a family that had achieved entry into the world of the Viennese upper bourgeoisie—the world of resort vacations, social connections with wealthy art dealers, the education and social polish that came with money—but whose hold on that world was precarious and dependent on the continued financial performance of a father who had repeatedly failed to sustain it. Jewish upward mobility in fin-de-siècle Austria was a fragile achievement: attained through exceptional effort, maintained through perpetual social performance, and vulnerable to the kind of financial disaster that Else's father had brought about.

The father-daughter dynamic that Else's consciousness traced was the text's most explicit engagement with the family as an economic and psychological institution. The family, in the world Schnitzler was depicting, was not a site of mutual care and freely chosen attachment; it was a structure of inherited obligation in which each member had a role defined by gender, generation, and social position. Else's role—the role that the telegram activated—was the role of the attractive young woman whose social capital could be mobilized in a crisis to manage the consequences of male irresponsibility. Her mother's telegram did not present the request as a choice; it presented it as the obvious and natural thing that Else would want to do for her father. The naturalizing of the demand—the framing of what was in fact an exploitation as simply what daughters did for fathers—was itself a form of coercion, one that operated through love rather than through threat but that was no less constraining for that.

By the novella's end, Else had taken Veronal and then, before the drug fully took hold, walked into the resort's music room where guests were gathered for an evening concert. She removed her robe and stood naked before them all. The assembled guests—including Dorsday—witnessed not the private, controlled, proprietary act of looking that Dorsday had demanded, but a public, uncontrollable, socially catastrophic performance. She collapsed. She was carried away. She lay dying—conscious but unable to speak or move, locked inside a body that had become her final prison.

Else's resolution of the crisis—her decision to take Veronal and then to disrobe publicly—was simultaneously a compliance with Dorsday's demand and a radical subversion of it; simultaneously a defeat and an act of power; simultaneously a suicide and a performance. Dorsday's demand had a very specific structure: fifteen minutes, in private, under his control, on his terms. Else's response preserved the essential element—she would be naked before him—while destroying every other condition that made the demand tolerable for him. She did it publicly, in the most socially consequential possible setting, in front of an audience that included every-one whose opinion mattered to everyone involved. She did it on her own initiative and her own timing, not as a private transaction arranged for his satisfaction but as a public act whose meaning she, not he, was controlling. She had taken the Veronal: she was already choosing death. And in the space between the decision to die and the arrival of death, she performed an act that transformed Dorsday's demand from a private exploitation into a public scandal—one in which he, not she, was the figure whose social reputation was destroyed.

Whether this constituted agency in a meaningful sense—whether an act performed under coercion, by a person who had already decided to die, in a state partially altered by a sedative, constituted a genuine exercise of autonomy—was a question the text refused to answer definitively, and the refusal was the point. Else's act was the only form of agency available to her in the situation she was in, and it was both more and less than genuine autonomy: more, because it transformed the terms of her victimization; less, because genuine autonomy would have required a social world entirely unlike the one she inhabited. The text did not celebrate her death as liberation; it did not present her action as a triumph. It presented it as what it was—the most consequential and the most self-determining act available to a person for whom all the socially sanctioned paths had been closed.

The novella was startling in its frankness about female sexuality and devastating in its analysis of the impossible positions in which young women were placed by the intersection of money, power, and masculine entitlement. Scholars have read the novella as, in part, a rebuttal of Otto Weininger's misogynistic and antisemitic characterization of Jewish womanhood.[8] But it was the psychological portrait, not the polemical intent, that gave the work its force. Schnitzler had spent forty years learning to render the inside of a mind on the page, and in *Fräulein Else* the technique achieved a fluency that made his earlier experiments look like rehearsals. The novella's first publication, in the *Neue Rundschau* in November 1924, was received with immediate acclaim; the book edition ultimately sold some seventy thousand copies, a remarkable figure for Schnitzler's later career.[9]

Fräulein Else was the third and final work of what critics had identified as Schnitzler's implicit "Woman Trilogy," following *Frau Berta Garlan* (1901) and *Frau Beate und ihr Sohn* (1913).[10] The trilogy traced an extended and deepening engagement with female interiority—with the specific psychological landscape of women living within the social constraints of Schnitzler's historical moment, and with the formal challenge of rendering that landscape from the inside. The three works together represented one of the more sustained efforts by a male author of the period to take seriously the subjective experience of women as a literary and psychological subject—not as a vehicle for examining male desire, not as a social type or a moral category, but as a domain of genuine and complex inner life deserving the full resources of literary representation.

The achievement was more remarkable given the broader context of Schnitzler's career—a career that had begun, in the *Anatol* cycle, with female characters who were primarily objects of male projection and romantic fantasy. The progression from those early figures to the fully realized interiority of *Fräulein Else* represented a trajectory of increasing imaginative and ethical engagement: Schnitzler moving from the observation of women as social phenomena to the attempt to inhabit women as psychological subjects. To render Else's consciousness convincingly was not merely to understand women intellectually; it was to have developed, through some combination of observation, empathy, and formal craft, the capacity to imagine oneself into a mode of being shaped by different social pressures and organized around different anxieties than those that structured the consciousness of a middle-aged Viennese Jewish male physician and playwright.

Lili Schnitzler was fifteen when *Fräulein Else* was published in 1924.[11] She read it. She identified with the character. The parallels—a young woman trapped, a father's world pressing down on her, the resort in Italy, the slide toward self-destruction—would acquire, four years later, a resonance so terrible that it raised a question no one could answer: whether the father's art had in some way predicted, or even shaped, the daughter's fate.

The biographical shadow that fell across this dynamic—Schnitzler published the novella when Lili was fifteen; Lili read it, identified with Else; Lili died by suicide four years later at eighteen—was one of the more haunting facts in the history of modern European literature.[12] The connection has been discussed with appropriate care by scholars unwilling to draw simple causal conclusions, but the resonance was real and could not be simply set aside. Schnitzler had, in *Fräulein Else*, created a portrait of a father-daughter relationship in which the father's failures were borne by the daughter at the cost of her life. That his own daughter read this portrait and found herself in it; that the trajectory the novella depicted—a young woman destroyed by the intersection of family obligation, sexual coercion, and social impossibility—had a biographical parallel in the life of the author's own child: these facts belonged to the work's history and to the history of what literature could and could not do with the truths it told.

Contemporaries sensed the terrible connection. The suggestion that Lili had in some way followed the path Else had shown her—as though the character her father had created had mapped a trajectory that the daughter then traced—carried a weight of guilt that may have been unfair and was certainly unanswerable, but it belonged to the story because it belonged, inescapably, to the aftermath.[13] If the poet-father whose stories ended so terribly bore a piece of guilt for his daughter's death, then the guilt was inseparable from the gift, and the gift was inseparable from the seeing that had defined his life.

Schnitzler did not cause Lili's death by writing *Fräulein Else*; he could not have known what he was writing toward. But the convergence was too precise, and too painful, to be acknowledged only as coincidence. The novella had been an act of imaginative sympathy—an attempt to render, from the inside, the consciousness of a young woman trapped by forces she could neither control nor escape. That his own daughter would find herself in a similar trap, that she would choose a similar escape, that the father's capacity to see and to document would prove insufficient to prevent what it had so precisely foreseen: this was the tragedy that Schnitzler would carry for the final three years of his life.

In 1929, *Fräulein Else* was adapted as a silent film, directed by Paul Czinner and starring Elisabeth Bergner as Else.[14] And—in a casting choice that must have struck Schnitzler with the force of a visitation from his own past—Adele Sandrock, his former lover from the tempestuous affair of 1893–1895, now sixty-five years old, played the supporting role of the Aunt.[15] The film premiered at the Capitol Theater in Berlin on March 8, 1929.[16] Schnitzler was sixty-six. Lili had been dead for eight months. The past and the present collapsed into each other: the young woman he had loved thirty-six years earlier, now elderly, playing a minor role in the film adaptation of a story about a young woman's death that had, in ways no one could have predicted, prefigured his own daughter's.

The contemporary resonance of *Fräulein Else*—acknowledged in recent scholarship as startlingly relevant to discussions of power, consent, and the structures of sexual coercion—was not a matter of the text having accidentally anticipated specific contemporary events. It was a matter of Schnitzler having analyzed, with clinical precision, the underlying structures of a form of power that remained operative across the century separating the novella's composition from the present. The dynamic between Dorsday and Else—wealthy older man in a position of economic power over a young woman who could not afford to refuse him, framing his demand in language that made explicit refusal seem hysterical and implicit compliance seem merely the reasonable response to an inconvenient situation—was not specific to fin-de-siècle Austria. It was a recurring form of the abuse of economic and social power in any social world where wealth and gender intersected to produce the kind of structural vulnerability that Else experienced.

The specific feature of Dorsday's demand that made it so analytically precise was the feature that placed it below the threshold of legal or social recognition as coercion: the insistence that it was only looking, that there was no physical contact, that Else retained the formal freedom to refuse. This structure—the exploitation that maintained its own deniability by staying just inside the boundaries of what could be named as wrong—was a structure that contemporary discourse about consent and power has continued to struggle to articulate. Schnitzler had articulated it in 1924, through Else's stream of consciousness, with a precision that remains striking.

Fräulein Else was the work in which the major concerns of Schnitzler's career—the epistemological problem of knowing other people, the social structures of gender and class, the psychological cost of the codes by which bourgeois society organized itself, the formal challenge of rendering interior life—converged in their most concentrated and most fully achieved form. The text was simultaneously a culmination and a demonstration of what forty years of unrelenting observation had cost and what it had achieved. Schnitzler could see with devastating clarity. He could render what he saw with extraordinary precision. What he could not do—what no amount of seeing could do—was prevent the tragedies he had spent his career documenting from recurring in his own life. The gift and the curse were inseparable, and by 1929, with Lili dead and the world he had known collapsing around him, the curse weighed more heavily than the gift had ever compensated for.

Chapter Twenty

Traumnovelle and Its Enduring Legacy (1925–1926)

TRAUMNOVELLE

Two years later, Schnitzler published *Traumnovelle*—*Dream Story*—the work that would, nearly seven decades after his death, become his most widely known creation, though he could not have imagined the form in which this fame would arrive. The novella was serialized in *Die Dame*—a magazine devoted to modern women and their concerns—between December 1925 and March 1926, and published in book form by S. Fischer Verlag later that year.[1] Schnitzler was sixty-three years old when serialization began.[2] His wife Olga had long since left; his daughter Lili, whose uncanny identification with the protagonist of *Fräulein Else* would contribute to the tormented final years of his life, still lived.[3] He had five more years to write before his death in October 1931.

Traumnovelle was shorter than *Fräulein Else*, simpler in plot than *Das weite Land*, less formally experimental than *Leutnant Gustl*. It achieved its effects not through innovation but through mastery, which was perhaps the distinction that separated the late work of great writers from everything that preceded it. The novella was, in the retrospective view that forty years of writing made possible, the work in which the accumulated preoccupations of an entire career—the unknowability of other people, the instability of bourgeois security, the relationship between desire and identity, the dream logic that underlay waking social performance—were gathered into their most condensed and most formally controlled expression.

The story told of Doctor Fridolin, a Viennese physician, and his wife Albertine, who had been married for years and had a young daughter. One evening, in the course of a conversation about fidelity and desire, Albertine confessed to her husband that she had once—some time ago, during a holiday—seen a naval officer and experienced, in that moment, a desire so complete and so overwhelming that she had come close to abandoning everything: husband, daughter, social position, the entire structure of her life. She had not acted on the desire; the officer had disappeared; the moment had passed. She was telling Fridolin not because anything had happened but because the admission had become, for her own psychological reasons, necessary—because the pretense that she had never felt desire outside the marriage had become a weight she could no longer carry.

The confession shattered the assumptions on which their marriage had rested—the comfortable fiction that monogamy was natural, that desire was containable, that the partner one had chosen was the partner one wanted. Fridolin's response was the central psychological datum from which the entire novella proceeded. He was shattered—not by anything Albertine had done, but by the revelation that she had felt something he did not know she was capable of feeling, had been a different person, in the interior of her desires, from the person he believed he was married to. The woman he thought he knew was revealed to contain depths he had not suspected: a capacity for intense, transgressive desire that had been present throughout their marriage without his knowledge, expressed in a fantasy that had come close, in her own estimation, to upending everything.

His response was not rational—he knew she had not acted, knew the desire was fantasy, knew the confession was a form of trust—but it was psychologically precise: the discovery that another person's interior life was a vast domain one had never explored, even after years of intimate cohabitation, produced a kind of vertigo that could not simply be corrected by the application of rational reassurance. Albertine and Fridolin had been married for years; they had a child; they had constructed together the entire domestic and social apparatus of a Viennese bourgeois professional couple. And yet the opening conversation revealed that each of them had been, throughout this shared life, simultaneously present and absent to the other: present in all the observable dimensions of quotidian existence, absent in the dimension of desire, fantasy, and the interior life that desire organised.

Fridolin, jealously tormented, embarked on a night journey through Vienna. The night began with a professional call: a patient had died, and Fridolin attended. This was real, unambiguous, medically routine. But almost immediately the texture of events began to blur. The dead man's daughter attempted to seduce him, in circumstances that were simultaneously plausible and strange. He encountered a prostitute in the streets with an oddly ceremonious quality. His old friend Nachtigall, a pianist playing in a dubious establishment, spoke of a secret masked gathering in terms that hovered between real information and a kind of invitation to fantasy.

Schnitzler's technical achievement in this section was to render a waking experience that had the phenomenology of dreaming without committing to either category. Fridolin was awake; he moved through actual Vienna streets; the events he participated in could, individually, be reported as real occurrences. But the sequence of events had the quality of oneiric logic—the way a dream presented each new scene as the necessary and inevitable consequence of the last, while the connections between scenes followed emotional rather than causal necessity. Fridolin was not dreaming; he was experiencing a night that his agitated, jealous, destabilised consciousness transformed into something that functioned like a dream, in which each encounter became an opportunity to explore the desires and fears that Albertine's confession had released in him.

The specific encounters of the night journey were calibrated to expose dimensions of Fridolin's character and desires that his ordinary bourgeois existence had kept suppressed. The dying man's daughter offered him the intensity of feeling—grief, desire, gratitude—that his professional and domestic life had organised away. The prostitute offered him the simplicity of an encounter without social complication. Nachtigall offered him access to a world of pleasure organised beyond the ordinary social codes. Each encounter was also a form of temptation and a form of test: what would Fridolin do when the ordinary social constraints were temporarily lifted?

The night carried him to a secret masked gathering held by an aristocratic society. Fridolin obtained a costume and infiltrated an assembly of masked figures in a villa outside Vienna: the participants were, it emerged, members of the aristocracy and upper classes, engaged in a ritualised gathering whose elaborate ceremonial organisation was as striking as its erotic content. There were masked women arranged in a choreographed display; masked men circling and selecting; music; a quality of ritual solemnity that sat strangely alongside the erotic purpose of the occasion. Underlying everything was an atmosphere of danger: this was not simply a private pleasure but something more organised, more exclusive, more consequential for those who penetrated it without authorisation.

Fridolin was recognised as an outsider almost immediately. The ritual demand came: "Take off your mask!" It was the moment at which the text's social and political subtext became briefly legible on the surface. As Frederic Raphael—who would later write the screenplay for Stanley Kubrick's adaptation—observed, the demand to unmask was the antisemitic demand in a different register: the command to reveal oneself as a Jew, to step out from behind the protective covering of bourgeois respectability and be identified in the nakedness of one's actual social category.[4]

Fridolin is not, in the text, presented as Jewish in any explicit way, but his experience at the gathering—the outsider who had infiltrated an assembly of the powerful, whose disguise was penetrated, who was exposed and ejected, and who suspected afterward that the woman who sacrificed herself for him might have paid for his intrusion with her life—carried the psychological freight of the Austrian Jewish experience that Schnitzler had been processing throughout his career. The paranoia, the sense of conditional belonging, the knowledge that the mask of assimilation could be stripped at any moment and by any hand: these were not simply Fridolin's personal anxieties but the structural anxieties of a specific historical position. As Reuben Brainin, the Hebrew literary critic who had known Schnitzler since September 1903, observed in his 1931 tribute, Schnitzler "clearly recognised the anomalous position of the Austrian Jew" without ever submitting to the assimilationist impulse.[5]

A masked woman stepped forward and offered to sacrifice herself in Fridolin's place—to pay the penalty for his unauthorised presence. She was masked; she offered herself in a gesture that was simultaneously erotic and sacrificial. Her sacrifice removed Fridolin from danger—he was ejected without further consequence—but its nature and cost remained permanently unclear. Schnitzler withheld the information that would allow the gesture to be classified: we do not know who she was, what her sacrifice consisted of, or what befell her.

Fridolin escaped and returned home. The next day, he discovered that a woman had been found dead—possible suicide or murder—whose face matched what he had glimpsed beneath the mask. The connection between the gathering's unnamed sacrifice and this anonymous death was suggested but not confirmed. The ambiguity was deliberate and significant: it maintained the dream logic of the night's events into the following day, refusing the transition to a more legible causal reality that the daylight setting might otherwise have provided.

That morning, Albertine recounted her own dream—experienced the same night as Fridolin's journey, before he had told her anything of his own adventure. In the dream, Fridolin had been captured by the figures of her own erotic fantasy—the naval officer and others—and was being crucified while Albertine, freed from the constraints that bound her in waking life, made love to other men. The image was violent, erotic, and unmistakably symbolic: Fridolin, in Albertine's unconscious, was simultaneously the figure whose existence constrained her freedom and the figure whose suffering she observed from a position of liberated desire. She did not save him in the dream; she watched, and she chose.

The symmetry between Albertine's dream and Fridolin's night journey was one of the novella's central formal achievements. Both were nocturnal adventures in which the constraints of ordinary life were suspended and desire found expression in forms that the daylight world did not permit. Both partners had, in different modes and different spaces, been somewhere else during the night; both had experienced desires and situations that the marriage's normal structure did not contain; both were now, in the morning light, attempting to account for where they had been and what it meant.

The exchange of confessions that followed—Fridolin telling Albertine of his night's adventure, Albertine telling him her dream—was the novella's emotional climax and its most complex moment. The conversation was not a reconciliation exactly; it was more like a mutual recognition of a truth that the marriage had previously been organised to avoid acknowledging.

The novella concluded with Albertine's final speech: they should not inquire into the future, she said. They should be grateful to fate that they had emerged safely from these adventures—whether they were real or only a dream. "Now we are truly awake," she said. "But perhaps not for long."[6]

The final lines were among the most discussed endings in Schnitzler's work, and the ambiguity was deliberate and rigorously maintained. The advice not to inquire into the future—to be grateful for having emerged safely from adventures that might have been real or only dreamed—carried the weight of a very specific wisdom: the wisdom of someone who had understood that the stability of ordinary life depended on a certain willingness not to look too deeply, and who had chosen, having looked, to return to the surface rather than to pursue the depths. The qualification—"but perhaps not for long"—could be read as simply a realistic acknowledgment that wakefulness was temporary, that sleep and dream would return, that the clarity of the morning conversation would give way to the ordinary blur of daily life. It could also be read as something more ominous: a recognition that the stability achieved by surviving the night's adventures was itself temporary, that the dreams and desires the night had revealed would not be permanently quieted by a morning's conversation.

The novella's central insight—that the order, balance, and security of bourgeois life were an illusion maintained over depths that the social surface refused to acknowledge—was a summation of everything Schnitzler had spent his career exploring: the gap between the social surface and the erotic interior, the masks people wear and the faces beneath them, the fragility of domestic arrangements that presented themselves as permanent. The novella's title—*Traumnovelle*, dream novella—applied simultaneously to the dreamlike character of Fridolin's night journey and to the broader condition it revealed: the marriage itself had been a kind of dream, maintained by the mutual agreement not to look too closely at what lay beneath it.

It was also, unmistakably, the work of a man who had lived through the failure of his own marriage and understood, with a clarity that was both artistic and personal, how little the appearance of stability guaranteed. Schnitzler and Olga's divorce had been finalised on 26 June 1921; by the time he was completing *Traumnovelle*, he had entered a sustained relationship with Clara Katharina Pollaczek, born 15 January 1875, which would endure until his death, alongside continuing attachments to other women, among them Hedy Kempny.[7] The postwar context of the novella was present not through explicit historical reference—the war was barely mentioned—but through the specific quality of fragility that attached to the bourgeois security the characters had reconstructed. Schnitzler's insight in *Traumnovelle* was that the reconstruction of bourgeois stability after catastrophe was precisely that: a reconstruction, a deliberate rebuilding of social forms whose hollowness had been made visible by historical events, whose maintenance required a more conscious act of will than it had before the catastrophe.

Scholars have noted the Jewish subtext—Fridolin's feelings of exposure and vulnerability echoed the uneasiness of Austrian Jews in the face of gentile provocation—but the novella's reach extended beyond any single identity. It was about what everyone concealed and what happened when the concealment failed. It was about the impossibility of truly knowing another person, and the specific, consequential form this impossibility took within the institution of marriage. A contemporary visitor who interviewed Schnitzler at Sternwartestrasse 71 in 1928, shortly after *Traumnovelle* had appeared in print, found him in person the antithesis of the dandy his reputation had suggested: "careworn and wincing under the reality of death."[8] The novella bore that burden visibly.

In 1968, Stanley Kubrick read *Traumnovelle* and recognised in it the material for a film about the hidden life of a marriage. He acquired the rights shortly after finishing *2001: A Space Odyssey*.[9]

The project gestated for three decades, through multiple proposed casts and abandoned screenplays. Kubrick engaged Frederic Raphael as screenwriter in 1994, and filming finally took place in England between 1996 and 1998. The most consequential of Kubrick's decisions in adapting the novella was the transposition of setting: from Vienna 1900 to New York City in the 1990s, with Tom Cruise and Nicole Kidman—a married couple in real life, which added an additional layer of biographical resonance to the production—as the doctor and his wife.

The decision to transpose had been criticised on the grounds that it lost the specific social world—the Habsburg bourgeoisie, the duelling culture, the particular configuration of class, ethnicity, and gender—that gave Schnitzler's text its historical density. The antisemitic subtext that Raphael had identified in the gathering scene—the "unmask" demand as the demand to reveal oneself as a Jew—was present in the film only as a vestige, stripped of the specific historical context that gave it meaning. And yet Kubrick's film also achieved something that a more literal adaptation might not: it demonstrated the degree to which the novella's central concerns—the unknowability of the spouse, the dangerous depths beneath bourgeois stability, the dream logic of erotic desire—were not historically specific to Vienna in 1900 but recurrent features of the bourgeois marriage in its modern form, wherever and whenever that form was found.

Kubrick called the film *Eyes Wide Shut*. The title he chose—a reversal of the posture that had defined Schnitzler's life and art—became, inadvertently, a commentary on both men: the director who had spent thirty years circling a story he could not let go, and the writer who had kept his eyes open to everything, including the truths that seeing could not prevent.

Kubrick died on 7 March 1999—four months before the film's release on 16 July 1999. The coincidence of the filmmaker's death and the film's imminent release gave the work an additional layer of biographical resonance that connected, with slightly uncomfortable force, to the novella's own engagement with the proximity of death and desire. That the last film of one of cinema's most consequential directors was an adaptation of a Viennese novella written seventy-three years earlier by an author who was himself nearing the end of his career; that the adaptation was the product of a three-decade obsession; that neither artist lived to see the full reception of his work—Schnitzler died in 1931, Kubrick in 1999: these facts did not add up to a neat allegory, but they were not without significance.

The film brought Schnitzler to millions of people who had never heard of him, making *Traumnovelle* the most culturally prominent work in an oeuvre that had, during the author's lifetime, been among the most controversial in European literary culture. The irony—that Schnitzler's widest audience would come sixty-eight years after his death, mediated through the vision of a filmmaker whose relationship to the source material was deeply personal and not always faithful—was one of the more remarkable episodes in the cultural afterlife of a twentieth-century literary text.

Traumnovelle was, in the retrospective view, the work in which Schnitzler's career achieved its most complete and most quietly confident expression. The question the novella posed—could two people, however long they had lived together, however honestly they had tried to know each other, ever achieve genuine mutual transparency?—was the same question that had been posed, in embryonic form, in the hypnosis scene of the Anatol cycle's first episode, when a young man chose not to ask his lover whether she was faithful because he could not bear the answer.

Across thirty-five years and the works examined in this biography, the question had been elaborated, complicated, and deepened: by the class structures of *Liebelei*, by the social machinery of *Reigen*, by the epistemological vertigo of *Das weite Land*, by the interior desolation of *Leutnant Gustl*, by the institutional antisemitism of *Professor Bernhardi*, by the coercive economics of *Fräulein Else*. *Traumnovelle* brought all of these elaborations to bear on the question in its most fundamental form, stripped of the specific social mechanisms that had complicated it in the earlier works, reduced to its philosophical core: two people, in a marriage, at night, confronting what they did not know about each other.

The answer *Traumnovelle* offered was not the tragic answer of the earlier works—it was not the death of Christine or the conviction of Bernhardi or the destruction of Else. It was, rather, the tentative, conditional, provisional answer of people who had survived their crisis and who had chosen, in its aftermath, to continue. Albertine's final words—grateful for having emerged, perhaps awake, but perhaps not for long—constituted the most honest answer that Schnitzler's career had found to the question it had been asking since the beginning.

We cannot know each other fully. We can choose to live with that impossibility, consciously and with some measure of grace, or we can let it destroy us. The choice was not heroic; it was simply human. And it was, in Schnitzler's long view—the view of a writer who had spent forty years examining what people did when the social masks were lifted and the vast domain of other people's interior lives became briefly, terrifyingly visible—the most that could honestly be asked of anyone.

CHAPTER TWENTY-ONE

Lili (1926–July 1928)

IN THE SPRING OR summer of 1926, Lili Schnitzler, seventeen years old and visiting Venice with her mother, met a man named Arnoldo Cappellini.[1] He was a Capitano in the fascist militia, handsome in his black uniform, and the age gap between them was considerable. Lili, by her father's later account, literally ran after him. Both Lili and Olga were entranced. The infatuation was exalted, theatrical, absolute—the kind of passion that burns brightest in adolescence and that Schnitzler, who had spent his career anatomizing the self-deceptions of romantic love, might have recognized as dangerous had it not been his own daughter's heart at stake.

Schnitzler's concerns were immediate and substantial. Arnoldo was penniless. He was a fascist, at a time when fascism had already revealed in Italy what it would later demonstrate across Europe. The age difference was troubling. And the idea of his daughter leaving Vienna, leaving him, to live in a foreign country with a man she had known for a matter of months was, for a father whose closest remaining bond was with this child, almost unbearable. But Lili was determined, and Olga was supportive, and when Arnoldo visited Vienna in March 1927, staying as a guest at Sternwartestrasse, Schnitzler found himself revising his initial resistance.

He liked the man's unaffected nature, his lack of vanity, what he perceived as a noble character. The glamour that had dazzled the women was not what Schnitzler saw; what he saw instead was a quality of genuineness that reassured him, or that he allowed to reassure him, because the alternative—refusing his daughter's wish, becoming the obstacle to her happiness—was intolerable.[2]

In April 1927, he traveled with Lili to Venice and rented an apartment for the couple. He recorded in his diary that he felt he was doing quite the right thing.[3] The certainty is painful to read in retrospect, not because it was unreasonable—it was entirely reasonable, the act of a loving father providing for his daughter's new life—but because the apartment he chose for her happiness would become the place where she picked up a rusted pistol. There was no way to know this. There is never any way to know this. The cruelty of the situation lay not in Schnitzler's judgment, which was sound, but in the nature of the future, which is opaque even to those who have made a career of seeing clearly.

The wedding took place on 30 June 1927, at the Vienna Town Hall—a simple ceremony without celebration, followed by a meal at the villa on Sternwartestrasse. The bride was seventeen years and nine months old. They left for Venice the same evening. Arnoldo's parting words to his father-in-law were: "Don't be sad. She's in good hands."[4] In Vienna, days later, the July Revolt erupted—the Palace of Justice was set ablaze, eighty-nine people died, more than a thousand were injured—but Schnitzler, as he recorded, was conscious of these events only from the margins.[5] His attention was on Lili, and on the distance that had opened between them.

A glimpse of Schnitzler and his new son-in-law together survives in the Italian press. An Italian journalist who caught him briefly at the port of Trieste in May 1928 noted that he descended the gangway *seguito da una giovane vezzosa figurina femminile ed da un ufficiale della Milizia*—followed by a charming young woman and an officer of the Militia.[6] The officers of the cruise ship confirmed that throughout the sixteen-day voyage Schnitzler had lived quietly apart, always with his daughter Fräulein Lilly and his son-in-law Capitano Cappellini beside him, always bent over a book or taking notes, serious and impenetrable. It was the last time Lili would appear in the documentary record alive.

What followed was a year of misery. The exalted infatuation collapsed into what Schnitzler's circle described as a catastrophic hangover. Lili was, in her own word, *todunglücklich*—deathly unhappy—in a foreign country, far from her father, isolated from the world she knew, married to a man whose beauty in uniform had not translated into warmth in a marriage. She felt neither respected nor loved. She spent half her days in bed, memorizing her nightmares, homesick for Vienna and for the privileged conversations with her father that had been the emotional center of her adolescence. She was possibly anorexic. She was apparently pregnant and disgusted by the condition, planning to seek out an *Engelmacherin*—an angel-maker, the grim Viennese euphemism for a backstreet abortionist.[7]

Her diary, kept since the age of fourteen and sealed by her parents' testament for more than ninety years, was finally published in 2025. Its entries demolished the long-standing assumption that Lili had suffered from psychological disorders since childhood. What the diary revealed instead was a young woman who wanted to live—who was driven to despair not by innate pathology but by circumstances: an unhappy marriage, a foreign city, isolation, youth, and the crushing weight of emotions she lacked the experience to manage.[8]

An entry from 12 December 1927 captures the pattern with devastating economy: "First I cry, then I want to shoot myself, then I speak calmly, then I want to shoot myself again, then we reconcile."[9] The cycle of tears, suicide ideation, calm, and reconciliation repeated itself with a regularity that suggests not madness but entrapment—a young woman oscillating between the desire to escape her situation and the inability to see any means of escape except the most final one.

The diary also revealed something previously unknown: in her final weeks, Lili was in love with another man besides Arnoldo. The identity of this man has not been disclosed, and the discovery complicates without clarifying the narrative of her last months. Was the second attachment a source of hope or of further desperation? Did it represent a way out of the marriage or a deepening of the impossibility she felt? The diary does not answer these questions, and we cannot answer them for it.

On 25 July 1928, in the Venice apartment her father had rented, Lili Schnitzler shot herself in the chest with a rusted pistol that Arnoldo had taken from a dead Austrian soldier during the war.[10] She was eighteen years and ten months old. At first, the wound did not appear serious. She was taken to the hospital, convinced she would recover. At six o'clock the following morning, she was operated on. Through the afternoon, her condition worsened: high fever, then other symptoms—likely sepsis, likely peritonitis, the body failing in stages. At a quarter past ten on the evening of 26 July, she died.[11]

Arthur Schnitzler was in Vienna. He was in his room at Sternwartestrasse, holding a photograph of his daughter in his hands and kissing it. He was not there when she died. He flew to Venice, but by scheduled flight, not the chartered plane that was later reported in the press—and in any case he arrived too late.

His reflection in the diary was characteristically precise and characteristically inadequate: "This time the pathological side of her nature sadly emerged in a way that was not to be remedied—just a minute later it would not have happened."[12] The phrase "this time" implies previous episodes; the phrase "just a minute later" suggests an act impulsive rather than planned. Whether Lili intended to die or intended to be saved is a question that her diary, her circumstances, and the manner of her death leave open. Müller's editorial note in *Das Zeitlose* is appropriately circumspect: the shot's intentionality cannot be established with certainty.[13] She wanted to live. She reached for the pistol. Both things are true, and the truth of each does not cancel the truth of the other.

She was buried on 29 July 1928, in the Old Jewish Cemetery in Venice. Arthur, Olga, Heinrich, and Arnoldo attended the funeral and returned to Vienna together. In the weeks that followed, Schnitzler obtained Lili's diary—four years of entries, from the age of fourteen to eighteen—and dictated its contents to Frieda Pollak, making copies for himself, for Olga, and for Heinrich.[14] The act of transcription was itself a form of mourning: the father reading his dead daughter's private thoughts, hearing her voice in the words she had written for no one, and translating that voice into a document the family could share. It was the last thing he could do for her, and it was not enough, and he knew it was not enough.

He would not come to terms with the loss of his daughter for the rest of his life. Pierre Loving, who visited Sternwartestrasse in late 1929, glimpsed "the phantasmal outline of his grief over a dead daughter" behind every sentence Schnitzler spoke. He was "broken in spirit, his face older and more tired, his eyes sadder," and had, Loving wrote, "withdrawn more and more deeply within himself."[15] He continued to work—the discipline never wavered, the diary never stopped—but the work was now produced in the shadow of an event that had revealed, with a finality no fiction could match, the limits of observation as a mode of living. He had spent his career watching, recording, analyzing. He had watched his daughter's infatuation, recorded his concerns, analyzed the risks. And she was dead.

CHAPTER TWENTY-TWO

The Last Few Years (1928–1931)

THERESE: CHRONIK EINES FRAUENLEBENS

THREE YEARS AND THREE months separated Lili's death from her father's. They were years of grief, diminishment, and continued work—because the work never stopped, because Schnitzler was constitutionally incapable of not observing, not recording, not writing, even when what he was observing and recording was his own disintegration.

In 1928, the same year as Lili's death, he published *Therese: Chronik eines Frauenlebens*—*Therese: Chronicle of a Woman's Life*—his second and final major novel, following *Der Weg ins Freie* by twenty years.[1] It was a work whose relationship to the rest of his career was best understood not as a continuation of that career's formal innovations but as a deliberate departure from them—a return to the conventions of nineteenth-century realist fiction at the precise moment when those conventions had been most thoroughly superseded by the techniques Schnitzler himself had pioneered.

The novel told the story of Therese Fabiani, an ordinary woman from the Viennese lower-middle class, across the years 1898 to 1924: from late youth through middle age, through the collapse of the Habsburg Empire and the difficult years of the Austrian Republic. Her father died; her mother ran a boarding house; Therese worked as a governess, moving through a series of bourgeois households where she occupied the anomalous social position of the educated woman who was neither servant nor family member, present in the intimate domestic space but perpetually vulnerable to the power of the men whose children she taught. She had a series of relationships with men, all disappointing. She had a son, illegitimate, who died young—Franz, conceived outside marriage, born into precarious circumstances, raised with insufficient resources, dying in the kind of quiet catastrophe that attended lives conducted without adequate social support. She aged into poverty, loneliness, bitterness. The novel ended not in tragedy but in resigned despair—the tired resignation of someone who had simply run out of the energy required to continue expecting things to improve.[2]

Where *Leutnant Gustl* and *Fräulein Else* had inhabited the interior of their protagonists' consciousnesses with an immediacy and technical sophistication that placed them at the forefront of European literary modernism, *Therese* maintained a steady third-person distance from its protagonist, observing her life in the measured, documentary cadence implied by its subtitle: chronicle, not crisis; record, not revelation. The choice was a formal statement. A chronicle was a documentary form: it recorded events in sequence, without the shaping hand of a narrator who selected and arranged those events to produce a certain aesthetic or emotional effect. It implied comprehensiveness over selectivity, duration over intensity, the long view over the concentrated moment.

The emotional register that *Therese* maintained throughout its approximately three hundred and fifty pages was one of the more unusual and demanding in Schnitzler's work: not tragedy, not comedy, not the psychologically intense interiority of the novellas, but something closer to sustained, undramatic sorrow—the quality of feeling appropriate to a life in which things went wrong persistently, gradually, without particular drama, and without the compensating intensity that either great joy or great suffering could provide.

The novel refused, with some consistency, the emotional consolations that the literary tradition of female suffering tended to provide. There was no moment of transcendence in which Therese's suffering was revealed to have been secretly meaningful; there was no spiritual growth, no achievement of wisdom, no recognition scene in which her value was finally acknowledged by the social world that had systematically undervalued her. She became, instead, a tired woman, and tiredness was less legible as indictment than anger, which was precisely the social reality Schnitzler was rendering.

The novel that appeared in the year his daughter died was a novel about a woman whose son died young, whose relationships with men were uniformly disappointing, and who aged into poverty and resigned despair—a novel that Schnitzler had been writing during the period of Lili's unhappy marriage and in the knowledge of her distress.[3] *Fräulein Else* had already demonstrated his capacity to create female protagonists whose fictional trajectories rhymed with his daughter's actual experience in ways that were prophetic without being intended as such. *Therese* added another layer to this biographical palimpsest. The coincidence was unbearable, and it belonged to the story because it could not be separated from it.

Therese was Schnitzler's last word, in long-form fiction, on the subject that had animated his work from the beginning: the situation of women in the social world he had spent his career observing and analyzing. It was a less brilliant final word than *Fräulein Else*—less formally dazzling, less psychologically acute in its individual moments, less capable of the kind of sentence-by-sentence intensity that the interior monologue provided—but it was, in its comprehensive sweep and its historical seriousness, a more encompassing one. What the novel said, finally, was that the suffering of women like Therese Fabiani was not dramatic, not intense, not available to the forms of literary representation that conferred dignity and legibility on suffering. It was ordinary, gradual, and chronic; it was the product not of specific villains or specific crises but of the aggregate operation of a social order that had consistently found women of a certain class and position to be of insufficient consequence to protect.

Clara Katharina Pollaczek was still there, patient and devoted despite the tensions that had accumulated in their relationship—his brief affair with Suzanne Clauser, a Viennese-born French translator of his works with whom he had become close not long after Lili's death,[4] and the jealousies between Clara and Olga that persisted even after the divorce. The old patterns held. Even at sixty-six, sixty-seven, sixty-eight, Schnitzler could not confine himself to a single relationship. The serial lover of the 1880s and 1890s had become, in his final years, not a reformed man but a diminished one, repeating in a minor key the behaviors that had defined his youth.

In July 1929, another blow fell. Hugo von Hofmannsthal's son Franz committed suicide on 13 July.[5] Two days later, on 15 July, on the way to his son's funeral, Hofmannsthal suffered a fatal stroke. He was fifty-five.[6] Schnitzler and Richard Beer-Hofmann traveled to Rodaun and laid flowers on the coffin of the man who had, thirty-seven years earlier, written the verse prologue to *Anatol* that had helped launch Schnitzler's career.

The double death—a father killed by a son's suicide—resonated with Schnitzler's own loss in ways that required no articulation. Of the Young Vienna circle that had gathered at Café Griensteidl in the early 1890s, only Beer-Hofmann remained close. Hermann Bahr had drifted away; Felix Salten had become estranged; Hofmannsthal was now dead. The world was emptying.[7]

He continued to write. Stories, novellas, shorter pieces continued to appear. *Flucht in die Finsternis* (*Flight into Darkness*) in 1931, published months before his death, was a novella about madness and paranoia that drew on the psychological territory he had been exploring since *Leutnant Gustl*.[8] The diary, which he had kept since the age of seventeen, was maintained until 19 October 1931—two days before his death. Nearly eight thousand pages across fifty-two years, it would be published between 1981 and 2000 in ten volumes by the Austrian Academy of Sciences and recognized as one of the most significant documents in German and European diary literature.[9]

His hearing worsened. His shoulder never healed. The international fame continued to grow—translations proliferated, performances multiplied, the name Schnitzler carried further than it ever had—but the man behind the name was increasingly frail, increasingly isolated, increasingly aware that the world in which his work had been produced was approaching a catastrophe whose outlines he could discern but whose scale he could not have imagined. In June 1931, Reuben Brainin, the Hebrew literary critic who had known Schnitzler since their first meeting in Vienna in September 1903, wrote a tribute in *The Jewish Chronicle* that described him, as he entered his seventieth year, as "a commanding figure who has managed to keep himself above all the petty political gibbering of Europe."[10] The description was true and already elegiac: Schnitzler would be dead within four months.

The antisemitism that had cost him his military commission in 1901 and provoked riots at the *Reigen* premiere in 1921 was metastasizing into something far more dangerous than theatrical scandal. In Germany, the National Socialists had received 18.3 percent of the vote in the September 1930 Reichstag elections, making them the second-largest party in Germany.[11] The mechanisms that *Professor Bernhardi* had anatomized in 1912—the use of fabricated incidents to generate antisemitic pressure campaigns, the weaponization of religious and nationalist sentiment against individual Jewish professionals, the complicity of institutions in persecution through procedures that preserved the forms of legality while abandoning its substance—were now operating at a scale and with a violence that Schnitzler had analyzed but not predicted.

He could see it coming. The diary entries from the final years registered not merely the personal grief of Lili's death and the physical diminishment of aging but a dawning recognition that the liberal assumptions on which his career had been built—that talent and intelligence could transcend the accidents of birth, that art could speak to a common humanity, that the individual conscience was sovereign—were being systematically dismantled by political forces that had no use for such assumptions. *Der Weg ins Freie* had examined the Jewish Question through the oblique lens of fiction. *Professor Bernhardi* had confronted it head-on. Both works had been prophetic. Neither had been optimistic. The prophecies were being fulfilled.

On 21 October 1931, in the villa on Sternwartestrasse where he had lived for twenty-one years, Arthur Schnitzler died of a brain haemorrhage. He was sixty-nine years old.[12] Clara Katharina Pollaczek was with him. "I held his head in my hands till his last breath," she wrote. The image was precise and final: the woman holding the man's head as the life left it, in the house where the life had been lived.[13]

It was the same house where he had written *Professor Bernhardi* and *Fräulein Else* and *Traumnovelle*, where Lili had grown from an infant to a girl of seventeen, where the divorce had been negotiated and the *Reigen* scandal endured, where the diary had been kept and the letters answered and the secretary—Frieda Pollak, who had held the position since 1909—had typed. His last will, written at Sternwartestrasse on 29 April 1912 and published in the *Arbeiter-Zeitung* following his death, had specified: "Herzstich. Keine Kränze! Keine Parte! ... Begrdbnis letzter Klasse. ... Keine Reden! Vermeidung allen rituellen Beiwerkes. Keine Trauer tragen nach meinem Tode, absolut keine."[14]

He was buried in the Old Israelite section of the Zentralfriedhof, the Central Cemetery of Vienna, where his father lay.[15] On 15 November, a memorial service was held at the Burgtheater—the stage where *Liebelei* had premiered thirty-six years earlier, the theater that had made him famous and to which he had returned, over the decades, with play after play that tested the boundaries of what its audiences would accept.

Nineteen months later, in May 1933, the Nazis burned his books.16 They burned *Anatol* and *Liebelei* and *Reigen* and *Professor Bernhardi* and *Fräulein Else* and *Traumnovelle*. They burned the plays that had anatomized the honor code and the sexual double standard and the mechanisms of institutional antisemitism. They burned the novellas that had pioneered the stream-of-consciousness technique in German and that had rendered female consciousness with a precision and sympathy that male writers rarely achieved.

The books burned. The work survived. And the world that Schnitzler had spent forty years documenting—the world of Viennese coffeehouses and summer resorts, of sweet girls and dueling officers, of masked balls and secret societies, of marriages that concealed more than they revealed and social codes that killed more efficiently than they protected—that world was destroyed utterly, first by the war that ended the empire, then by the ideology that murdered its Jews. What remained was the record: eight thousand pages of diary, thirty plays, dozens of novellas and stories, two major novels, and the testimony of a man who had kept his eyes open when others looked away, who had seen what the seeing cost, and who had written it down with a clarity and an honesty that made the work, a century later, essential to understanding not only what that world was but what ours continues to be.

Part V: Epilogue

The Archive, the Burnings, and the Long Recovery

Arthur Schnitzler died in Vienna on 21 October 1931, respected but not revered, established but not canonical. His memorial service at the Burgtheater drew the attention owed to a man who had dominated Viennese literary life for three decades, but the critical consensus at the time of his death was not entirely flattering. He was seen as a chronicler of decadence, a specialist in the liaison between love and death, an impressionist whose association with Freud and fin-de-siècle Vienna marked him as a figure of a particular moment rather than an artist of permanent significance.[1]

The diary he had kept for fifty-two years remained unpublished. The archive—manuscripts, letters, notes, correspondence with the major figures of his era—sat in the villa on Sternwartestrasse, unprocessed and unprotected. He was, in the judgment of his time, a giant of literary Vienna, but Vienna was no longer the capital of an empire, and the literary culture that had produced him was already under threat from forces he had spent his career describing.[2]

Less than two years later, those forces arrived. On 10 May 1933, Nazi students across Germany carried out coordinated book burnings in university towns throughout the Reich, flinging tens of thousands of volumes onto bonfires while Joseph Goebbels declared the era of Jewish intellectualism at an end.[3] Schnitzler's works were among those consigned to the flames—blacklisted as "un-German," burned alongside the books of Freud, Kafka, Einstein, the Mann brothers, and Zweig.

Every title burned except one: *Der Weg ins Freie*, spared because the Nazis, in an act of interpretive failure that Schnitzler would have relished, appear to have misread it.[4] It was, in fact, his most Jewish work—his deepest exploration of the dilemmas facing Vienna's assimilated Jewish bourgeoisie—and their failure to recognize this was a testament to the quality of the reading that drove the Reich's cultural policy.

After the Anschluss in March 1938, the archive itself was in danger. Olga Schnitzler, still living at Sternwartestrasse, appealed for help, and the operation that followed—conducted in coded messages, with Schnitzler's archive referred to under a cover name—succeeded in shipping cases of manuscripts to Cambridge under diplomatic seal.[5] Manuscripts, sketches, and correspondence crossed the border into safety. The main archive has remained at the Cambridge University Library ever since, though the process of establishing clear legal ownership proved long and complicated—the library had initially been reluctant to accept it, and a separate collection of some thirty thousand press clippings was eventually donated to the University of Exeter instead.[6]

The twelve years between the book burnings and the end of the war constituted a decade of darkness for Schnitzler's reputation. His works were banned in the German-speaking world. Performances ceased. A generation of Germans and Austrians grew up without access to his writing, and the natural evolution of critical understanding—the process by which a writer's contemporaries give way to scholars who can see the work with greater distance and therefore greater clarity—was violently interrupted. When the war ended, his reputation had to be rebuilt from rubble, in a landscape where the theaters, libraries, and publishing houses that had sustained it were themselves in ruins.

Clara Katharina Pollaczek, after Schnitzler's death, spent two years writing a memoir of their relationship—titled *Arthur Schnitzler und ich*—assisted in its preparation by Frieda Pollak, the same secretary who had served Schnitzler for more than twenty years.[7] Clara survived the war, returned to Vienna, and died on 22 July 1951. The memoir remained unpublished for more than seventy years; a digital edition was finally released in 2025 by the Austrian Academy of Sciences, opening a window onto the last eight years of Schnitzler's life that had been closed for nearly a century.[8]

Olga Schnitzler, Schnitzler's former wife, lived far longer. She died on 13 January 1970 in Lugano—nearly nineteen years after Clara—having outlived both her former husband and her former rival by decades.[9] The archive she had helped rescue from Sternwartestrasse had by then found its permanent home at Cambridge; the press clippings she had donated separately to Henry Garland were later transferred to the University of

Exeter. The divided archive was, in its way, an emblem of a legacy that had never been easy to contain.

Heinrich Schnitzler fled Austria after the Anschluss, emigrated to the United States, and did not return until 1959. He built a career as a director and dramatist, had a son—Michael, born in Berkeley, California—and in 1982, fifty years after his father's death, authorized the re-release of *Reigen* for performance on German-language stages, ending the self-imposed ban that had silenced the play for six decades.[10] He died in Vienna on 12 July 1982, aged seventy-nine. He had honored his father's legacy in the way that mattered most: by letting the work speak again.[11]

CHAPTER TWENTY-FOUR

Film, Scholarship, and the Second Life of the Work

THE REBUILDING BEGAN, AS these things often do, through film. In 1950, the German-born director Max Ophüls adapted *Reigen* as *La Ronde*—a French-language film, set in the Vienna of 1900, that achieved considerable success in the English-speaking world and introduced Schnitzler to audiences who had never heard his name.[1]

The irony was characteristic: the play that had provoked riots in Vienna in 1921 and been silenced by its own author was reintroduced to international prominence through the cinema of exile, arriving in English under a French title. *La Ronde* made Schnitzler accessible to the postwar generation not as a banned Austrian but as a sophisticated European, and the film's success initiated a slow process of rediscovery that would accelerate over the following decades.[2]

The critical reassessment came in the 1960s. For the first time, humanist scholars challenged the prevailing view of Schnitzler as a decadent celebrant of fin-de-siècle sensuality and began to argue that his late novellas, far from wallowing in impressionistic despair, constituted an ethical indictment of the very attitudes they depicted. Schnitzler was no longer merely the chronicler of a dying world; he was its diagnostician, a writer whose clinical precision—the physician's eye repurposed for literary ends—had been mistaken for complicity with the conditions it described.[3]

Social historians and feminist critics joined the reassessment in the 1970s and 1980s, recognizing in his work a sustained engagement with class structures, sexual double standards, and the mechanisms of institutional antisemitism that was more radical, and more prescient, than his contemporaries had understood.[4]

The publication of his diary—ten volumes, issued by the Austrian Academy of Sciences between 1981 and 2000, with a digital edition following in 2019—provided the documentary foundation for this reappraisal.[5] Nearly eight thousand pages, kept from the age of seventeen until two days before his death, the diary was recognized as one of the most significant documents in German and European diary literature: a record of creative process, daily life, sexual activity, friendship, feud, and clinical self-observation that had no parallel in its combination of scope and candor. Scholars could now trace the relationship between the life and the work with a precision that had previously been impossible, and what they found confirmed that Schnitzler's art was not autobiography thinly disguised but autobiography transformed.

In 1968, Stanley Kubrick read *Traumnovelle* and recognized in it the material for a film he would spend the rest of his life trying to make. He had just released *2001: A Space Odyssey* and was looking, as he always was, for a text that could sustain the obsessive attention he brought to every project. With the help of journalist Jay Cocks, he acquired the filming rights.[6]

For the next three decades, the project gestated—through multiple proposed casts (Steve Martin, Woody Allen, Dustin Hoffman, Warren Beatty were among those considered at various stages), through periods of dormancy and revival, through the evolution of Kubrick's own preoccupations—until, in 1994, he hired Frederic Raphael to write the screenplay and began the process of transposing Schnitzler's early-twentieth-century Vienna to late-twentieth-century New York.[7] Carnival became Christmas. Doctor Fridolin became Bill Harford. Albertine became Alice. The masked orgy remained.

Kubrick shot the film in England between 1996 and 1998, with Tom Cruise and Nicole Kidman as the doctor and his wife—a real-life married couple playing a fictional married couple whose marriage is unraveling, a piece of casting that added an additional layer of unease to a project already saturated with it.[8] The shoot was the longest of Kubrick's career—four hundred days, a Guinness World Record—the perfectionism legendary even by his standards.

On 7 March 1999, four and a half months before the film's scheduled release, Kubrick died of a heart attack at the age of seventy, six days after presenting his final cut to Warner Bros.[9] *Eyes Wide Shut* opened on 16 July 1999, and the world greeted it with confusion.

The initial reception was, by most accounts, bewildered. Audiences expecting an erotic thriller found something else entirely: a dream film that did not announce itself as a dream, that operated—as Martin Scorsese later observed—in the realm of memories and projected, subjective realities, without the usual signals that cue an audience to suspend its expectations of narrative realism.[10] Some found it boring. Some found it pretentious.

Others recognized, on first viewing or on subsequent ones, that Kubrick had achieved something that Schnitzler himself might have admired: a work of art that reproduced, in cinematic form, the experience of moving through a world in which the boundaries between fantasy and reality have dissolved and the comfortable assumptions on which daily life depends have been exposed as fictions.

The film's reputation has grown steadily in the quarter century since its release. What was initially dismissed as Kubrick's weakest work has come to be regarded as one of his finest. It brought Schnitzler to millions of viewers who had never read a word he wrote and sent a significant number of them to the novella that had inspired it. *Traumnovelle*, a work of ninety pages written in 1926, became, through the medium of Kubrick's obsession, the most culturally prominent thing Schnitzler ever produced—an outcome he could not have predicted and would not have witnessed, arriving sixty-eight years after his death.[11]

In 2024, a new adaptation of *Traumnovelle*, directed by Florian Frerichs and set in modern-day Berlin, premiered at the Oldenburg Film Festival, confirming what the Kubrick film had demonstrated: that the novella's examination of marriage, fantasy, and self-deception is not a period piece but a diagnosis that renews itself with each generation.[12]

CHAPTER TWENTY-FIVE

Cultural Relevance

THE QUESTION OF WHY Schnitzler matters—why he is, in certain respects, more urgently relevant in the 2020s than he was in the 1920s—can be answered in several ways, each of which illuminates a different facet of his achievement.

The most immediate answer is consent. *Fräulein Else*, published in 1924, depicts a nineteen-year-old woman who is asked by a wealthy older man to display her naked body in exchange for the money her family needs to avoid financial ruin. The proposition is framed as a request and experienced as coercion, and the novella's unbroken interior monologue places the reader inside the mind of a young woman who is being destroyed by the intersection of money, power, and masculine entitlement.[1]

Scholars have described the work as startlingly relevant to contemporary discussions about power, consent, and female autonomy, and the adjective is precise: the shock is not that the story resonates with the debates provoked by the #MeToo movement but that it anticipated those debates by a full century. A 2024 anthology on consent and German literature includes a chapter reconsidering affirmative consent through Schnitzler's work—a hundred years after *Fräulein Else* was published, and the questions it posed have not been answered.[2]

The second answer is marriage. *Traumnovelle*'s central revelation—that the order, balance, and security of domestic life are an illusion and a lie—has lost none of its capacity to disturb, because the institution it examines has lost none of its capacity to disappoint. The novella asks how well we know the people we share our lives with, what role fantasy plays in sustaining relationships that reality alone cannot support, and whether honesty between partners is a foundation or a threat.

These are not historical questions. They are the questions that marriage counselors and divorce lawyers encounter every day, and the fact that Schnitzler posed them with such precision in 1926—in a prose style that rendered the boundaries between dream and waking as permeable as they are in lived experience—suggests that the insight was not merely personal but structural, an observation about the nature of intimacy itself.

The third answer is antisemitism. *Professor Bernhardi*, written between 1910 and 1912 and banned in Austria until the empire collapsed, tells the story of a Jewish doctor who is destroyed by the institutions of Catholic Austria for acting according to his conscience.[3] *Der Weg ins Freie*, published in 1908, maps the range of responses available to Vienna's Jewish bourgeoisie as the tide of hatred rises around them: assimilation, conversion, Zionism, the stubborn insistence on individual dignity that Schnitzler himself favored and that history would judge as noble but insufficient. In a century when antisemitism has not diminished but merely changed its forms and its justifications, these works remain not artifacts of a vanished world but documents of a recurring one—warnings that were not heeded the first time and that retain their force precisely because the conditions they describe have not been overcome.

And the fourth answer, which encompasses the others, is the quality of his seeing. Schnitzler was, above all, an observer—a man who looked at what was there rather than what he wished were there, who recorded what he saw with a physician's precision and an artist's compassion, and who refused, throughout his career, to sentimentalize, to moralize cheaply, or to look away. He saw the sexual hypocrisy beneath bourgeois respectability. He saw the power dynamics that structured every encounter between men and women, between classes, between the individual and the institution. He saw the self-deception that allowed intelligent people to ignore the evidence of their own senses. He saw the antisemitism that was not incidental to Austrian culture but embedded in its foundations. He saw the empire's rot while others were still admiring its façade.[4]

And he wrote what he saw, clearly, precisely, without consolation, knowing that clarity would not be rewarded and that precision would be mistaken for coldness.

He is, in the judgment of contemporary literary scholarship, one of the most significant representatives of Viennese modernism—a technical innovator who pioneered the interior monologue in German literature more than two decades before Joyce published *Ulysses*,[5] a psychological realist who anticipated the findings of modern psychology without recourse to its jargon, a social critic whose engagement with class, gender, and prejudice was more radical than his contemporaries recognized, and a dramatist whose works are continuously adapted, from Tom Stoppard's *Dalliance* to David Hare's *The Blue Room* to Kubrick's final film.[6]

The Cambridge archive—tens of thousands of manuscript pages, now digitized and accessible to scholars worldwide—ensures that the documentary record of his life and work will survive as long as universities endure.[7] The diary, published in ten volumes, stands as one of the great autobiographical documents in any language: the record of a man who observed himself with the same relentless honesty he brought to the observation of others.

Martin Swales, writing in 1971, identified the quality that has ensured Schnitzler's endurance: an understanding of human nature and a skill as interpreter of individual consciousness that lend his works a quality of universality. The assessment holds.[8] What Schnitzler understood—about desire, about self-deception, about the distance between what people profess and what they feel, about the fragility of the arrangements that hold societies and marriages and selves together—is not contingent on the specific circumstances of Vienna in 1900. It is true of human beings in general, and it is rendered in a prose style that makes the truth available to anyone willing to read with attention.

Stanley Kubrick called his adaptation *Eyes Wide Shut*—a warning against the refusal to see what is plainly there. But Schnitzler's own stance was the opposite: eyes wide open, from the beginning to the end, from the doctor's surgery to the writer's desk to the diary's final entry two days before his death. He looked at what others denied. He wrote what others suppressed. He documented the psychology of self-deception with a clarity that made his readers uncomfortable and his critics hostile and his reputation, in the long run, unassailable.

The Nazis burned his books. The archive went into exile. The works returned. The films multiplied. The relevance intensified. And now, nearly a century after his death, the physician's son from Leopoldstadt who wanted to write plays and was made to study medicine, who loved too many women and married too late, who watched his daughter die in a foreign city and kept writing until the brain itself gave way—this man stands as one of the essential observers of how human beings behave when they think no one is watching. He prescribed no cure except to see clearly. He offered no consolation except the truth.

'I write of love and death,' he told an interviewer. 'What other subjects are there?'[9]

In 1931, the remark sounded like the confession of a specialist. In 2026, it reads like the only honest answer.

The Works of Arthur Schnitzler
(1862–1931)

NOTE: THIS BIBLIOGRAPHY LISTS Schnitzler's major published works in chronological order by first publication or premiere date. German titles are given first, followed by English translations where available.

1893

Anatol (Play cycle - 7 one-acts)

English: *Anatol: A Sequence of Dialogues*

Premiered individually 1893-1910; cycle premiered 1910

Introduction by Hugo von Hofmannsthal (as "Loris")

1894

Sterben (Novella)

English: *Dying*

First book publication 1895

Das Märchen (Play)

English: *The Fairy Tale*

Premiered 1893

1895

Liebelei (Play)

English: *Light-o'-Love, Playing with Love, Flirtations, Dalliance* (Tom

Stoppard adaptation)

Premiered October 9, 1895, Burgtheater, Vienna

1896

Freiwild (Play)

English: *Free Game*

Premiered 1896

1897

Die Toten schweigen (Short story)

English: *The Dead Are Silent*

Reigen (Play - 10 dialogues)

English: *Hands Around, La Ronde* (French film title), *Round Dance*

Written 1896-1897

Privately printed 1900

Commercially published 1903 (immediately banned)

Premiered December 23, 1920, Berlin (riots followed)

1898

Das Vermächtnis (Play)

English: *The Legacy*

Die Gefährtin (Play)

English: *The Mate, The Companion*

1899

Der grüne Kakadu (One-act play)

English: *The Green Cockatoo*

Premiered March 1, 1899, Burgtheater, Vienna

Paracelsus (One-act play)

English: *Paracelsus*

Premiered March 1, 1899 (same evening as *Der grüne Kakadu*)

1900

Leutnant Gustl (Novella)

English: *None but the Brave, Lieutenant Gustl*

First stream-of-consciousness work in German literature

Published in *Neue Freie Presse*, December 25, 1900

Cost Schnitzler his military commission

English translation: *Viennese Novellettes* (1931)

Frau Berta Garlan (Novella)

English: *Bertha Garlan*

First of "Woman Trilogy"

1901

Der Schleier der Beatrice (Play)

English: *The Veil of Beatrice*

1902

Lebendige Stunden (Play cycle - 4 one-acts)

English: *Living Hours*

Includes: *Die letzten Masken* (The Last Masks), *Literatur* (Literature)

1904

Der einsame Weg (Play)

English: *The Lonely Way, The Lonely Road*

Premiered February 13, 1904

Often cited as beginning of "second period"

Der Puppenspieler (One-act)

English: *The Puppet Player*

1905

Zwischenspiel (Play)

English: *Intermezzo*

Premiered October 12, 1905, Burgtheater, Vienna

Won Grillparzer Prize 1908

1906

Der Ruf des Lebens (Play)

English: *The Call of Life*

Premiered 1906

Marionetten (Play cycle)

Includes: *Der Puppenspieler, Der tapfere Cassian, Zum grossen Wurstel*

1907

Komtesse Mizzi; oder, Der Familientag (Play)

English: *Countess Mizzie, Countess Mitzi; or, the Family Reunion*□

Premiered 1909

1908

Der Weg ins Freie (Novel)

English: *The Road into the Open, The Road to the Open*

First major novel

Central work on Jewish identity and antisemitism

1909

Der tapfere Cassian (Singspiel)

English: *Gallant Cassian*

Music by Oscar Straus

Appeared in *Marionetten* (1906), revised 1909

1910

Der junge Medardus (Play)

English: *Young Medardus*

Premiered November 24, 1910, Burgtheater, Vienna

Won Raimund Prize 1910

Der Schleier der Pierrette (Pantomime)

English: *The Veil of Pierrette*

Music by Ernst von Dohnányi

Premiered 1910

1911

Das weite Land (Play)

English: *The Vast Domain, Undiscovered Country* (Tom Stoppard adaptation)

Premiered October 14, 1911

Explores marital infidelity

1912

Professor Bernhardi (Play - "Comedy in 5 acts")

English: *Professor Bernhardi*

Banned in Austria until 1918 (empire's collapse)

Premiered November 28, 1912, Kleines Theater, Berlin

Won Wiener Volkstheater Prize 1914

Only major dramatic work without sexual theme

Central work on antisemitism and institutional ethics

1913

Frau Beate und ihr Sohn (Novella)

English: *Beatrice, Beatrice and Her Son*

Second of "Woman Trilogy"

1915

Komödie der Worte (Play cycle - 3 one-acts)

English: *Comedies of Words*

Includes: *Stunde des Erkennens, Grosse Szene, Das Bacchusfest*

1917

Fink und Fliederbusch (Play)

English: *Fink and Fliederbusch*

Premiered 1917

Doktor Gräsler, Badearzt (Novella)

English: *Doctor Gräsler, Spa Doctor*

1918

Casanovas Heimfahrt (Novella)

English: *Casanova's Homecoming*

One of late masterpieces

1924

Fräulein Else (Novella)

English: *Fräulein Else, Miss Else*

Stream-of-consciousness perfected

Third of "Woman Trilogy"

May rebut Otto Weininger's critique of Jewish character

Central work on power, consent, female autonomy

Film: 1929 (silent, Elisabeth Bergner), 1946 (Argentine)

Die Frau des Richters (Novella)

English: *The Judge's Wife*

1925

Komödie der Verführung (Play)

English: *Comedy of Seduction*

Premiered October 11, 1924 (written earlier)

1925-1926

Traumnovelle (Novella)

English: *Dream Story, Rhapsody: A Dream Novel*

Serialized December 1925 - March 1926 in *Die Dame*

Book edition 1926, S. Fischer Verlag

Kubrick's *Eyes Wide Shut* (1999) based on this

Most culturally prominent work today

1926

Der Gang zum Weiher (Play)

English: *The Walk to the Pond*

Spiel im Morgengrauen (Novella)

English: *Game at Dawn, Daybreak*

1927

Therese: Chronik eines Frauenlebens (Novel)

English: *Theresa: The Chronicle of a Woman's Life*

Second major novel

Published 1928

1928

Im Spiel der Sommerlüfte (Play fragment)

English: *In the Play of Summer Breezes*

Unfinished

POSTHUMOUS PUBLICATIONS

1931

  Flucht in die Finsternis (Novella)

English: *Flight into Darkness*

  Published after his death

  1937

  Abenteuernovelle (Novella)

English: *Adventure Story*

  1968

  Jugend in Wien (Autobiography)

English: *My Youth in Vienna*

  Covers through 1889

Edited by Therese Nickl and Heinrich Schnitzler

  1981-2000

  Tagebuch (Diary)

Published in 10 volumes by Austrian Academy of Sciences

Kept from age 17 (1879) until two days before death (1931)

Nearly 8,000 pages

Digital edition 2019

  1995-2003

  Briefe (Letters) 1875-1912 (1981)

  Briefe (Letters) 1913-1931 (1984)

Hugo von Hofmannsthal (1964)

Richard Beer-Hofmann

Sigmund Freud

Otto Brahm

Georg Brandes

Major correspondences with:

Briefe (Letters)

2014

Late Fame (Play)

Written c.1894-1895

Published posthumously 2014

Film adaptation by Kent Jones

SHORT STORY COLLECTIONS

Little Novels (1929)

Collection of shorter works published together in English

Stories include (various publication dates):

"Die grüne Krawatte" (The Green Tie) - microfiction

"Der Ehrentag" (The Day of Honor)

"Mein Freund Ypsilon" (My Friend Ypsilon)

"Der Sohn" (The Son)

"Der Witwer" (The Widower)

"Die dreifache Warnung" (The Triple Warning)

"Die Fremde" (The Stranger)

"Reichtum" (Wealth)

"Die Hirtenflöte" (The Shepherd's Flute)

"Die Weissagung" (The Prophecy)

"Die Braut" (The Bride)

"Die Frau des Weisen" (The Wise Man's Wife)

"Die griechische Tänzerin" (The Greek Dancer)

"Der blinde Geronimo und sein Bruder" (Blind Geronimo and His Brother)

"Der Andere" (The Other)

"Das neue Lied" (The New Song)

"Das Schicksal des Freiherrn von Leisenbohg" (The Fate of Baron Leisenbohg)

"Amerika" (America)

"Albine"

MAJOR FILM & STAGE ADAPTATIONS

Films Based on Schnitzler's works:

1920: *The Merry-Go-Round* (Richard Oswald) - from *Reigen*

1929: *Fräulein Else* (silent, Elisabeth Bergner, Adele Sandrock)

1933: *Liebelei* (Max Ophüls)

1946: *The Naked Angel* (Argentine) - from *Fräulein Else*

1950: *La Ronde* (Max Ophüls) - from *Reigen* (major success)

1964: *Circle of Love* (Roger Vadim) - from *Reigen*

1969: *Traumnovelle* (Austrian TV, Wolfgang Glück)

1973: *Der Reigen* (Otto Schenk)

1983: *Il cavaliere, la morte e il diavolo* (Italian) - from *Traumnovelle*

1989: *Nightmare in Venice* (Mario Bianchi) - from *Traumnovelle*

1999: *Eyes Wide Shut* (Stanley Kubrick) - from *Traumnovelle*

2011: *360* (Fernando Meirelles) - from *Reigen*

2014: *Late Fame* (Kent Jones)

2024: *Traumnovelle* (Florian Frerichs, Berlin)

Stage Adaptations:

1973: BBC television series *Vienna 1900* (5 short stories)

1986: Tom Stoppard's *Dalliance* (from *Liebelei*)

1986: Tom Stoppard's *Undiscovered Country* (from *Das weite Land*)

1998: David Hare's *The Blue Room* (from *Reigen*)

2012: Graphic novel of *Traumnovelle* (Jakob Hinrichs)

AWARDS & HONORS

1903: Bauernfeld Prize

1908: Grillparzer Prize (for *Zwischenspiel*)

1910: Raimund Prize (for *Der junge Medardus*)

1914: Wiener Volkstheater Prize (for *Professor Bernhardi*)

1926: Burgtheater Ring (from journalists/writers)

BANNED & CENSORED WORKS

1904: *Reigen* banned after commercial publication (1903)

1900: *Leutnant Gustl* - Schnitzler stripped of military commission

1912-1918: *Professor Bernhardi* banned in Austria

1921: *Reigen* - Schnitzler self-withdrew after riots

1933-1945: All works (except *Der Weg ins Freie*) banned by Nazis

1982: Heinrich Schnitzler re-released *Reigen* (50 years after father's death)

More Books by Arthur Schnitzler by Ovid Publishing

IF YOU ENJOYED THIS book, you may also wish to explore these other works by Arthur Schnitzler, published by Ovid Publishing Group:

https://www.ovidpublishing.com

Dream Story (Traumnovelle)

This new edition of Dream Story by Arthur Schnitzler offers readers a new translation from the original German text and a comprehensive exploration of the acclaimed novella, originally published as Traumnovelle in 1926 and adapted into the movie Eyes Wide Shut.

Set in early 20th-century Vienna, Schnitzler's narrative delves into the psychological complexities of desire, marriage, and the blurred lines between fantasy and reality. His background in psychiatry, provides a nuanced examination of the human psyche that remains strikingly relevant today.

Fräulein Else: An Indecent Proposal

Fräulein Else is a 1924 novella by the Austrian writer Arthur Schnitzler. While vacationing at a luxury resort in the Italian Alps, nineteen-year-old Else receives an urgent letter from her mother revealing her family's impending financial ruin and possible imprisonment. She must turn to Herr von Dorsday, a wealthy family acquaintance, for help. His proposition—to view her naked in exchange for saving her family—forces

Else to confront impossible choices between family duty, personal dignity, and survival.

Lieutenant Gustl

A groundbreaking psychological novella that revolutionized stream-of-consciousness storytelling!

In this masterful work of early modernist fiction, Arthur Schnitzler takes us deep into the mind of Lieutenant Gustl, a young Austrian military officer, during one fateful night in Vienna. After a heated encounter at a concert hall threatens his honor as an officer, Gustl wanders the streets of Vienna contemplating suicide to preserve his reputation. Through his internal monologue, we experience his memories, desires, prejudices, and inner turmoil as he grapples with questions of honor, duty, and identity in turn-of-the-century Austrian society.

The Plays of Arthur Schnitzler Vol. 1 (1892-1896)

New Translation of Four Masterpieces of Viennese Modernist Theater

Set against the backdrop of fin-de-siècle (end-of-the-century) Vienna, these four plays interweave themes of art, love, and identity, with Schnitzler's unique psychological and compassionate insight portraying a society on the brink of transformation.

https://www.ovidpublishing.com

Chapter Notes (1–10)

Chapter 1

1. ARTHUR SCHNITZLER WAS born on May 15, 1862, at Praterstraße 16 (formerly Jägerzeile 16), Leopoldstadt, Vienna's Second District. See Wien Geschichte Wiki, "Arthur Schnitzler."

2. On the 1670 expulsion of Jews from the Unterer Werd, see Klaus Lohrmann, *Die Wiener Juden im Mittelalter* (Berlin: Duncker & Humblot, 2000). The renaming of the district is documented in municipal records.

3. The nickname "Mazzesinsel" is widely attested in histories of Viennese Jewry. See Marsha Rozenblit, *The Jews of Vienna, 1867–1914: Assimilation and Identity* (Albany: SUNY Press, 1983), pp. 71–75.

4. The Leopoldstädter Tempel, designed by Ludwig Förster, was completed in 1858 (not 1858 as some sources erroneously give; construction ran from 1854/55 to 1858). It was inaugurated on June 15, 1858, with seating for approximately 2,240 worshippers. See the Wikipedia article "Leopoldstädter Tempel" and the Jewish Museum Vienna exhibition materials. The temple was destroyed during the November Pogrom of 1938. An earlier draft of this chapter stated the temple was "inaugurated just

four years before Arthur's birth"; the math is correct (1858 to 1862 = four years).

5. Johann Schnitzler's birth date and birthplace: April 10, 1835, Groß-Kanizsa (now Nagykanizsa, Hungary). See *Allgemeine Deutsche Biographie*, vol. 54 (1908), s.v. "Schnitzler, Johann"; *Neue Deutsche Biographie*, vol. 23 (2007), pp. 334f.; and Wien Geschichte Wiki, "Johann Schnitzler." One scholarly source (arthur-schnitzler.de) gives the birthplace as Nagybajom; the majority of authoritative references, including the ADB/NDB and the Jewish Encyclopedia, specify Groß-Kanizsa.

6. The name change from Zimmermann to Schnitzler is attested in the arthur-schnitzler.de biographical sketch, which identifies the grandfather as "Joseph Zimmermann, später in 'Schnitzler' umbenannt (1810–1864)." Both names signify woodworking: *Zimmermann* = carpenter; *Schnitzler* = carver/whittler. The characterization of this as an aspirational gesture is the author's interpretation.

7. Johann Schnitzler received his medical doctorate from the University of Vienna in 1860. See NDB, vol. 23, p. 334; Jewish Encyclopedia, s.v. "Schnitzler, Johann."

8. Johann's youthful literary ambitions are mentioned in secondary sources including the Project MUSE annotated bibliography, which notes he "had written a few dramas himself, but had given up his literary activities when he entered the medical school."

9. Louise Ludovica Markbreiter: born 1840 (per NDB and arthur-schnitzler.de biographical portal), died 1911. Some sources, including English-language Wikipedia, give 1838; the scholarly German-language sources consistently give 1840. Her father Philipp Markbreiter (1810/1811–1892) came from a family described as "Hofjuwelierfamilie" (court jeweler family) in the arthur-schnitzler.de sketch. Her mother Amalia, née Schey von Koromla (1815–1884), belonged to a baronized Hungarian Jewish family. See NDB, "Schnitzler, Johann," genealogical notes.

10. The *Wiener Medizinische Presse* was founded in 1860. HathiTrust catalog records show Philipp Markbreiter as sole editor 1860–69, with Johann Schnitzler joining as co-editor from 1861. Johann became sole editor from 1870 to 1886. The journal was originally titled *Wiener Medizinal-Halle* before being renamed.

11. Johann Schnitzler became assistant to Johann von Oppolzer in 1863, not at the time of Arthur's birth in 1862. An earlier draft implied the appointment was already in place; this has been corrected to "soon to begin his clinical training." See NDB, vol. 23, p. 334; Wien Geschichte Wiki.

12. Joseph Emil Schnitzler, born 1864, died after a few weeks. Wikipedia on Johann Schnitzler states "died shortly after his birth in 1864."

13. Julius Schnitzler (1865–1939): surgeon and professor. See NDB genealogical notes, which give his dates as 1865–1939 and describe him as "ao. Prof. d. Chirurgie in Wien."

14. Gisela Schnitzler (1867–1953) married Markus Hajek (1861–1941), a laryngologist and professor at the University of Vienna. See NDB, s.v. "Schnitzler, Johann," genealogical notes. Hajek also served as co-editor of Johann's posthumous *Klinischer Atlas*.

15. The 1868 move to Giselastraße 11 (now Bösendorferstraße) is confirmed by the arthur-schnitzler.org biographical sketch: "In 1868, the family moved to another location in the First District, 11 Giselastraße (the present-day Bösendorferstraße)."

16. The arrangement of a combined home and medical practice is confirmed by the arthur-schnitzler.org biographical sketch: "Arthur's father ran his practice from their home address, so that his son already had contact with patients from childhood."

17. Adolf von Sonnenthal (1834–1909) and Charlotte Wolter (1834–1897) as patients of Johann Schnitzler: confirmed by Wien Geschichte Wiki ("Johann Schnitzler") and multiple biographical sources. See also the German-language biographical portal de-academic.com

: "Adolf von Sonnenthal, Charlotte Wolter und viele Sänger der Hofoper ließen sich bei ihm behandeln."

18. Johann Schnitzler co-founded the Vienna General Polyclinic (Allgemeine Poliklinik Wien) in 1872 and became head of its laryngological department. See NDB, vol. 23, p. 334; ADB, vol. 54, p. 137.

19. Johann received the title of titular professor in 1878, was appointed associate professor (unbesoldeter a.o. Professor) in 1880, and became medical director of the Polyclinic in 1884. Sources differ slightly on the sequence of titles. See Jewish Encyclopedia (which says 1878 for titular professor, 1880 for assistant professor); NDB (1878 tit. a.o. Prof., 1880 unbesoldeter a.o. Prof.); and ADB (1882 for Regierungsrat).

20. The *Klinischer Atlas der Laryngologie* was published posthumously in 1895, co-edited by Markus Hajek and Arthur Schnitzler. See Wien Geschichte Wiki; NDB. Johann Schnitzler died on May 2, 1893, at the family apartment, Burgring 1.

21. Berta Lehmann's engagement as governess in 1870: confirmed by the arthur-schnitzler.org biographical sketch: "Berta Lehmann, who was employed as a governess from 1870, encouraged Arthur's interest in literature and theatre from an early age."

22. The first dramatic work, *Aristokrat und Demokrat*: "Her brother inspired him to write his first drama, Aristocrat and Democrat (*Aristokrat und Demokrat*)." See arthur-schnitzler.org.

23. *The passage about Schnitzler's later reflections on childhood certainties is indebted to JiW, where Schnitzler discusses the atmosphere of liberal confidence in which he was raised. Readers should consult JiW directly for Schnitzler's own words on this subject.*

24. The 1871 move to Burgring 1: confirmed by the Schnitzler Tagebuch digital edition, which lists "Wohnung und Ordination Johann Schnitzler Burgring 1" as Arthur's address from this period. See also diary entry of March 3, 1879, which contextualizes the Burgring address via the Wiener Schnitzler project.

25. Arthur entered the Akademisches Gymnasium in autumn 1871. He completed the Matura on July 8, 1879. See Wien Geschichte Wiki, "Arthur Schnitzler"; arthur-schnitzler.org biographical sketch. On Friedrich von Schmidt as architect of the school building at Beethovenplatz, see the Akademisches Gymnasium Wikipedia article.

26. The alumni list: Nestroy, Schubert, Altenberg, Hofmannsthal, Beer-Hofmann, Schrödinger, Mises, Meitner—all confirmed by the Akademisches Gymnasium's own published records and the arthur-sch nitzler.org biographical sketch. The claim that "roughly half the student body would be Jewish" by the twentieth century is based on Rozenblit, *The Jews of Vienna*, and school enrollment statistics.

27. The first love with Franziska ("Fännchen") Reich: "In the spring of 1875 Arthur, now 13, fell in love for the first time. His love was also reciprocated by Fanny." See arthur-schnitzler.org biographical sketch. The September 1878 resumption is likewise documented there. *See Ji W for a fuller account.*

28. Matura with distinction, July 8, 1879: confirmed by Wien Geschichte Wiki ("Matura mit Auszeichnung") and arthur-schnitzler.org.

29. The Amsterdam trip and the travel report *Von Amsterdam nach Ymuiden*: "Arthur schreibt auf Wunsch des Vaters einen Reisebericht, den dieser in der Wiener medizinischen Presse ... veröffentlicht." See arthur-s chnitzler.de biographical sketch.

30. The diary: Schnitzler began his Tagebuch in March 1879, at the age of seventeen. The first surviving entry in the published edition is dated March 3, 1879. The digital edition comprises 16,407 entries span- ning 1879–1931. See Arthur Schnitzler: *Tagebuch 1879–1931*. Digitale Ausgabe, herausgegeben von ACDH der Österreichischen Akademie der Wissenschaften (schnitzler-tagebuch.acdh.oeaw.ac.at). The fragment of an earlier juvenile diary is preserved in the appendix of the final volume of the printed edition (2000). A half-year after beginning the diary, the young

Schnitzler took stock of his literary output to that point, as noted in the arthur-schnitzler.de biographical sketch.

31. By Praterstern - Own work, CC BY-SA 3.0, https://commons.wik imedia.org/w/index.php?curid=31344268

32. By Josef Székely - Österreichische Nationalbibliothek, Bildarchiv Austria, Inventarnr. AS 68 B, Public Domain, https://commons.wikim edia.org/w/index.php?curid=15682059

Chapter 2

1. Arthur Schnitzler, *Tagebuch 1879–1892*, ed. Peter Michael Braunwarth et al., Vienna: Verlag der Österreichischen Akademie der Wissenschaften, 1987, entry of 27 October 1879. Also available in the CC-licensed digital edition: https://schnitzler-tagebuch.acdh.oeaw.ac.at. The German original reads: "Ich fühle es schon, die Wissenschaft wird mir nie das bedeuten, was die Kunst mir schon jetzt ist."

2. Arthur Schnitzler, "Von Amsterdam nach Ymuiden," *Wiener Medizinische Presse* 20 (1879). Johann Schnitzler and Philipp Markbreiter co-founded the journal in 1860. See the biographical sketch at the Arthur Schnitzler Portal, https://www.arthur-schnitzler.org/bio-bibliography/b iographical-sketch/.

3. Arthur Schnitzler, *Jugend in Wien. Eine Autobiographie*, ed. Therese Nickl and Heinrich Schnitzler, Vienna/Munich/Zurich: Fritz Molden, 1968. The phrase in German is "mehr aus Gewohnheit als aus Neigung."

4. Schnitzler, *Tagebuch 1879–1892*, entry of 27 October 1879 (see note 1). This is from the published diary, which is in the public domain. The digital edition of the diary data is available under a Creative Commons license at https://github.com/arthur-schnitzler/schnitzler-tagebuch-data.

5. Schnitzler, *Tagebuch 1879–1892*, entry from approximately spring 1880. The Arthur Schnitzler Portal cites this as occurring about half a year after enrollment. The German reads: "ich habe demnach bis zum heutigen

Tage 23 Dramen fertig geschrieben und 13 angefangen, soweit ich mich erinnere."

6. On the medical faculty during this period, see Erna Lesky, *Die Wiener medizinische Schule im 19. Jahrhundert*, Graz: Böhlau, 1978. Theodor Billroth (1829–1894) was professor of surgery; Hermann Nothnagel (1841–1905) held the chair of internal medicine from 1882; Theodor Meynert (1833–1892) was professor of psychiatry and directed the psychiatric clinic.

7. On Johann Schnitzler's career: see "Johann Schnitzler," Wikipedia, and the Deutsche Biographie entry. He was named titular professor in 1878, associate professor ("unbesoldeter ao. Prof.") in 1880, and became director of the Polyclinic in 1884. See also the Jewish Encyclopedia entry, s.v. "Schnitzler, Johann."

8. Johann's father was Joseph Zimmermann (1810–1864), who later took or was assigned the name Schnitzler. See Schnitzler, *Jugend in Wien*, opening pages; also Arthur Schnitzler Portal, biographical sketch. The Schnitzler/Zimmermann genealogy is discussed in the autobiography's first chapter.

9. That Johann Schnitzler originally harbored literary ambitions is stated in the Arthur Schnitzler Portal biographical sketch: "Johann originally wanted to be a writer, but ultimately decided to study medicine." This detail also appears in *Jugend in Wien*.

10. The interpretation of the psychological dynamics between Johann and Arthur—Johann's possible recognition of his own abandoned dreams in his son's ambitions—is a widely discussed theme in Schnitzler scholarship. See Hartmut Scheible, *Arthur Schnitzler in Selbstzeugnissen und Bilddokumenten*, Reinbek: Rowohlt, 1976 (13th ed. 2003), and Konstanze Fliedl, *Arthur Schnitzler*, Stuttgart: Reclam, 2005. The framing here is the present author's synthesis; however, readers should be aware that Scheible and Fliedl develop this argument in detail.

11. Schnitzler, *Tagebuch 1879–1892*, entry of 25 November 1881. The Arthur Schnitzler Portal confirms: "On 25 November 1881, Schnitzler met Gusti, a singer from a theatre chorus living in the suburbs, fell in love and recognised in her the type of the 'sweet young girl' (süßes Mädel)."

12. Schnitzler first used the term "süßes Mädel" in his diary in September 1887, in connection with Jeanette Heeger. See the German Wikipedia article "Süßes Mädel," which cites the diary entry and provides the relevant passage. Also see Schnitzler, *Tagebuch 1879–1892*, entry for September 1887. The Arthur Schnitzler Portal confirms that Heeger's relationship began in September 1887.

13. Schnitzler, *Jugend in Wien*, Siebentes Buch (Seventh Book). The German reads: "In der Rückerinnerung eines solchen Morgens war es, daß ich dieses Schmeichelwort vom süßen Mädel zum erstenmal in mein Tagebuch schrieb, ohne zu ahnen, daß es bestimmt war, einmal gewissermaßen literarisch zu werden." The full passage is available at Zeno.or g (http://www.zeno.org/Literatur/M/Schnitzler,+Arthur/Autobiograp hisches/Jugend+in+Wien/Siebentes+Buch).

14. Arthur Schnitzler Portal, biographical sketch. See also Schnitzler, *Tagebuch 1879–1892*, entries from October 1882.

15. Arthur Schnitzler Portal, biographical sketch: "[He] passed the officers' examination and turned his back on the military."

16. *Leutnant Gustl* was first published in the *Neue Freie Presse*, 25 December 1900. The military disciplinary proceedings are documented in Otto P. Schinnerer, "Schnitzler and the Military Censorship: Unpublished Correspondence," *Germanic Review* 5 (1930): 238–246. The committee's finding was issued in June 1901. See also Konstanze Fliedl, ed., *Arthur Schnitzler: Leutnant Gustl* (historisch-kritische Ausgabe), and the review in *Modern Austrian Literature* (MUSE). The novella is in the public domain.

17. Arthur Schnitzler Portal, biographical sketch: "At the end of May 1885 Schnitzler graduated as 'doctor in general medicine.'" See also Schnitzler, *Tagebuch 1879–1892*.

18. Arthur Schnitzler Portal: "[He] began practical training to become an assistant doctor at the General Hospital and as an aspirant at the Viennese Polyclinic. During this time, he occasionally deputised for his father in his practice." Freud trained at the Vienna General Hospital from 1882 to 1885.

19. By Josef Székely - http://www.zeno.org/Literatur/M/Schnitzler,+Arthur, Public Domain, https://commons.wikimedia.org/w/index.php?curid=6004497

Chapter 3

1. Arthur Schnitzler Portal, biographical sketch: "In April 1886, when Schnitzler was staying in Merano with suspected tuberculosis, he met Olga Waissnix (1862–1897)." See also Schnitzler, *Tagebuch 1879–1892*, entries from April 1886; and *Jugend in Wien*. The Merano encounter is also discussed in Elisabeth-Joe Harriet, *Die unvollendete Geliebte: Olga Waissnix & Arthur Schnitzler*, Vienna: Amalthea, 2015.

2. On the Thalhof and Olga Waissnix's background: "Waissnix (Waißnix), Olga (I.); geb. Schneider," *Österreichisches Biographisches Lexikon*, vol. 15 (2018), pp. 429–430. The Thalhof in Reichenau is described as a "Nobelhotel" frequented by the upper classes. Peter Altenberg was a known guest (see ÖsterreichWiki entry on Olga Waissnix).

3. Olga Waissnix to Arthur Schnitzler, 1886. The German reads: "Du geliebtes Meran, wie die längst versunkene Zauberstadt Vineta steigst Du vor mir herauf, wenn ich an Dich denke." Published in Nickl/Schnitzler, eds., *Liebe, die starb vor der Zeit* (1970). Waissnix's letters are in the public domain (she died 1897); the editorial apparatus of the 1970 edition remains under copyright. The NZZ (Zurich) quoted this passage in 2002.

4. Schnitzler, *Tagebuch*. The German: "Nie red ich mit einem Frauenzimmer so gescheidt wie mit der." Cited in the APA report on Elisabeth-Joe Harriet's biography (Tiroler Tageszeitung, 29 April 2015) and in multiple secondary sources.

5. Hans Weigel, foreword to *Liebe, die starb vor der Zeit* (1970): "Ohne sie wäre er vielleicht kein Schriftsteller und gewiss nicht dieser Schriftsteller geworden." Confirmed by the ÖsterreichWiki article on Olga Waissnix.

6. Nickl, Therese, and Heinrich Schnitzler, eds. *Liebe, die starb vor der Zeit: Arthur Schnitzler und Olga Waissnix. Ein Briefwechsel.* Vienna: Molden, 1970. The title translates as "Love That Died Before Its Time."

7. On the meeting with Jeanette Heeger: The details—the Pferderennbahn, the whistling, her profession as Kunststickerin, four siblings, modest apartment, weak health—are confirmed by the Oper Stuttgart blog (20 May 2016, "Reigen // Arthur Schnitzler und die Frauen 2"), citing diary sources. The blog states she was born in 1865. The Arthur Schnitzler Portal dates the relationship's start to "the start of September 1887" and describes her as carrying out "sewing work for luxury shops."

8. On Schnitzler's sexual bookkeeping: Wikipedia and multiple secondary sources confirm that "for a period of some years he kept a record of every orgasm" (see Andrew C. Wisely, *Arthur Schnitzler and Twentieth-Century Criticism*, Camden House, 2004, ch. 6). Peter Gay, *Schnitzler's Century* (2001), discusses this practice extensively. A Star Tribune review (2007) summarizes: "Sexually active to a degree, he kept count of his orgasms and then totaled them up at the end of each month."

9. Arthur Schnitzler Portal: the Heeger relationship "was to last around two years." The affair's deterioration and the suicide threats are described in the Oper Stuttgart blog (2016) and are consistent with diary entries.

10. Schnitzler, *Tagebuch 1879–1892*, entry from 1890 (precise date to be confirmed against the published diary). The German: "Ich habe ein sonderbares Bedürfnis, mich psychologisch festzuhalten. Warum? Um ein wenig Ordnung in mein gequältes Nervensystem zu bringen? Aus Eigen-

liebe? Aus literarischem Interesse?" This passage is widely cited in Schnitzler scholarship.

11. Arthur Schnitzler Portal: Schnitzler "joined the editorial team" of the *Internationale Klinische Rundschau*. Encyclopedia.com states he "edited" it from 1887 to 1894. The Schnitzler Portal dates this to 1886: "[He] regularly published medical articles and reviews in the Internationale Klinische Rundschau, the editorial team of which he had also joined."

12. On Schnitzler's engagement with hypnosis research: Freud translated Charcot's *Leçons sur les maladies du système nerveux* (published 1886) and Bernheim's *De la suggestion* (1888–89).

13. Freud to Schnitzler, 14 May 1922. The full German text is available under CC license at freudedition.net (https://www.freudedition.net/en/briefe/freud-sigmund/schnitzler-arthur/1922/05/14). Freud wrote: "Ich meine, ich habe Sie gemieden aus einer Art von Doppelgängerscheu." The letter was first published in English in Kupper, H. I., and Rollman-Branch, H. S., "Freud and Schnitzler—(Doppelgänger)," *Journal of the American Psychoanalytic Association* 7 (1959): 109–126. Also published in *Letters of Sigmund Freud*, ed. Ernst L. Freud. The TIME article "Medicine: Freud's Doppelgänger" provides an English translation. Freud did not simply "call" Schnitzler his Doppelgänger; he confessed to a "Doppelgängerscheu"—a fear or reluctance to meet his double.

14. Schnitzler, "Über funktionelle Aphonie und deren Behandlung durch Hypnose und Suggestion," *Internationale Klinische Rundschau* 3 (1889). Cited in the Arthur Schnitzler Portal biographical sketch.

15. Schnitzler, *Tagebuch 1879–1892*, entry from May 1886. The German: "Es war eine Rieseneselei von mir – Mediziner zu werden, und es ist leider eine Eselei, die nicht mehr gut zu machen ist." Cited in the Arthur Schnitzler Portal biographical sketch (German version). Public domain.

Chapter 4

1. The interpretive framework here—liberal culture in retreat, the rise of Lueger, Schönerer, and ethnic nationalisms within the Habsburg Empire—follows Carl Schorske, *Fin-de-Siècle Vienna: Politics and Culture* (New York: Knopf, 1980), especially ch. 1–3. This is standard historiography but readers should be aware of the interpretive lineage.

2. On the gathering at Café Griensteidl from around 1890: Wikipedia, "Young Vienna"; Springer, "Schnitzler und Jung Wien" (citing diary entry of 26 February 1891: "Das junge Oesterreich. Im Griensteidl"); Arthur Schnitzler Portal, biographical sketch: "In Café Griensteidl, where a circle of young writers, soon to be known as 'Jung Wien' ('Young Vienna'), had gathered since around 1890, he got to know among others the young Hugo von Hofmannsthal as well as others of his own generation." The café was located in the Palais Herberstein (sometimes called Palais Dietrichstein) at Michaelerplatz.

3. Bahr published *Die Überwindung des Naturalismus* in 1891. The Gustav Klimt Database confirms he "became the central figure of the literary circle Jung-Wien" and "published a collection of his reviews in 1891 under the title of Die Überwindung des Naturalismus." On his background: Bahr was born in Linz in 1863, traveled through Berlin and Paris, and returned to Vienna in the early 1890s.

4. Beer-Hofmann met Schnitzler in the autumn of 1890, probably at the Café Griensteidl. See Eugene Weber, review of *Briefwechsel 1891–1931* (ed. Konstanze Fliedl), *Modern Austrian Literature* 6, no. 3/4 (1973): 40. Beer-Hofmann was born in 1866, moved to Vienna in 1880, studied at the Akademisches Gymnasium, and took a law degree in 1890. Both Beer-Hofmann and Schnitzler attended the Akademisches Gymnasium—the oldest secondary school in Vienna—but years apart.

5. Altenberg's association with Café Central is one of the most famous anecdotes of Viennese coffeehouse culture. The Café Central article on

the Gustav Klimt Database lists Altenberg among the regulars who moved there after Griensteidl's closure in 1897.

6. Hofmannsthal was born on 1 February 1874 and was thus sixteen when introduced to the Jung-Wien group in late 1890. He published under the pseudonym "Loris" (short for "Loris Melikow") because students were not permitted to publish under their own names. See Wikipedia, "Hugo von Hofmannsthal"; Abigail Gillman, *Viennese Jewish Modernism* (Penn State UP, 2009): "Hofmannsthal, a sixteen-year-old student who published under the name Loris, was introduced to the group late in 1890." Schnitzler's first impressions are recorded as noting "significant talent... authentic artistry, unheard of for his age."

7. Schnitzler, *Tagebuch 1879–1892*, entry of 9 October 1891: "Loris, Salten, Beer-Hofmann und ich werden nämlich schon als Clique betrachtet." Cited by the Arthur Schnitzler Portal.

8. Schnitzler, *Tagebuch 1879–1892*, entry of 5 February 1891: "literarische Anerkennung beginnt." Cited by the Arthur Schnitzler Portal.

9. Müller, Martin Anton, ed. *Arthur Schnitzler: "Das Zeitlose ist von kürzester Dauer."* Band 1, No. 4: "Wiener Porträts. XLVI. Hermann Bahr" (1903). CC BY 4.0. In this joint interview, Bahr declared he had been in the Griensteidl with Schnitzler and Hofmannsthal together only twice. Schnitzler was irritated ("geärgert") at being called a "Kaffeehausdichter" in magazines. The interviewer concluded: "Das mit dem Café Griensteidl und den großen Schlagworten, die dort von Bahr ausgegeben worden sein sollen, ist Erfindung und Eselei." Schnitzler also interjected characteristically when the interviewer's question to Bahr seemed too blunt, saying in his "fine, well-modulated voice": "Is that not a little too crude?" ("Ist das nicht ein bißchen zu grob?")

10. Schnitzler, *Tagebuch*. The Arthur Schnitzler Portal (German version) quotes: "Vertrage Griensteidl nicht; die Atmosphäre [...]"

11. Schnitzler, *Später Ruhm*. Written c. 1894–95, published posthumously: Arthur Schnitzler, *Später Ruhm*, ed. Wilhelm Hemecker and

David Österle (Vienna: Zsolnay, 2014). Confirmed as a satire of the Jung-Wien circle by the Arthur Schnitzler Portal and by Scheffel, "Später Ruhm," in Schnitzler Handbuch, pp. 245–247. The English Wikipedia article on Young Vienna notes: "The group was satirized by Arthur Schnitzler, one of its members, in his novella Late Fame, which was written c. 1894–1895, but not published until 2014."

12. Karl Kraus, "Die demolirte Literatur," *Wiener Rundschau* 1, no. 1 (1897). The essay used the demolition of the Griensteidl as a satirical framework. See Wikipedia, "Young Vienna."

13. On the Salten-Kraus incident: "According to Schnitzler's diary, Felix Salten, angry with a negative review Kraus had given him, attacked the young journalist in the café." Cited in the English-language Wikipedia article on Young Vienna and in the Primidi encyclopedia entry.

14. Müller, Band 1, No. 1: "Arthur Schnitzler. Verfasser der 'Liebelei'" (1897). Originally published in Danish; German translation in Müller's edition. CC BY 4.0. The interview describes Schnitzler as "sicherlich derzeit der prominenteste Mann des jungen Österreichs, im engeren Sinne des jungen Wiens" and characterizes him as "Heiter und sentimental, ein eleganter Mann von Welt und ein rebellischer Spötter." It notes his summer trip to Copenhagen with Beer-Hofmann and Paul Goldmann, describing their friendship as marked by "eine blinde, fast schuljungenhafte Zuneigung füreinander."

15. Müller, Band 1, No. 2 or 3 (1903 interview). Schnitzler on the art of suggestion: "Diese Kunst der Andeutung ist nicht nur eine Consequenz unserer feineren Nerven, sondern auch eine Reaction gegen den Naturalismus." CC BY 4.0. The interview discusses the audience's imaginative participation in modern theater.

Chapter 5

1. Johann Schnitzler (10 April 1835 – 2 May 1893). Arthur Schnitzler Portal, biographical sketch: "At the end of April Schnitzler's father developed erysipelas in his face and died on 2 May after blood poisoning." Confirmed by Wikipedia ("Johann Schnitzler"), Jewish Encyclopedia, and Geni.com. He was buried in Vienna's Zentralfriedhof.

2. Arthur Schnitzler Portal: "In August Schnitzler left the Polyclinic and from then on only saw a limited number of patients in private practice. He also moved in with his mother at her Frankgasse address."

3. *Anatol* was published in book form by the Verlag des Bibliographischen Bureaus, Berlin. German Wikipedia ("Anatol [Schauspiel]"): "Als Buchausgabe erschien er im Herbst 1892, vordatiert auf das Jahr 1893." He published under his pseudonym "Loris," as school regulations prohibited students from publishing under their own names. See Wikipedia, "Anatol (play)" and "Hugo von Hofmannsthal."

4. Arthur Schnitzler Portal: "Johann originally wanted to be a writer, but ultimately decided to study medicine and settled in Vienna as a laryngologist."

5. Arthur Schnitzler Portal: "1893 was a hard year for Schnitzler. In the March of that year Mizi Glümer's confession of infidelity left him in a fury, even if he had been unfaithful to her on multiple occasions." The diary records his admission: "I berate and hit her." *Das Märchen* premiered at the Deutsches Volkstheater in early December 1893 with Adele Sandrock as Fanny Theren. The Portal notes it "prompted a theatre scandal and was curtailed after only two performances. However, the diva Sandrock began an exalted affair with Schnitzler."

6. German Wikipedia, "Tagebuch (Schnitzler)": "In seiner zu Lebzeiten unveröffentlichten Autobiografie Jugend in Wien schildert Schnitzler, wie sein Vater Johann Schnitzler 1879 heimlich sein Tagebuch las und ihm dann wegen der darin geschilderten sexuellen Handlungen eine Strafpredigt zu Geschlechtskrankheiten hielt. Dieser Vertrauensbruch des Vaters dürfte die Ursache darstellen, dass von den frühen Aufzeichnungen

nur Bruchstücke überliefert sind." (In his posthumously published autobiography Jugend in Wien, Schnitzler describes how his father secretly read his diary in 1879 and delivered a lecture on venereal disease; this breach of trust likely explains why only fragments of the early diary survive.)

7. Müller, Martin Anton, ed. *Arthur Schnitzler: "Das Zeitlose ist von kürzester Dauer." Interviews, Meinungen und Proteste 1891–1931*. Band 1. CC BY 4.0. DOI: https://doi.org/10.46500/83535471. Copenhagen interview (1920s). Schnitzler's German: "Ich war Arzt – und das bin ich ja auf eine Art noch immer, wie es mein Vater und mein Großvater waren und wie es mein Bruder und mein Schwager und mehrere meiner Verwandten sind. Wir bilden eine ganze Ärztefamilie, und ich bin der Medizin nie ganz entkommen." On why he writes: "Das ist sehr schwer zu beantworten. Bewusst schreibe ich keine Tendenzbücher, die einen bestimmten Zweck verfolgen. Ich schreibe, um Menschen zu schildern und Figuren zu formen."

8. Müller, Band 1. Tribute in the *Wiener Medizinische Wochenschrift* on Schnitzler's 60th birthday (15 May 1922). CC BY 4.0. The passage argues: "Vielleicht würde man, wüßte man von dieser Tatsache nicht, urteilen dürfen, dieser Dichter hätte auch Arzt sein können. Und das nicht etwa deshalb, weil in seinen Schriften Probleme, die auch den Arzt beschäftigen, Situationen, die auch dieser kennt, eindringlich dargestellt werden ... sondern weil die ganze Art der Erfassung des Menschen irgendwie an den Standpunkt des Arztes erinnert." (Even without knowing the biographical fact, one could judge that this writer might also have been a physician—not because his writings vividly depict problems and situations familiar to doctors, but because his entire manner of apprehending the human being recalls the physician's standpoint.)

9. Wikipedia, "Johann Schnitzler": "His son Arthur perpetuated parts of his life in the 1912 drama Professor Bernhardi." Beniston, in the *Schnitzler-Handbuch* (2022), confirms: "die im Jahr 1872 vom Vater Johann Schnitzler mitgegründeten Allgemeinen Poliklinik, die das Vorbild für das

von der Titelfigur geleitete ›Elisabethinum‹ liefert" (the General Poly-clinic co-founded by Johann in 1872, which provides the model for the "Elisabethinum" run by the title character). The Portal notes the play was "refused by the censors" in Vienna, with the premiere at the Kleines Theater in Berlin on 28 November 1912.

10. Diary entry, 27 March 1918. Cited in Beniston, "Professor Bernhar-di. Komödie in fünf Akten (1912)," *Schnitzler-Handbuch* (2022): "Es gibt Sachen von mir die ich lieber habe, – aber mich hab ich nirgends lieber als im Bernhardi." (There are works of mine that I like better—but there is none in which I like myself better than in Bernhardi.) The Tagebuch digital edition is available at https://schnitzler-tagebuch.acdh.oeaw.ac.at. The diary is in the public domain; the Tagebuch was published 1987–2000 by the Austrian Academy of Sciences.

Chapter 6

1. *Anatol* published by Verlag des Bibliographischen Bureaus, Berlin, autumn 1892 (predated to 1893). Verse prologue by Hugo von Hof-mannsthal ("Loris"). Johann Schnitzler died 2 May 1893; Arthur left the Polyclinic in August 1893. See Arthur Schnitzler Portal, biographical sketch.

2. Arthur Schnitzler to Richard Beer-Hofmann, March 11, 1892. In: Arthur Schnitzler: Correspondence with Authors. Digital Edition. Edited by Martin Anton Müller with Gerd Hermann Susen, Laura Untner and Selma Jahnke, https://schnitzler-briefe.acdh.oeaw.ac.at/L00079.html (ac-cessed March 2, 2026)

3. Süßes Mädel definition: from *Jugend in Wien* (1968). The orig-inal German: "verdorben ohne Sündhaftigkeit, unschuldsvoll ohne Jungfräulichkeit, [...] als Bürgertöchterchen immerhin nicht ganz wohl geraten, aber als Liebchen das bürgerlichste und uneigennützigste Geschöpf, das sich denken lässt."

4. Freud's letter to Schnitzler, 14 May 1922. Available at https://w
ww.freudedition.net (CC BY-NC-ND 4.0). Freud wrote that Schnitzler
had arrived through intuition—or rather through sensitive self-observation—at everything Freud had laboriously uncovered through work on
other people ("alles das, was ich in mühseliger Arbeit an anderen Menschen aufzudecken hatte").

5. Full *Anatol* cycle first staged 3 December 1910 at the Lessing Theater,
Berlin, with simultaneous premiere at the Wiener Volkstheater. Wikipedia,
"Lessing Theater."

6. A 1912 Broadway production, *The Affairs of Anatol*, introduced
American audiences to Viennese literary culture.

7. Adele Sandrock (19 August 1863 – 30 August 1937). Born in Rotterdam, daughter of a Prussian officer and a Dutch stage actress. IMDB
biography. Müller, Band 1 (1908 interview, CC BY 4.0) confirms Sandrock
as "die erste Darstellerin der Christine" in *Liebelei*.

8. Arthur Schnitzler wrote "Ich hasse dieses Weib" ("I hate this woman")
about Adele Sandrock in a letter to Mizzi Glümer on November 18,
1892, after her performance evoked strong negative emotions in him. Renate Wagner, Frauen um Arthur Schnitzler (Frankfurt am Main: Fisch-
er-Taschenbuch-Verlag, 1983), 84. | Andrea Weinmann, *Arthur Schnitzler
und Adele Sandrock* (Munich: GRIN Verlag, 2001), https://www.grin.c
om/document/103750.

9. Meeting date of 24 October 1893. Arthur Schnitzler Portal confirms:
"The diva Sandrock began an exalted affair with Schnitzler."

10. "a female friend" who could enter "the cooler and more sublime
realms of your mind, and who would feel at home there": diary, December
17, 1893. Arthur Schnitzler: Diary. Digital Edition, Sunday, December 17,
1893, https://schnitzler-tagebuch.acdh.oeaw.ac.at/entry__1893-12-17.h
tml (accessed February 23, 2026), PID: http://hdl.handle.net/21.11115
/0000-000B-E798-5.

11. *Das Märchen* premiered Deutsches Volkstheater, Vienna, December 1893. Arthur Schnitzler Portal: "a production which prompted a theatre scandal and was curtailed after only two performances."

Chapter 7

1. *Liebelei* timeline: Wikipedia ("Liebelei [play]"). First act written autumn 1893, originally set in a dance school. Discarded after criticism from Beer-Hofmann, Hofmannsthal, Salten, and Schwarzkopf. Rewritten three times. Final three-act form begun 13 September 1894, completed mid-October 1894.

2. Richard Alewyn, Probleme und Gestalten: Essays (Frankfurt am Main: Insel Verlag, 1974), 163.

3. "Es wird was Hübsches zum Erinnern sein" ("It will be something nice to remember"). Diary entry during Schnitzler's relationship with Jeanette Heeger, likely 1887–1889. Confirmed by getAbstract Liebelei summary. Public domain diary. Digital edition: https://schnitzler-tageb uch.acdh.oeaw.ac.at.

4. Submitted to Burgtheater late October 1894; accepted January 1895. Director Max Burckhard (Burgtheater director 1890–1898). Wikipedia, "Liebelei (play)."

5. Premiered 9 October 1895, Burgtheater, Vienna, with Adele Sandrock as Christine. Wikipedia, "Liebelei (play)." Müller, Band 1 (1908 interview, CC BY 4.0): "Adele Sandrock, die erste Darstellerin der Christine."

6. Friedrich Torberg, "Schnitzler," in Das fünfte Rad am Thespiskarren (Wien: Georg Müller Verlag, 1966), 218–31.

7. Film adaptations: Max Ophüls, *Liebelei* (1933), starring Magda Schneider. Pierre Gaspard-Huit, *Christine* (1958), starring Romy Schneider. Tom Stoppard, *Dalliance* (1986), premiered Lyttelton Theatre, National Theatre, London, 27 May 1986. Wikipedia, "Dalliance."

8. S. Fischer Verlag published *Liebelei* in 1896. *Sterben* also published by Fischer, 1895.

Chapter 8

1. Arthur Schnitzler Portal, biographical sketch: "Then, in the summer of 1894 the singing teacher Marie 'Mizi' Reinhard (1871–1899) was treated by Schnitzler, and they fell in love, making plans for a future together." The Portal describes her as a Gesangspädagogin (voice teacher). https://www.arthur-schnitzler.org/bio-bibliography/biographical-sketch/.

2. German Wikipedia, "Maria Reinhard." Father's position and linguistic abilities confirmed. Broken engagement, depression, and psychiatric stay also confirmed. Born 1871, making her 23 in July 1894.

3. Renate Wagner, *Arthur Schnitzler: Eine Biographie* (Vienna: Fritz Molden, 1981).

4. German Wikipedia, "Maria Reinhard": 230 letters survive in the Deutsches Literaturarchiv Marbach (DLA). See also: Arthur Schnitzler, "Arthur Schnitzler an Marie Reinhard (1896)," *Modern Austrian Literature* 10, nos. 3/4 (1977): 23–68.

5. Schnitzler Portal: "Marie Reinhard realised in January 1897 that she was pregnant. As nobody was to know of this in Vienna, she left the city in order to bring the child into the world elsewhere."

6. Stillborn child confirmed as Paul Schnitzler, born and died 24 September 1897 in Mauer bei Wien. Wikidata entity Q125245739. Cousin Ludwig Mandl as birth attendant confirmed by Schnitzler Portal and German Wikipedia.

7. Schnitzler Portal: "Schnitzler was shattered and noted the 'deep feeling of a connection between the death of the child and my lack of interest for the child before the birth.'" Diary entry, autumn 1897. Public domain. https://schnitzler-tagebuch.acdh.oeaw.ac.at.

8. *Reigen* written November 23, 1896 – February 24, 1897, under the working title *Liebesreigen*. See Met Museum catalogue entry for publication: "Reigen. Zehn Dialoge, geschrieben Winter 1896/97." Private printing of 200 copies, spring 1900. Public edition: Wiener Verlag, 1903. First authorized performance: Kleines Schauspielhaus, Berlin, 23 December 1920.

9. German Wikipedia, "Maria Reinhard": "Im Januar 1899 kam es zu einer neuerlichen Schwangerschaft."

10. Diary entry, 12 February 1899: "Abd. mit Mz. Rh., ... Sie war wieder verstimmt, weil ich das Heir. auf die lange Bank schiebe. Ich ärgerte mich." Cited in Rolf-Peter Lacher, *Der Mensch ist eine Bestie* (2014), and confirmed by Project MUSE review. See also diary entry 2 February 1899: "Vm. bei Mz Rh.—Wieder neuen Sorgen." Public domain diary, digital edition.

11. Triple bill premiere confirmed: 1 March 1899, Burgtheater, Vienna. German Wikipedia, "Der grüne Kakadu"; "Paracelsus (Schnitzler)"; English Wikipedia, "Die Gefährtin."

12. English Wikipedia, "Die Gefährtin": "Die Gefährtin is a one-act play by Arthur Schnitzler, which premiered on 1 March 1899 at the Burgtheater in Vienna. ... Schnitzler had already developed the material of a husband who has to revise his view of marriage after the death of his wife in the novella Der Wittwer published in 1894."

13. Müller, Band 1, 1904 Danish interview (CC BY 4.0): "Dazu muss ich sagen: Das Problem ist in dem genannten Stück nur berührt. Es ist mehr Stimmung als eigentliche Ausarbeitung des Problems. Es steckt mehr darin, als man in einem Akt ausgestalten kann."

14. Müller, Band 1, 1903 *Neues Wiener Journal* interview (CC BY 4.0): "Was es mit meinem ›Kakadu‹ für eine Bewandtniß hat? Ich kann hier nur Andeutungen geben. Er wurde nach siebenmaliger Aufführung abgesetzt, anfangs nur ›nicht erlaubt◻ und erst später – verboten."

15. Julius Schnitzler's expertise: German Wikipedia, "Maria Reinhard": "Julius Schnitzler war in Wien führend in der Behandlung der Appendicitis, insbesondere in der Technik der Appendektomie." Ludwig Mandl identified as the gynecologist. Museum of Contraception and Abortion article confirms both were consulted.

16. Diary gap: the Tagebuch digital edition shows entries through mid-March 1899, then a gap until early April. The last pre-death entry appears to be around 12 March 1899 (Sonntag, 12. März); the next is Montag, 3. April 1899. Approximately three weeks of silence.

17. Schnitzler Portal: "Four days after her death, he described the feeling of loss as a 'loneliness without compare – I have to think of how I have always tried to depict people who lose what is dearest to them – for there is something that cannot be expressed – just like eternity, infinity: – loneliness, having been made lonely; being made to be lonely.'" Diary entry c. 22 March 1899. Public domain diary.

18. Rolf-Peter Lacher, *Der Mensch ist eine Bestie: Anna Heeger, Maria Chlum, Maria Reinhard und Arthur Schnitzler* (2014). Title from Schnitzler's diary entry, 24 December 1889.

19. The Project MUSE review (2015) calls Lacher's evidence "inference, innuendo, and circumstantial evidence" and notes that "a far more balanced approach to the writer's stormy affairs can be found in Ulrich Weinzierl's *Arthur Schnitzler: Lieben Träumen Sterben* (1994)." German Wikipedia: "Von der akademischen Schnitzlerforschung blieb das Buch bislang unberücksichtigt oder wurde abschlägig beurteilt."

20. German Wikipedia, "Maria Reinhard": Schnitzler told Karoline Burger on 25 May 1903 that Marie had died "an einer durch keine Anzeichen vorhersehbaren Blinddarmentzündung."

21. German Wikipedia, "Maria Reinhard": "Am 25. Juli 2014 erklärte die Stadt Wien das Grab (Gruppe 71 B Reihe 20, Nr. 68) zum Historischen Grab und zur Stätte der Erinnerung."

22. Schnitzler Portal: "At the end of March 1899 Schnitzler was awarded the Bauernfeld Prize for his novellas and dramatic works."

23. Schnitzler Portal: "In January 1902 Olga Gussmann turned twenty, was pregnant once more and wished to be married to Schnitzler. As in the case of Marie Reinhard, Schnitzler was evasive and searched for a small house outside Vienna where Olga could give birth in the summer."

24. Schnitzler Portal: "Schnitzler would hold the anniversary of Marie Reinhard's death in remembrance until the end of his life."

25. Paul Wilhelm, "Bei Artur Schnitzler," 1908 (Müller, Band 1, CC BY 4.0): "Er wurde zum Dichter des süßen Mädels ... Man wies ihm seinen Platz an in der Literatur, und – da gedankenloses Einschachteln nun einmal in der Wiener Art liegt, – so übersah man lange, daß der Dichter ... durchaus nicht stehen geblieben war. Er sah tiefer in die Probleme des Lebens und in die menschliche Seele."

26. Müller, Band 1, 1921 *Illustrirtes Wiener Extrablatt* interview (CC BY 4.0): "Die Dialoge wurden vor achtzehn Jahren geschrieben, sie sind ein Jugendwerk."

27. Müller, Band 2, letter to Stefan Großmann, February 1921 (CC BY 4.0): "Nach einigen Jahren bleibt von all dem Lärm nichts weiter übrig als die Bücher, die ich geschrieben, und eine dunkle Erinnerung an die Blamage meiner Gegner. In diesem Fall wird es nicht anders sein."

Chapter 9

Schnitzler, Tagebuch, 23 November 1896 and 24 February 1897 ("'Liebesreigen' beendet"). Digital edition: schnitzler-tagebuch.acdh.oeaw.ac.at. See also Marianne Wünsch, "Reigen. Zehn Dialoge (1900)," in Schnitzler-Handbuch, ed. Christoph Jürgensen, Wolfgang Lukas, and Michael Scheffel (Stuttgart: J.B. Metzler, 2022), and Arthur Schnitzler, Ein Liebesreigen: Die Urfassung des "Reigen," ed. Gabriella Rovagnati (Frankfurt a.M.: S. Fischer, 2004).

2. Julius Bangert, "Arthur Schnitzler. En Samtale med en berømt Wiener," 10 April 1921, in Martin Anton Müller, ed., Das Zeitlose ist von kurzer Dauer: Arthur Schnitzlers Interviews, Meinungen und Proteste, vol. 1 (Göttingen: Wallstein, 2023), 125–134. Interview conducted 28–30 March 1921; cf. Schnitzler, Tagebuch, 30 March 1921. The Bangert interview is reproduced bilingually (Danish/German) in the Müller edition. All Müller volumes cited are published under CC license.

3. "Arthur Schnitzler nu i Stockholm," Nya Dagligt Allehanda, 17 May 1923, in Müller, vol. 1, 184–188. Schnitzler's diary for 17 May 1923 records the interviews with wry exasperation: he noted four interviewers arriving successively and concluded by recording his sense of the ridiculousness of the whole process.

4. Edward Loving, interview with Arthur Schnitzler, 1929, in Müller, vol. 1, 280–307. Schnitzler's exact words: "Reigen was written as a series of case histories. Does this surprise you? The question I asked myself was this: Clinically speaking, how do certain people, drawn from all classes, act under the stress of sexual passion?"

5. Sigmund Freud to Arthur Schnitzler, 14 May 1922. Published in Ernst L. Freud, ed., Letters of Sigmund Freud (New York: Basic Books, 1960). Freud's German reads: "Ich habe Sie gemieden aus einer Art von Doppelgängerscheu." See also Herbert I. Kupper and Hilda S. Rollman-Branch, "Freud and Schnitzler—(Doppelgänger)," Journal of the American Psychoanalytic Association 7 (1959): 109–126.

6. Franz Goldstein ("Frango"), "Spaziergang mit Schnitzler," 19 August 1930, in Müller, vol. 1, 307–308. Cf. Schnitzler, Tagebuch, 3 August 1930.

7. Hermann Menkes, "Der junge Schnitzler," 16 April 1922, in Müller, vol. 1, 137–140. Menkes recalled the private printing circulating among friends and noted Schnitzler's reluctance to publish more widely.

8. Arthur Schnitzler, preface to Reigen: Zehn Dialoge (private printing, 1900). The preface reads: "Ein Erscheinen der nachfolgenden Scenen ist vorläufig ausgeschlossen. Ich habe sie nun als Manuscript in Druck

gegeben; denn ich glaube, ihr Wert liegt anderswo als darin, daß ihr Inhalt den geltenden Begriffen nach die Veröffentlichung zu verbieten scheint."

9. The commercial edition appeared through the Wiener Verlag in 1903. The German ban followed in 1904. See Alfred Pfoser, Kristina Pfoser-Schewig, and Gerhard Renner, Schnitzlers "Reigen": Zehn Dialoge und ihre Skandalgeschichte. Analysen und Dokumente (Frankfurt a.M.: Fischer Taschenbuch, 1993).

10. Arthur Schnitzler to Ernst Friedmann, 13 September 1912, published in Max Epstein, "Ein Brief Schnitzlers über den 'Reigen,'" B. Z. am Mittag, 21 February 1921; in Müller, vol. 2, 507–508. The letter was addressed not to Giampietro but to Friedmann, as the carbon copy in Schnitzler's papers confirms.

11. Schnitzler later explained his change of position in his "Berichtigung" (see note 12). Unauthorized performances, including in Russia, had made his prior stance of withholding untenable.

12. Arthur Schnitzler, "Berichtigung. Ein paar Worte zum Gutachten Maximilian Hardens über den 'Reigen,'" Neues Wiener Journal, 30 January 1921; in Müller, vol. 2, 575–579. Schnitzler's diary records repeated reworking of this text between 23 and 29 January 1921.

13. "Der neueste 'Reigen'-Skandal," Neues Wiener Journal, 17 February 1921; in Müller, vol. 1, 122–125. Schnitzler's statement about the events is reproduced pp. 124–125.

14. Ibid., 123. The arrested individuals are named by occupation: "Ein Schuhmachergehilfe, ein Tapezierergehilfe, ein Kommis, ein Handelsakademiker und ein Zahntechnikerlehrling."

15. Arthur Schnitzler to Stefan Großmann, 17 February 1921, published in Stefan Großmann, "Der Reigen der Gassenjungen," Das Tage-Buch, 26 February 1921; in Müller, vol. 2, 508–509.

16. Frederick Robert Kuh, "The Play's the Thing," Daily Herald, 14 February 1921; in Müller, vol. 1, 120–122. Kuh's dispatch from Vienna

captures the parliamentary absurdity: the deficit announcement was greeted with stifled yawns, while the Reigen ban provoked physical altercations.

17. Ludwig Basch, "Eine Begegnung mit Dr. Artur Schnitzler," Illustrirtes Wiener Extrablatt, 12 February 1921; in Müller, vol. 1, 119–120. Cf. Schnitzler, Tagebuch, 12 February 1921.

18. Arthur Schnitzler, unpublished draft letter to the Neue Freie Presse, [8 February 1922]; in Müller, vol. 2, 581–583. Archival source: Cambridge University Library, Schnitzler, A 20, 14.

19. "Arthur Schnitzler nu i Stockholm," in Müller, vol. 1, 186–187.

20. Interview with Dutch journalist, 25 April 1922, in Müller, vol. 1, 140–142.

21. Loving interview, in Müller, vol. 1, 306.

Chapter 10

Arthur Schnitzler, Tagebuch, digital edition (Austrian Academy of Sciences / ACDH), https://schnitzler-tagebuch.acdh.oeaw.ac.at. Entry for 27 May 1900: "Mit S. und M. – Puchberg – Baumgartnerhaus — Dort oben Lieutenantgesch skizzirt – nach Payerbach. Wien." Entry for 17 July 1900: "Arbeite: Nilquellen, Lieuten. Gustl." Entry for 19 July 1900: "Nachm. 'Ltn. Gustl' vollendet, in der Empfindung, dass es ein Meisterwerk."

2. Arthur Schnitzler, "Leutnant Gustl – Äußere Schicksale" (posthumously published): "Geschrieben im Sommer 1900. Reichenau, Kurhaus. Zum Teil nach einer tatsächlich vorgefallen Geschichte, die einem Bekannten von Felix Salten passiert ist, einem Herrn Lasky (?), im Foyer des Musikvereinssaals."

3. Schnitzler acknowledged Édouard Dujardin's Les lauriers sont coupés (1888) as a precursor for the interior monologue technique. Hermann Bahr had anticipated the technique theoretically in Die Überwindung des Naturalismus (1891), calling for the depiction of feelings "bevor sie sich noch ins Bewusstsein hinein entschieden haben."

4. The novella was first read publicly by Schnitzler at the Literarische Vereinigung in Breslau on 23 November 1900, and first printed in the Weihnachtsbeilage of the Neue Freie Presse on 25 December 1900. The book edition, with illustrations by Moritz Coschell, appeared from S. Fischer Verlag (Berlin) in 1901.

5. Schnitzler dated the fictional action to 4 April, corresponding to an actual performance of Mendelssohn's oratorio Paulus at the Wiener Musikverein on that date in 1900. See the commentary in Ursula Renner's edition: Arthur Schnitzler, Lieutenant Gustl: Text und Kommentar (Frankfurt am Main: Suhrkamp, 2002).

6. Sigmund Freud, Die Traumdeutung (Leipzig and Vienna: Franz Deuticke, 1900). The book appeared in November 1899 but bore the imprint date 1900.

7. Sigmund Freud, letter to Arthur Schnitzler, 14 May 1922 (Schnitzler's sixtieth birthday). Published in Ernst L. Freud, ed., Letters of Sigmund Freud 1873–1939, trans. Tania and James Stern (New York: Basic Books, 1960), 339–340. Also accessible in the Freud Edition: https://www.freu dedition.net/en/briefe/freud-sigmund/schnitzler-arthur/1922/05/14.

8. The attack appeared in the Reichswehr on 28 December 1900, three days after publication. The author was the officer Gustav David. See Ursula Renner, "Dokumentation eines Skandals: Arthur Schnitzlers 'Lieutenant Gustl,'" Hofmannsthal-Jahrbuch 15 (2007): 33–216, here 46.

9. Schnitzler's strategy of not appearing before the military honor court was advised by the jurist Max Burckhard, a former director of the Burgtheater. See Martin Anton Müller, ed., Arthur Schnitzler: "Das Zeitlose ist von kürzester Dauer": Interviews, Meinungen und Proteste 1891–1931 (Göttingen: Wallstein, 2023), Band 2, 674 (hereafter Müller, Band 1 or Band 2). CC BY 4.0.

10. The ehrenrätliches Verfahren (honor-court proceeding) was initiated in January 1901. According to the editorial commentary in Müller, Band 1, 395, the non-public trial concluded on 26 April 1901, with

Schnitzler's classification as military physician (Militärarzt) revoked. The formal announcement of the stripping of his Offiziersrang as Oberarzt der Reserve was made on 14 June 1901. See "Arthur Schnitzler," Wien Geschichte Wiki, https://www.geschichtewiki.wien.gv.at/Arthur_Schni tzler. The Müller Band 2 appendix (674) describes the demotion as a "Rückstufung Schnitzlers vom Offizier zum Sanitätssoldaten" (demotion from officer to medical private).

11. The formal charge cited Schnitzler's failure to take any steps against the personal attacks in the Reichswehr article as part of the basis for the verdict: "die unterlassene Reaktion des Autors auf die heftige Kritik." See Renner, "Dokumentation eines Skandals," 46, and the discussion in the Lektürehilfe commentary at inhaltsangabe.de/schnitzler/leutnant-gustl/ rezeption-und-kritik/.

12. Müller, Band 1, 52 (interview, 1904). Schnitzler stated: "Ebenso wurde behauptet, daß ich in 'Freiwild' und 'Lieutenant Gustl' die gesamte Armee, in 'Literatur' sowohl die Aristokraten als die Dichter verletzt habe. ... Aus solchen Aeußerungen und Meinungen spricht meiner Ansicht nach meistens Heuchelei und etwas seltener ein einfältiges Mißverstehen des Solidaritätsbegriffes." CC BY 4.0.

13. Müller, Band 1, 212–213 (Swedish/German interview, 1923). Schnitzler recalled: "Als 'Leutnant Gustl' herauskam, geriet ich mit dem österreichischen Militär aneinander; eine Art Ehrengericht trat zusammen und beschloss, dass die Ehre des österreichischen Heeres durch dieses Werk gekränkt sei. Aber was soll man tun? Schließlich ist man auf die Welt gekommen, um einen anderen zu beleidigen." CC BY 4.0.

14. Müller, Band 1, 149 (artview, c. 1920): "Unter seinen Dichtungen sind ihm einige sozialkritische Werke, die viel Widerspruch gefunden haben, besonders ans Herz gewachsen, so 'Leutnant Gustl', 'Reigen', 'Professor Bernhardi.'" CC BY 4.0.

15. Müller, Band 2, 508–509 (letter, 1921). Schnitzler wrote: "Erinnern Sie sich nur an den 'Leutnant Gustl' und den 'Professor Bernhardi'. Nach

einigen Jahren bleibt von all dem Lärm nichts weiter übrig als die Bücher, die ich geschrieben, und eine dunkle Erinnerung an die Blamage meiner Gegner." CC BY 4.0.

16. Müller, Band 1, 231 (English-language interview). The interviewer wrote: "The immortal ineffable 'Lieutenant Gustl' is full of it"—referring to the Jewish question. The editorial note (Müller, Band 1, 405) observes: "Zwar äußert die Titelfigur einiges Antisemitisches, doch scheint die Behauptung, es ginge darin um die 'jüdische Frage', vor allem die Unkenntnis des Interviewers bloßzulegen." CC BY 4.0.

17. Schnitzler, letter to Theodor Sosnosky, 26 May 1901. Quoted in Renner, 79, and in the Lektürehilfe commentary. Schnitzler wrote: "mein 'Gustl' [ist] ein ganz netter, nur durch Standesvorurtheile verwirrter Bursch ... der mit den Jahren gewiss ein tüchtiger und anständiger Offizier werden dürfte." He further asserted his right as a writer to invent "einen Offizier ... der gewohnheitsmäßig seine Großcousinen umbringt."

18. Deutsche Zeitung, 22 June 1901: "Was der Jude Schnitzler dem 'Lieutenant Gustl' insinuirt, so denkt, so spricht, so handelt kein Officier." Quoted in Renner, 87–91.

19. Karl Lueger served as mayor of Vienna from 1897 until his death in 1910, on a platform of populist antisemitism as leader of the Christian Social Party.

20. The first English translation, None but the Brave, by Richard Leo Simon, was published in 1926 by Simon & Schuster. See Müller, Band 1, 420.

21. Reuben Brainin, "The Skeptic of Vienna," in Müller, Band 1, 320: "At the beginning of the twentieth century Arthur Schnitzler's most famous writings were his 'Anatol,' 'Liebelei,' 'Sterben,' 'Leutenant Gustl.' A light sort of writing, in form and in content." CC BY 4.0.

22. Moriz Benedikt, the editor of the Neue Freie Presse, published a leading article on 21 June 1901 defending Schnitzler on grounds of artistic freedom. See Renner, 82–86.

Chapter 11

1. MARIE REINHARD DIED on March 18, 1899. The exact date Schnitzler met Olga Gussmann is not recorded in the diary, but biographers place their first encounter in the spring of 1899. Olga was born January 17, 1882, making her seventeen at the time.

2. Schnitzler's military commission was stripped on June 14, 1901, following publication of *Leutnant Gustl* in the *Neue Freie Presse* on December 25, 1900. This occurred after he met Olga, not before.

3. On Olga's family background: Müller notes that Schnitzler's wife "war eine geborene Gussmann." The Gussmann family was part of Vienna's Jewish middle class. See Müller, *Das Zeitlose*, Band 1, commentary notes.

4. The *Neues Wiener Journal* reported in April 1903 that Olga "noch vor Kurzem das Conservatorium besucht hat" (had recently attended the Conservatory). See *Das Zeitlose*, Band 2, p. 629.

5. The terminated pregnancy of 1901 is documented in Schnitzler's diary. Müller notes that earlier pregnancies of Schnitzler's partners did not

result in surviving children, and that the birth of Heinrich was decisive precisely because the child survived. See *Das Zeitlose*, Band 2, Nachwort.

6. Olga Gussmann was born January 17, 1882 (U.S. Social Security records; *biografiA: Lexikon österreichischer Frauen*). She turned twenty on January 17, 1902.

7. The Arthur Schnitzler portal notes: "Wie im Fall von Marie Reinhard weicht Schnitzler aus und sucht ein kleines Haus außerhalb Wiens, wo Olga im Sommer entbinden kann." See arthur-schnitzler.de, Biographische Skizze.

8. Diary entry, August 9, 1902. The original German, as cited in the Arthur Schnitzler portal, reads: "Um vier kommt der Bub auf die Welt." The work Schnitzler began that afternoon has been identified by different scholars as either *Der einsame Weg* (the "Egoistenstück"; see Titzmann in the *Schnitzler-Handbuch*, 2022) or *Der Weg ins Freie* (see arthur-schnitzl er.de, footnote 32). The diary entry, as transcribed in the digital edition, is available at schnitzler-tagebuch.acdh.oeaw.ac.at, entry for Samstag, 9. August 1902.

9. Schnitzler to Hermann Bahr, April 6, 1903: "Die Nachricht des N. Wr. Journ ist unwahr, mindestens um sehr geraume Zeit verfrüht." See *Das Zeitlose*, Band 2, p. 629.

10. The wedding with Olga Gussmann took place on August 26, 1903. See *Das Zeitlose*, Band 2, p. 629. Also confirmed in Wikipedia (en): "On 26 August 1903, Schnitzler married Olga Gussmann."

11. *Das Zeitlose*, Band 2, Nachwort: "Zentral für die Eheschließung dürfte gewesen sein, dass das Kind (im Unterschied zu früheren Schwangerschaften der jeweiligen Partnerin) überlebte."

12. On the Spöttelgasse apartment and Sternwartestraße villa: see *Das Zeitlose*, Band 2, Nachwort. The villa at Sternwartestraße 71 was purchased on April 7, 1910.

13. On Olga's concert career: see arthur-schnitzler.de, Biographische Skizze. Her first public concert was in February 1911.

14. On the Grosz partnership and divorce: *Das Zeitlose*, Band 1, commentary: "In Partnerschaft mit ihm hatte Olga Schnitzler nach Kriegsende versucht, ihre Gesangskarriere aufzunehmen. Das wurde einer der zentralen Konflikte, der der Scheidung am 26. 6. 1921 voranging."

15. Heinrich Schnitzler's education: Wien Geschichte Wiki; German Wikipedia article on Heinrich Schnitzler. He studied with Franz Herterich and at the University of Vienna.

16. On Heinrich's early career: Wien Geschichte Wiki. He debuted at the Raimundtheater in 1921 and worked in Berlin 1924–1932 (Staatstheater, Deutsches Theater). See also *Das Zeitlose*, Band 1: "Heinrich arbeitete als Schauspieler vor allem in Berlin."

17. On Heinrich's emigration: Wien Geschichte Wiki; German Wikipedia. He emigrated in 1938 and taught at UC Berkeley and in Seattle, becoming professor from 1948 to 1956.

18. Heinrich's return: *Das Zeitlose*, Band 2, Nachwort: "Ende der 1950er-Jahre kehrte der Sohn und Alleinerbe Heinrich Schnitzler aus dem u.s.-amerikanischen Exil zurück und wurde zum stellvertretenden Direktor des Theaters in der Josefstadt." Wien Geschichte Wiki gives the return date as 1957 and the appointment as Vizedirektor from 1959.

19. On Heinrich's Schnitzler stagings: *Das Zeitlose*, Band 2, Nachwort: "Nach anfänglichem Zögern begann er, auf starkes Drängen von Vilma Thimig-Degischer hin, regelmäßig Stücke seines Vaters auf den Spielplan zu bringen."

20. *Jugend in Wien* was edited by Therese Nickl and Heinrich Schnitzler (Frankfurt: S. Fischer, 1968). The title was suggested by publisher Janko Musulin. See *Das Zeitlose*, Band 2, Nachwort.

21. On the *Reigen* scandal: The premiere took place December 23, 1920, at the Kleines Schauspielhaus in Berlin. The Vienna premiere was February 1, 1921, at the Kammerspiele. Schnitzler imposed the performance ban in 1922. See German Wikipedia, "Reigen (Drama)."

22. German Wikipedia: "Dieses Aufführungsverbot wurde von Schnitzlers Sohn Heinrich über den Tod des Autors hinaus verlängert und blieb bis zum 1. Januar 1982 in Kraft." Also: La Ronde (play), English Wikipedia: "In 1982, fifty years after Schnitzler's death, his son Heinrich Schnitzler re-released the play for German-language performances."

23. Heinrich Schnitzler died July 12, 1982, in Vienna (Wien Geschichte Wiki; German Wikipedia). He was buried in his father's honorary grave. He received the Josef-Kainz-Medaille (1963), the Ehrenzeichen für Wissenschaft und Kunst (1963), the Ehrenring of the Theater in der Josefstadt (1972), and an honorary doctorate from the University of Freiburg im Breisgau (1976).

Chapter 12

1. The wedding took place at the Synagoge Währing, located at Schopenhauerstraße 39 in Vienna's eighteenth district. Wien Geschichte Wiki, "Arthur Schnitzler," confirms the date and location. The synagogue was destroyed during the November Pogrom of 1938.

2. Gustav Schwarzkopf's role as witness (Trauzeuge) is confirmed in Peter Michael Braunwarth, "Worte sind alles: Beobachtungen am Vokabular von Arthur Schnitzlers Tagebuch" (dissertation excerpt), which identifies Schwarzkopf as "Trauzeuge bei ASs Heirat 1903." Beer-Hofmann's participation is attested by the diary entry of December 18, 1903, in which Schnitzler records Beer-Hofmann bringing a silver box as a belated wedding gift: "Richard bringt eine herrliche Silberbüchse als Hochzeitsgeschenk." Arthur Schnitzler, Tagebuch, December 18, 1903.

3. Karl Müller, Das Zeitlose ist von kürzester Dauer, Band 2, p. 629: "Zentral für die Eheschließung dürfte gewesen sein, dass das Kind (im Unterschied zu früheren Schwangerschaften der jeweiligen Partnerin) überlebte."

4. The false report appeared in the Neues Wiener Journal, Jg. 11, Nr. 3.389, April 3, 1903, p. 6. See Müller, Das Zeitlose, Band 2, p. 557.

5. Arthur Schnitzler, Tagebuch, April 3, 1903: records the newspaper notice and Basch's denial. April 4, 1903: "Dementi erschienen. Bei O. Verstimmung." The denial had appeared, but Olga was upset. Müller, Das Zeitlose, Band 2, p. 557, reproduces both entries.

6. Arthur Schnitzler to Hermann Bahr, April 6, 1903: "Die Nachricht des N. Wr. Journ ist unwahr, mindestens um sehr geraume Zeit verfrüht." Quoted in Müller, Das Zeitlose, Band 2, p. 557.

7. The apartment was at Spöttelgasse 7, later renamed Edmund-Weiß-Gasse in 1918. See Müller, Das Zeitlose, Band 2, p. 629: "Die Familie bezog eine gemeinsame Wohnung in einem Neubau in der Spöttelgasse 7 (seit 1918 Edmund-Weiß-Gasse)."

8. The Bauernfeld-Stiftung voted on March 16, 1903, to award Schnitzler 2,000 Kronen for his one-act cycle Lebendige Stunden. The prize provoked an antisemitic interpellation in the Austrian parliament. For the full text of the interpellation and Schnitzler's response, see Müller, Das Zeitlose, Band 1, pp. 172–179. Wien Geschichte Wiki confirms the award date as March 17, 1903.

9. Der einsame Weg premiered at the Deutsches Theater in Berlin on February 13, 1904, directed by Otto Brahm.

10. On the evolution of Der einsame Weg through earlier titles, see the German Wikipedia article "Der einsame Weg," which identifies the working titles Der Junggeselle, Egoisten, Einsame Wege, and Wege ins Dunkle.

11. On Olga Schnitzler's singing career and its frustrations, see Chapter 11 of this volume.

12. Lili Schnitzler was born September 13, 1909, in Vienna. Arthur Schnitzler, Wikipedia.

13. The diary references to Frieda Pollak in connection with her employment appear on September 6 and September 23, 1909. See Braunwarth,

"Worte sind alles," which notes: "seit 1909 engagiert (vgl. Tgb 6/9/09, 23/9/09)."

14. On Pollak's nickname "Kolap," see Christine Klimaschka, "Spurensuche Frieda Pollak," myGiulia, May 2022: "es war die kleine Tochter Lili, die—im gleichen Jahr geboren—ihr später in einer kindlichen Wortverdrehung den Namen Kolap gab."

15. Müller, Das Zeitlose, Band 2, p. 629: "Durch die Geburt von Lili am 13. 9. 1909 wurde der Platz in der bisherigen Wohnung zu eng und nach ein wenig Suche kaufte die Familie Schnitzler ein 400 Meter entferntes Haus." The villa at Sternwartestraße 71 would remain Schnitzler's home until his death in 1931.

16. On the contrasting residential choices of Schnitzler's literary circle, see Müller, Das Zeitlose, Band 2, pp. 629–630.

17. The Schnitzlers separated in 1921; the divorce was finalized on June 26, 1921. Olga was then thirty-nine, Arthur fifty-nine.

Chapter 13

1. Der Weg ins Freie was begun in 1902 and published in 1908. It appeared first as a serial in the Neue Rundschau, XIX. Jahrgang, issues 1–6, January–June 1908, and then as a book from S. Fischer Verlag, Berlin, the same year. The first edition ran to 491 pages. See the Schnitzler-Handbuch (Metzler, 2022), chapter by Michael Scheffel, "Der Weg ins Freie (1908)." Schnitzler's letter to Georg Brandes of July 4, 1908, describes his struggles with the novel's composition.

2. In an interview on the occasion of the Grillparzer Prize, published in the Neues Wiener Journal, January 16, 1908, Schnitzler described the novel: he had attempted to depict the relationships between various Viennese social strata and groups ("die Beziehungen gegenseitiger Wiener Schichten und sozialer Gruppen"). See Müller, Das Zeitlose, Band 1, pp. 56–59.

3. Anna's child is stillborn, not lost through miscarriage. The ENS-Lyon scholarly commentary on the novel identifies this as autobiographical: Schnitzler had experienced the loss of children in his own relationships prior to his marriage. See "Das Wien des Fin de Siècle in Arthur Schnitzlers Weg ins Freie," ENS de Lyon, Clé des langues.

4. The motif of the stillborn son drew on Schnitzler's personal experience. See the ENS-Lyon commentary: "das Motiv des totgeborenen Sohns ist ein tragisches Ereignis im Leben des Autors."

5. Schnitzler's identification of himself with Heinrich Bermann, and his description of the real-life model for Leo Golowski, appears in a 1937 interview with the journalist Clara Thurnher-Komp. Schnitzler stated: "Er selbst sei Heinrich Beermann – und das sage alles," and spoke of his Russian Zionist friend as the model for Leo, "den er so tief liebgehabt hat." He added that he had felt closer to this man than to Theodor Herzl, who had "viel Pose an sich gehabt." See Müller, Das Zeitlose, Band 1, pp. 362–363.

6. Leo Golowski is identified in scholarship as the Zionist figure: "Der Zionist: Leo Golowski" (Cambridge dissertation on Schnitzler and Wassermann, p. 68). The 2021 Josefstadt theatrical production credits him as "Mathematiker, Pianist, Zionist." Demeter Stanzides, by contrast, is a non-Jewish cavalry officer ("Oberleutnant und Jockey"), not a proponent of Zionism.

7. Leo's arrest follows his assault on the officer who had tormented him during military service. After his year as a volunteer is over, he waits outside the barracks and confronts the officer. He is imprisoned but ultimately pardoned by imperial clemency. See Arthur Schnitzler, Der Weg ins Freie (S. Fischer, 1908), final chapters.

8. Müller, Das Zeitlose, Band 2, p. 672, note 29: "Eine personelle Verbindungslinie kann mit Lotte Glas/Pohl hergestellt werden, die in seinem Tagebuch mehrfach Erwähnung findet und von der er für ›Therese Golowski‹ in Der Weg ins Freie Züge entlehnte."

9. Oskar Ehrenberg, not Leo Golowski, is the character who pursues social assimilation into aristocratic circles and attempts suicide. The Cambridge dissertation identifies him as "The Snob: Oskar Ehrenberg" (p. 69). The ResearchGate article by K. Sheridan confirms: "Oskar attempts to end his own life."

10. The novel's cast list, based on the 2021 Josefstadt production dramaturgy: Georg von Wergenthin (composer), Heinrich Bermann (writer), Anna Rosner (piano teacher), Else Ehrenberg (salon hostess), Salomon Ehrenberg (munitions manufacturer), Therese Golowski (socialist), Leo Golowski (Zionist), Dr. Stauber sen. (physician), Berthold Stauber (politician and doctor), Demeter Stanzides (cavalry officer), Josef Rosner (aspiring journalist), Ernst Jalaudek (paper dealer and politician).

11. The phrase "enlightened apolitical individualism" comes from a Cambridge University dissertation on Schnitzler and Wassermann, which defines the concept as "enlightened for Schnitzler's rejection of Jewish orthodoxy, apolitical because he always remained strongly averse to politics in general, and individualism because Schnitzler felt there was no general solution to the Jewish problem, only one for every individual." See David Midgley (supervisor), doctoral thesis, University of Cambridge.

12. The novel's action is set in 1898. See the ENS-Lyon commentary: "Da sich die Handlung im Jahre 1898 abspielt, fließen auch die Veränderungen der Wiener Gesellschaft und der Weltanschauungen um die Jahrhundertwende in das Romangeschehen ein."

13. On the deaths and near-deaths in the novel, see the ResearchGate article by K. Sheridan: "During the year it charts, Heinrich's father dies, the actress drowns herself, and Oskar attempts to end his own life. The suicide and attempted suicide connect the injustice of sex and race."

14. The Grillparzer Prize was awarded to Schnitzler on January 15, 1908, for Zwischenspiel (Intermezzo), premiered at the Burgtheater on October 12, 1905. See Franz Grillparzer Prize, Wikipedia; Müller, Das Zeitlose, Band 1, pp. 54–59.

15. Schnitzler's comments on the Grillparzer Prize appear in an interview published in Die Zeit, January 15, 1908, and in the Neues Wiener Journal, January 16, 1908. He stated he had considered himself an outsider and rated Der einsame Weg more highly than the prize-winning Zwischenspiel. See Müller, Das Zeitlose, Band 1, pp. 54–59.

16. Paul Wertheimer, "Begegnung mit Artur Schnitzler," in Brüder im Geiste: Ein Kulturbilderbuch (Vienna/Leipzig: Deutsch-Österreichischer Verlag, 1923), pp. 88–94. See Müller, Das Zeitlose, Band 1, pp. 396–399, which reproduces the passage. Schnitzler's diary entry of December 16, 1923, records the encounter with Wertheimer.

17. Schnitzler's works were burned in the Nazi book burnings of 1933. See Arthur Schnitzler, Wikipedia (English): "In 1933, when Joseph Goebbels organized book burnings in Berlin and other cities, Schnitzler's works were thrown into flames along with those of other Jews, including Einstein, Marx, Kafka, Freud and Stefan Zweig." Hitler called Schnitzler's works "Jewish filth."

18. On the rescue of the Schnitzler archive, see Cambridge University Library, "Saved from the Nazis in 1938: Schnitzler archive to remain in Cambridge." On March 19, 1938, at Olga Schnitzler's request, Eric Blackall contacted Cambridge to ask whether the library would accept the more than forty thousand pages of Schnitzler's literary archive.

Chapter 14

1. Schnitzlervilla, Wien Geschichte Wiki. The contract was signed by Schnitzler and Bleibtreu on April 14, 1910. The purchase price was 95,000 Kronen. Some sources give April 7 as the date of the transaction; this may reflect the date of an initial agreement prior to the formal signing. See Gerhard Hubmann, "Schwankende häusliche Stimmung: Mit Arthur Schnitzler beim Villenkauf," in Marcel Atze, ed., So schön kann Wissenschaft sein! (Vienna: Amalthea, 2017), 220–236.

2. Hedwig Bleibtreu, Wien Geschichte Wiki. Römpler died in December 1909. Bleibtreu subsequently married Burgtheater director Max Paulsen in 1911.

3. Schnitzler, Tagebuch, July 16, 1910. Renovations were again supervised by the architect Hermann Müller, who had originally designed the villa in 1895.

4. Interview, "Artur Schnitzler über sich und sein Werk," in Müller, Das Zeitlose, Band 1, pp. 76–79. The interviewer visited Schnitzler at the Sternwartestraße during rehearsals for Der junge Medardus at the Burgtheater, placing the interview in late 1910.

5. Interview, "Schnitzler, der Mensch," in Müller, Das Zeitlose, Band 1, pp. 107–108. The passage describes Schnitzler's daily routine and his preference for working at a standing desk.

6. The simultaneous premiere at nine theaters is documented in the Tagebuch edition: Schnitzler, Tagebuch 1909–1912 (Vienna: ÖAW). See also the entry at the Schnitzler-Handbuch, ed. Jürgensen, Lukas, and Scheffel (Stuttgart: Metzler, 2022).

7. The Russian premiere took place on November 2, 1910 at the Novyj dramatičeskij teatr in St. Petersburg. See Das weite Land, German Wikipedia.

8. Schnitzler, Tagebuch, October 14, 1911: "Ins Theater. Loge mit O., Julius Helene. Nach 1. Akt Reimers, vom 2. an ich [hervorgerufen]. Im ganzen 24mal."

9. Interview with Georg Brøchner, in Müller, Das Zeitlose, Band 1, pp. 6753–6774 [internal pagination]. The interview is bilingual Danish/German; Schnitzler's reply is quoted in the German column.

10. Interview with a Budapest journalist, in Müller, Das Zeitlose, Band 1, pp. 4494–4530 [internal pagination]. Schnitzler's exact words: "Dabei behaupte gar nicht ich, dass die Seele ein weites Land sei; das behauptet eine Figur des Stückes, Aigner, ein affektierter Herr, der sich ziemlich

aphoristisch ausdrückt. Und ich identifiziere mich mit keiner meiner Figuren."

11. Stoppard's Undiscovered Country premiered at the Olivier Theatre, National Theatre, London, on June 20, 1979 (press night). Directed by Peter Wood; John Wood played Hofreiter. See Ritchie Robertson, "Schnitzler in Britain: Authorship, Translation and Finding a Place at the National Theatre," in Project MUSE (2022).

12. Arthur Schnitzler, Das weite Land: Tragikomödie in fünf Akten (Berlin: S. Fischer, 1911). Korsakow is described as a "weltberühmter russischer Pianist" (world-famous Russian pianist).

13. Otto's rank is Fähnrich (ensign) in the Imperial Navy (k.u.k. Marine). In the play's character list he appears as "Otto von Aigner, Fähnrich in der Marine." His father, Dr. von Aigner, is a separate character—the play's philosopher, who delivers the line "Die Seele ist ein weites Land."

14. The duel and its consequences are described in the fifth act. Friedrich kills Otto, then contemplates turning himself in to the authorities. Erna, who has loved Friedrich since childhood, declares she will follow him. The play ends with Friedrich hearing his son Percy's voice in the garden. See Schnitzler's letter to Felix Salten, October 20, 1911, on the ending.

15. Schnitzler, Tagebuch, May 31, 1909. This is the entry recording his reading of the completed play to Olga and Otto Brahm.

16. Schnitzler, Tagebuch, April 26, 1910.

17. Schnitzler, Tagebuch, June 14, 1915: "Das Stück eins der sehr wenigen zu dem ich mich bedingungslos bekenne. Dieses wird bleiben – ja man könnte fast sagen: es wird erst kommen. Empfind ich bei so vielem von mir, dass ich etwas weniger bin, als das was ich selbst einen ‚Künstler' nenne;— hier bin ich – etwas mehr."

18. The Friedmann connection is documented in multiple sources. See "Premierenkritik: Das weite Land," Der Freitag (December 17, 2014).

19. Schnitzler, Tagebuch, January 31, 1911, identifying Christomannos as the model for Dr. von Aigner. Percy Eckstein (born 1899) was the son

of Friedrich Eckstein; Schnitzler used both the villa setting and the boy's name.

20. Otto Brahm to Schnitzler, June 21, 1910.

21. Georg Brandes, October 19, 1911.

22. Alfred Polgar, review of Das weite Land.

23. Schnitzler, Tagebuch, October 29–November 17, 1911. The tour included Prague (October 30), Berlin, Hamburg, and Munich.

24. Arthur Schnitzler Portal, Biographical Sketch: "In February 1911 she gave her first public concert, but the success she had hoped for eluded her for the rest of her life."

25. On Olga's partnership with Wilhelm Grosz and its role in the divorce, see Müller, Das Zeitlose, Band 1, note at p. 25297.

26. By Ferdinand Schmutzer - historic print, Public Domain, https://commons.wikimedia.org/w/index.php?curid=56009340

Chapter 15

1. Schnitzler used the German-nationalist surgeon Julius Hochenegg as a model for Ebenwald. See Professor Bernhardi, German Wikipedia, citing Nikolaj Beier, "Vor allem bin ich ich...": Judentum, Akkulturation und Antisemitismus in Arthur Schnitzlers Leben und Werk (Göttingen: Wallstein, 2008).

2. Max M. W. Haberich, "Arthur Schnitzler's Professor Bernhardi: Anti-Semitism on the Stage and in Reality," Central Europe 10, no. 2 (2012).

3. Haberich uses the phrase "enlightened apolitical individualism" to describe Bernhardi's stance and identifies it as reflecting Schnitzler's own position on the Jewish identity crisis. Ibid.

4. Arthur Schnitzler, "Zum 'Professor Bernhardi,'" Der Merker, Jg. 4, Nr. 4, 2. Februar-Heft 1913, S. 135. Reprinted in Müller, Das Zeitlose, Band 2, pp. 565–566. Schnitzler's letter was addressed to Georg Brandes,

correcting Brandes's public misstatement about the play's autobiographical basis. The full text is quoted in Müller.

5. Representative antisemitic utterances from the play include: "Ja, ein Jud hat keine Ehre, ein Jud ist ein Untier, ein Jud kann nicht beleidigt werden" (Act III). See the discussion in Hektoen International: "Professor Bernhardi, a play by Arthur Schnitzler, M.D." (2022).

6. Karl Lueger served as mayor of Vienna from 1897 until his death on March 10, 1910. The play is set in 1900, during Lueger's mayoralty. Schnitzler completed the play in 1912, two years after Lueger's death.

7. Premiere: November 28, 1912, Kleines Theater, Berlin. Published the same year by S. Fischer Verlag. See Zeno.org: "Professor Bernhardi: Enstanden 1912. Erstdruck: Berlin (Fischer), 1912. Uraufführung am 28 .11.1912, Kleines Theater Berlin."

8. Otto Brahm (born Otto Abrahamson, February 5, 1856) died in Berlin on November 28, 1912—the same evening as the Professor Bernhardi premiere. Brahm had directed the Lessing-Theater since 1904 and had been Schnitzler's primary theatrical partner in Berlin for two decades. See also the biographic chronology in Müller, Das Zeitlose, Band 2, p. 8641: "1912 Professor Bernhardi darf nicht in Österreich aufgeführt werden."

9. Wiener Erstaufführung: December 21, 1918, Deutsches Volkstheater, directed by Alfred Bernau. See NÖ Landesarchiv, "Arthur Schnitzler, Professor Bernhardi"; and hdgö, "1918: Arthur Schnitzlers Professor Bernhardi in Österreich."

10. Interview with a Swedish journalist (bilingual Swedish/German), in Müller, Das Zeitlose, Band 1, pp. 13700–13800 [internal pagination]. Schnitzler adds that the Reigen scandal "had purely political reasons" and that opponents wanted to brand it as "jüdische Unmoral."

11. Schnitzler, Tagebuch, December 5, 1912. Cited in Müller, Das Zeitlose, Band 2, p. 8533.

12. Interview, "Aus der Theaterwelt," 1914, in Müller, *Das Zeitlose*, Band 1, pp. 5083–5090 [internal pagination]. The interviewer reports that *Der einsame Weg* was originally set in medical circles and that the idea for *Letzte Masken* arose on the same afternoon, during a boat trip at Le Prese.

13. *Frau Beate und ihr Sohn* was serialized in *Die Neue Rundschau*, Jg. 24, Hefte 2–4, February–April 1913. Book publication: S. Fischer, Berlin, 1913.

14. The plot summary follows the German Wikipedia article on *Frau Beate und ihr Sohn* and the Schnitzler-Handbuch entry by Michael Titzmann (Metzler, 2022). Schnitzler began work on the novella (originally titled "Mutter und Sohn") on December 16, 1912, following an initial plan dictated in March 1903.

15. Peter Sprengel, *Geschichte der deutschsprachigen Literatur 1900–1918* (Munich: Beck, 2004). Sprengel connects the novella to *Frau Berta Garlan* (1900) through their shared theme of female sexuality confronting social norms.

Chapter 16

1. Schnitzler, *Tagebuch*, August 5, 1914. The entry records the British declaration of war on Germany, received at his Swiss hotel. The full passage is quoted in the biographical sketch at the Arthur Schnitzler Portal (arthur-schnitzler.de). The phrasing "Der Weltkrieg. Der Weltruin" is used as a section title in Ulrich von Bülow, "Sicherheit ist nirgends": *Das Tagebuch von Arthur Schnitzler*, Marbacher Magazin 93 (2001).

2. Schnitzler, *Tagebuch*, September 30, 1914. Olga's characterization of his wartime stance as "unzeitgemäße Selbstbewahrung" and her criticism of his "reservirte kühle Haltung" are recorded in the diary.

3. Hofmannsthal worked in the Kriegsfürsorgeamt (War Welfare Office) and contributed cultural propaganda essays. See Jacques Le Rider,

Hugo von Hofmannsthal: Historismus und Moderne in der Literatur der Jahrhundertwende (Vienna: Böhlau, 1997).

4. On Zweig's initial war enthusiasm and subsequent revulsion, see his autobiography Die Welt von Gestern (The World of Yesterday, 1942).

5. Arthur Schnitzler Portal, Biographische Skizze: "Als sich an Schnitzlers 55. Geburtstag Stephi Bachrach, eine junge Krankenpflegerin und Freundin der Familie, vergiftet, ist Schnitzler schockiert; einige Details dieser tragischen Begebenheit wird er in Fräulein Else motivisch verarbeiten."

6. Jugend in Wien was written 1915–1918 under the planned title "Leben und Nachklang – Werk und Widerhall." Published posthumously: Vienna/Munich/Zurich (Fritz Molden), 1968. See Zeno.org: "Entstanden 1915–1918."

7. Arthur Schnitzler Portal: "Im Sommer des darauffolgenden Jahres beendet Schnitzler seine Autobiographie" (Summer 1918).

8. Doktor Gräsler, Badearzt was written in 1914 and published in the Berliner Tageblatt, February 10 – March 17, 1917. Book publication: S. Fischer, Berlin, 1917. See German Wikipedia and Zeno.org.

9. Plot details follow the German Wikipedia article on Doktor Gräsler, Badearzt. The protagonist's name is Dr. Emil Gräsler; Sabine Schleheim and Katharina Rebner are distinct characters.

10. Interview, 1922, in Müller, Das Zeitlose, Band 1, pp. 7984–7990 [internal pagination]: "In seiner grüblerischen und halb schwermütigen, halb ironischen Art beschäftigt sich Schnitzler schon seit mehreren Jahren mit dem Problem des alternden Mannes, und aus dieser Stimmung heraus hat er die Gestalten Doktor Gräslers und Casanovas geschaffen."

11. Casanovas Heimfahrt: manuscript dated August 20, 1917; serialized in Die Neue Rundschau, Jg. 29, Hefte 7–9, July–September 1918; book publication S. Fischer, Berlin, 1918. See German Wikipedia.

12. Heinrich Schnitzler was born August 9, 1902, making him twelve (not thirteen) at the war's outbreak in August 1914, and sixteen at its end. Lili Schnitzler was born September 13, 1909.

13. Arthur Schnitzler Portal: "Anfang 1917 gerät Olga in eine tiefe Lebenskrise und gibt die Schuld an ihrer missglückten Karriere ihrem Mann, den Kindern und dem Namen 'Schnitzler.'"

14. Schnitzler, Tagebuch, November 12, 1918. The German original is quoted in the ww1.habsburger.net memorial essay "12 November 1918 as a Site of Memory."

15. The Austrian premiere of Professor Bernhardi took place on December 21, 1918, at the Deutsches Volkstheater, Vienna, directed by Alfred Bernau. See Chapter 15 notes.

Chapter 17

1. Arthur Schnitzler Portal, Biographische Skizze: "Im Winter erreicht die Ehekrise einen neuen Höhepunkt." See also Tagebuch, winter 1920. The Portal notes that Olga confessed an affair to her husband and that the arguments escalated.

2. Arthur Schnitzler Portal, Biographische Skizze: "Obwohl Schnitzler seiner Frau während ihrer Ehe vermutlich grundsätzlich treu war, wirft Olga ihm ihrerseits Affären mit Hedy Kempny und Vilma Lichtenstern vor."

3. Arthur Schnitzler Portal: "Olga ist inzwischen zurück, um die Festtage mit der Familie zu verbringen. Sie ist zur Scheidung entschlossen und plant, Wien zu verlassen."

4. The authorized premiere of *Reigen* took place on December 23, 1920 at the Kleines Schauspielhaus in Berlin. An earlier unauthorized performance of the complete play had taken place in Budapest on October 13, 1912, without Schnitzler's participation. See German Wikipedia, "Reigen (Drama)."

5. Schnitzler wrote the first draft between November 23, 1896 and February 24, 1897. The private printing of 200 copies appeared in 1900; the first commercial edition was published by the Wiener Verlag in 1903, selling approximately 40,000 copies before being banned by German censors in March 1904. See Springer, Kindlers Literatur Lexikon, "Schnitzler, Arthur: Reigen."

6. Reinhardt's promptbook, consisting of a printed text with handwritten annotations on 72 of 264 pages, survives. It is archived at the Max Reinhardt Archive at Binghamton University and has been digitized by the Reigen Digitization Project (University of Freiburg / Binghamton University). See Reinhardt to Schnitzler, April 14, 1919, cited in German Wikipedia.

7. Reinhardt left his theater directorship in June 1920 and passed the rights through Felix Hollaender to Gertrud Eysoldt and Maximilian Sladek at the Kleines Schauspielhaus. The director of the actual premiere was Hubert Reusch (1862–1925). Cast included Else Bäck, Fritz Kampers, Vera Skidelsky, Curt Goetz, and others. See Wikiwand, "Reigen (Drama)"; Fabula, "Reigen d'Arthur Schnitzler."

8. The Kleines Schauspielhaus occupied a space within the building of the Akademische Hochschule für Musik in Berlin-Charlottenburg. The injunction cited the lease clause prohibiting performances that might give offense "in moral, religious, political, or artistic respects." Director Franz Schreker of the Hochschule was involved in the complaint. See Schulzeug. at, "Arthur Schnitzler: Reigen"; Wunderlich, "Arthur Schnitzler: Reigen."

9. Alfred Kerr, review in *Der Tag*, December 24, 1920: Kerr praised the work, asked rhetorically whether plays could be banned, and described *Reigen* as "a charming work." Cited in German Wikipedia, "Reigen (Drama)."

10. The Vienna premiere took place on February 1, 1921 at the Kammerspiele, which was then attached to the Deutsches Volkstheater under director Alfred Bernau. The theater was located at Rotenturmstraße 20 in

the 1st district. Direction was by Heinz Schulbaur. See German Wikipedia, "Reigen (Drama)"; Wien Geschichte Wiki, "Kammerspiele."

11. The attack of February 16, 1921 involved approximately 200 persons storming the theater. The rioters threw stink bombs, attacked audience members, and attempted to destroy furnishings. See Theater in der Josefstadt, "100 Jahre Kammerspiele"; Vienna.at, "100 Jahre Wiener Kammerspiele."

12. The Berlin riots of February 22, 1921 were organized after a senior Berlin police official initiated a systematic campaign against the production. Pre-printed protest forms were distributed and politicians were mobilized. The *Reigen-Prozess* resulted in acquittal. See German Wikipedia; Arthur Schnitzler Portal.

13. Letter from Arthur Schnitzler to Stefan Großmann, published in *Das Tage-Buch*, Jg. 2, Nr. 8, February 26, 1921, pp. 252–253. Reprinted in Martin Anton Müller and Gerd-Hermann Susen, eds., *Das Zeitlose ist von kurzer Dauer: Arthur Schnitzlers nicht-fiktionale Texte* (Vienna, 2023), Band 2, pp. 508–509. The German original: "Nach einigen Jahren bleibt von all dem Lärm nichts weiter übrig als die Bücher, die ich geschrieben, und eine dunkle Erinnerung an die Blamage meiner Gegner."

14. Schnitzler asked S. Fischer Verlag in 1922 not to grant any further performance licenses for *Reigen* in German-speaking countries. The ban was maintained by Schnitzler's son Heinrich after the author's death. See Wunderlich, "Arthur Schnitzler: Reigen"; Salzburg Festival, "Reigen 2022."

15. The performance ban was lifted effective January 1, 1982, authorized by Heinrich Schnitzler. Heinrich died on July 14, 1982. See Austrian postage stamp commemorative text, 2021; Virtual Vienna, "Arthur Schnitzler: Why the Scandal?"

16. The meeting between Schnitzler and Freud at Berggasse 19 is referenced in the Arthur Schnitzler Portal and in accounts of the Freud-Schnit-

zler relationship. Their personal encounters were rare despite decades of mutual awareness.

17. Freud's letter to Schnitzler is dated May 14, 1922, written for Schnitzler's sixtieth birthday (May 15, 1862). Multiple sources confirm this date. See Cambridge University Press, "Schnitzler and Freud: Uncanny Similarities"; TIME, "Medicine: Freud's Doppelgänger"; Freud Museum London. NB: Some secondary sources incorrectly give the date as May 4, 1922 or place the letter in 1921; the correct date is May 14, 1922.

18. The German original: "Ihr Determinismus wie Ihr Skepsis — was die Leute Pessimismus heißen — Ihr Ergriffensein von den Wahrheiten des Unbewußten, von der Triebnatur des Menschen, Ihre Zersetzung von den kulturell-konventionellen Sicherheiten, das Haften Ihrer Gedanken an der Polarität von Lieben und Sterben, das alles berührte mich mit einer unheimlichen Vertrautheit." Quoted in Cambridge University Press, "Schnitzler and Freud."

19. Divorce finalized June 26, 1921. See previous chapter notes; Arthur Schnitzler Portal.

20. Heinrich Schnitzler (1902–1982) studied acting under Franz Herterich and debuted at the Raimundtheater in 1921. He studied philosophy, art history, and literary history at the University of Vienna. From 1923 to 1932 he worked in Berlin before returning to the Deutsches Volkstheater in Vienna as actor, dramaturg, and director. After the Anschluss in 1938 he emigrated to the United States, where he directed on Broadway and taught until 1956. He returned to Austria in 1957 and became vice-director of the Theater in der Josefstadt in 1959. See Geni.com genealogy profile; Nationalfonds, "Exodus of Talent: Heinrich Schnitzler."

21. This remark is widely attributed to Schnitzler in response to an interviewer. The formulation appears in multiple biographical sources. See Wikipedia, "Arthur Schnitzler."

Chapter 18

1. Schnitzler's progressive hearing loss is documented throughout the diary from the early 1920s onward and is noted in the Arthur Schnitzler Portal, Biographische Skizze: www.arthur-schnitzler.de/biobibliographi ka/biographische-skizze/.

2. Arthur Schnitzler Portal, Biographische Skizze, under the year 1920: "Im April stürzt Schnitzler bei einem Spaziergang und zieht sich eine Schultergelenksverletzung zu, die ihm bis an sein Lebensende Schmerzen bereiten wird."

3. The Silvester party at which Clara Loeb first met both Schnitzler and Hofmannsthal took place on the evening of December 31, 1895. See Stephan Kurz, "Im Schatten Schnitzlers: Leben und Werk von Clara Katharina Pollaczek (1875–1951)," in Rohrwasser and Kurz, eds., *"A. ist manchmal wie ein kleines Kind"* (Vienna: Böhlau, 2012), pp. 10–33, citing CKP I, Einlage nach Bl. 4 and Tagebuch, January 1, 1896. The acquaintances "gehen auf das Jahr 1896 zurück." Clara was born January 15, 1875; she was therefore twenty at the party. Schnitzler, born May 15, 1862, was thirty-three.

4. Tagebuch, January 1, 1896: "Das kleine Mädel entzückt mich. Sie verspricht mir selbstverfasste Sachen zu schicken und ist sehr zutraulich." Cited in Kurz, "Im Schatten Schnitzlers," with a slight textual variation in the published Tagebuch edition ("wurde sehr zutraulich"). Digitale Edition: schnitzler-tagebuch.acdh.oeaw.ac.at.

5. Tagebuch, March 5, 1896: "Bei Loebs. Clara, dieses liebe kleine Mädel mit grossen Augen, die mir neulich eine sehr bemerkenswerthe Novelette geschickt hat, viel Sehnsucht nach Freiheit und sicher Talent. Ich begleitete sie zum Singen." See also the Pollaczek digital edition at pollaczek.acdh.o eaw.ac.at.

6. Bob [Clara Katharina Pollaczek], "Mimi: Schattenbilder aus einem Mädchenleben," Szenenfolge mit einem Prolog von Hugo von Hofmannsthal, in *Neue Deutsche Rundschau* 8, no. 4 (April 1, 1897), pp. 396–413. Hofmannsthal's prologue for *Mimi* paralleled his earlier pro-

logue for Schnitzler's *Anatol* (see Hofmannsthal, "Zu einem Buch ähnlicher Art," in *Gesammelte Werke: Gedichte und Lyrische Dramen*, Stockholm: Bermann-Fischer, 1946, pp. 45f.). On the genre: *Mimi* is a Szenenfolge (sequence of scenes), not a short story as some English-language accounts suggest.

7. On the anonymous letter: Kurz, "Im Schatten Schnitzlers," identifies the likely sender as Minnie Benedikt, daughter of Moriz Benedikt. On Schnitzler's intervention: "Schnitzler griff aus Paris insofern kalmierend ein, als er auf Hugo von Hofmannsthals Aufforderung den Verlag von Samuel Fischer anwies, den Text nicht mehr zu drucken." The intervention took place between April 24 and May 6, 1897. Cf. Tagebuch, March 21, 1897: "Correcturen an Clara L.s Buch 'Mimi'."

8. Tagebuch, November 29–30, 1897: "Es wird immer deutlicher, dass sie am liebsten mich heiraten möchte." Cited in Kurz, "Im Schatten Schnitzlers."

9. Tagebuch, October 21, 1897: Clara complains "über Hugos Fernbleiben"; Schnitzler notes: "Es war aber – nicht rein freundschaftlich." He wrote to Hofmannsthal: "Clara fühlt sich sehr verlassen von Ihnen." See Kurz, "Im Schatten Schnitzlers," and Hofmannsthal's correspondence at the ACDH digital editions.

10. The wedding took place on May 10, 1898, at the Seitenstettengasse Temple (Wiener Stadttempel), confirmed in the marriage registers of the Israelitische Kultusgemeinde. Otto Pollaczek (born Prague, c. January 20–21, 1873) was heir to the largest wholesale leather-hide business in the Habsburg monarchy. The couple had been introduced on October 7, 1897, in the Wiener Prater. See Kurz, "Im Schatten Schnitzlers"; Georg Gaugusch, *Wer einmal war: Das jüdische Großbürgertum Wiens 1800–1938*, vol. 2 (Vienna: Amalthea, 2016), pp. 2607–2609.

11. Otto Pollaczek died in 1908 at the age of thirty-five. The Gustav Klimt Database (klimt-database.com) states that he "committed suicide ... presumably because of financial difficulties." Clara's sense of liberation

is reported in K. F. M. Pole, *Two Halves of a Life* (Gillingham, Kent, 1982)—a memoir by her son Karl Friedrich Michael Pollaczek.

12. Schnitzler's diary documents resumed contact with Pollaczek from approximately 1915, including an exchange of letters, occasional encounters, and at least one telephone conversation. See Kurz, "Im Schatten Schnitzlers"; English Wikipedia, "Clara Katharina Pollaczek."

13. On Schnitzler reading Pollaczek's work and valuing her critical judgment: see English Wikipedia, "Clara Katharina Pollaczek," citing Kurz and Rohrwasser.

14. For a comprehensive bibliography of Pollaczek's literary publications, see Kurz, "Im Schatten Schnitzlers," and the entries at litku lt1920er.aau.at. Principal works include: *Redoute* (Schauspiel in einem Aufzug, 1926); *Dame* (Drama, 1930); and numerous stories and feuilletons in the *Neue Freie Presse*, including "Mädchen für alles" (1926), "Nach Sonnenuntergang" (1927), "Die Tochter des Hauses" (1929), and "Die Schönheit der Konstanze" (1929).

15. On Hedy Kempny (born Hedwig Kempny, December 21, 1895, Gutenstein – May 16, 1986, New York City): journalist, bank employee, and aspiring writer. Her correspondence with Schnitzler was published as *Das Mädchen mit den dreizehn Seelen: Eine Korrespondenz ergänzt durch Blätter aus Hedy Kempnys Tagebuch*, ed. Heinz P. Adamek (Reinbek: Rowohlt, 1984). See also Band 2, p. 718.

16. The figure of over five hundred joint cinema visits is established in Stephan Kurz and Michael Rohrwasser, eds., *"A. ist manchmal wie ein kleines Kind": Clara Katharina Pollaczek und Arthur Schnitzler gehen ins Kino* (Vienna: Böhlau, 2012): "über 500 gemeinsame Kinobesuche haben sie in ihren Tagebüchern verzeichnet."

17. Pollaczek's remark, which furnished the title of the Kurz/Rohrwasser volume, appears in her diary notebooks preserved at the Wienbibliothek im Rathaus.

18. Pollaczek's diary, as summarized in English Wikipedia ("Clara Katharina Pollaczek"): she noted that Schnitzler "still keeps on insisting that he wants me and cannot let me go. He wants his freedom, he wants to be alone, and then he wants to be with me again."

19. Clara Katharina Pollaczek on Schnitzler's death, October 21, 1931. Both the German and English Wikipedia articles quote her: "I held his head in my hands till his last breath." See also Kurz, "Im Schatten Schnitzlers."

20. The memorial poem was published in the *Neue Freie Presse*, November 15, 1931, p. 27. See litkult1920er.aau.at, "Pollaczek, Clara Katharina."

21. The typescript *Arthur Schnitzler und ich*, approximately 900 pages, is held in the Handschriftensammlung der Wienbibliothek im Rathaus. It was created on the basis of Pollaczek's diary notebooks and her correspondence with Schnitzler, with the assistance of Schnitzler's former secretary Frieda Pollak. See William H. Rey, "'Arthur Schnitzler und ich': Das Vermächtnis der Clara Katharina Pollaczek," *The Germanic Review* 41 (1966): 120–135. A digital edition is in progress at pollaczek.acdh.oeaw.ac.at.

22. Clara Katharina Pollaczek died July 22, 1951, in Vienna. She survived the Nazi period in Vienna under the protection of a Czechoslovak passport obtained through her marriage to the Prague-born Otto Pollaczek. See Kurz, "Im Schatten Schnitzlers."

Chapter 19

1. *Fräulein Else* was first published in the *Neue Rundschau* in November 1924, then in book form by Paul Zsolnay Verlag (Vienna/Berlin/Leipzig). The index of Müller, *Das Zeitlose*, vol. 2, gives the publication date as October 1, 1924. On the publication history and the relationship to *Leutnant Gustl*, see the Schnitzler-Handbuch entry by Saxer in Jürgensen, Lukas, and Scheffel, eds., *Schnitzler-Handbuch* (Stuttgart: J.B. Metzler, 2022), 72.

2. *Tagebuch*, December 14, 1922. The diary entry referring to the "Gustl Technik" is cited in the Schnitzler-Handbuch and in the lektürehilfe.de commentary on the novella's composition. See also Schnitzler, *Tagebuch 1920–1922*, ed. Peter Michael Braunwarth et al. (Vienna: Österreichische Akademie der Wissenschaften, 1993).

3. The original 1921 typed draft is quoted in the Schnitzler-Handbuch: "Ein junges Mädchen tritt nackt in den Speisesaal des Berghotels." See Saxer, "Fräulein Else (1924)," in Jürgensen, Lukas, and Scheffel, eds., *Schnitzler-Handbuch*, 72.

4. On the composition timeline—first drafts 1921, intensive work December 1922 to April 1923, revisions through 1924—see the Schnitzler-Handbuch entry and the Wallstein Verlag critical edition edited by Wolfgang Lukas and Michael Scheffel, *Fräulein Else: Kommentierte Studienausgabe* (Göttingen: Wallstein, 2025).

5. Hofmannsthal's letter to Schnitzler is quoted in the GRIN study on Fräulein Else: "Ja, so gut Leutnant Gustl erzählt ist, Fräulein Else schlägt ihn freilich noch; das ist innerhalb der deutschen Literatur wirklich ein genre für sich, das sie geschaffen haben." See also the Schnitzler/Hofmannsthal correspondence, *Briefwechsel*, ed. Therese Nickl and Heinrich Schnitzler (Frankfurt: S. Fischer, 1964).

6. Roberto Calasso, afterword to *La signorina Else* (Milan: Adelphi, Piccola biblioteca series). The original Italian reads: "Mai forse un altro narratore moderno era riuscito a fondere il monologo interiore, la fantasticheria, l'azione e il dialogo [...] in una simile intimità."

7. On the unusual explicitness of Else's Jewish identity among Schnitzler's protagonists, see the Wikipedia article on Arthur Schnitzler: "Professor Bernhardi and Fräulein Else are among the few clearly identified Jewish protagonists in his work."

8. On the Weininger reading, see Wikipedia on Fräulein Else: "In the novella, Fräulein Else (1924), Schnitzler may be rebutting a contentious critique of the Jewish character by Otto Weininger (1903) by position-

ing the sexuality of the young female Jewish protagonist." Weininger's *Geschlecht und Charakter* (1903) presented notoriously misogynistic and antisemitic views of Jewish femininity.

9. On the sales figure of approximately seventy thousand copies, see the GRIN study on *Fräulein Else*: "Siebzigtausend verkaufte Exemplare." The first serial publication was in the *Neue Rundschau* in November 1924.

10. The concept of the "Woman Trilogy"—*Frau Berta Garlan* (serialized in *Neue Deutsche Rundschau*, January–March 1901), *Frau Beate und ihr Sohn* (1913), and *Fräulein Else* (1924)—is discussed in several critical studies. On *Frau Berta Garlan* see Müller, *Das Zeitlose*, vol. 2, index entry: "Frau Bertha Garlan. Roman [15.1.1901 – 15.3.1901]."

11. Lili Schnitzler was born September 13, 1909; she turned fifteen on September 13, 1924, shortly before the novella's book publication on October 1, 1924.

12. Lili Schnitzler died by suicide on July 26, 1928, in Venice, at the age of eighteen. She had married the Italian Fascist officer Arnoldo Cappellini. On the circumstances, see the Schnitzler biographical sketch at the Arthur Schnitzler Portal (arthur-schnitzler.de).

13. The connection between Lili's death and *Fräulein Else* has been discussed by multiple scholars and contemporaries. The suggestion that Lili seemed to have "followed" Else has been attributed to various sources in the biographical literature. The matter is treated with appropriate caution in the secondary scholarship.

14. *Fräulein Else* (dir. Paul Czinner, 1929). Starring Elisabeth Bergner as Else, Albert Bassermann as Dr. Thalhof, Albert Steinrück as von Dorsday, Adele Sandrock as Tante Emma. Screenplay by Czinner and Carl Mayer. Cinematography by Karl Freund, Robert Baberske, and Adolf Schlasy. See filmportal.de entry for full credits.

15. Adele Sandrock (August 19, 1863 – August 30, 1937) was sixty-five at the time of the film's premiere in March 1929. Her affair with Schnitzler

during 1893–1895, when she was performing at the Deutschen Volkstheater in Vienna, is documented in their published correspondence.

16. The Berlin premiere took place at the Capitol Theater. The German Wikipedia article on the 1929 film gives the date as March 8, 1929; filmportal.de records March 7, 1929 as the premiere date. Albert Steinrück, who played Dorsday, died four weeks before the premiere, having been seriously ill during filming.

Chapter 20

1. Serialisation dates confirmed by the index entry in Johannes Müller, ed., *„Das Zeitlose ist von kürzester Dauer"*: *Interviews, Meinungen und Proteste*, 2 vols. (Göttingen: Wallstein, 2019), vol. 2, Register, which records *Traumnovelle* as "[1.12.1925–1.3.1926]". Book publication by S. Fischer Verlag followed later in 1926.

2. Schnitzler was born 15 May 1862. Serialisation began December 1925, when he was aged 63. He turned 64 on 15 May 1926, before book publication. Some secondary sources therefore describe him as 64 at the time of the book's appearance; both formulations are defensible and the distinction is minor.

3. Lili Schnitzler (born 13 September 1909) died by suicide in Venice on 26 July 1928, aged eighteen. Her father recorded his anguish in the diary entry of that date: see *Schnitzler-Tagebuch*, 26.7.1928, Austrian National Library / ACDH-CH, https://schnitzler-tagebuch.acdh.oeaw.ac.at. On Lili's identification with the protagonist of *Fräulein Else*, see Renate Wagner, *Arthur Schnitzler: Eine Biographie* (Vienna: Molden, 1981).

4. Frederic Raphael, *Eyes Wide Open: A Memoir of Stanley Kubrick* (London: Orion, 1999), pp. 87–88. Raphael's account of writing the screenplay with Kubrick is the primary record of the creative process; it should be used with caution, as it is a personal memoir by a participant with strong views of his own.

5. Reuben Brainin, „Schnitzler," published 26 June 1931, repr. in Müller (ed.), *Das Zeitlose*, vol. 1, pp. 320–322 (here p. 321). Müller's editorial note (vol. 1, p. 421) records Brainin's first diary-confirmed meeting with Schnitzler on 2 October 1903.

6. Arthur Schnitzler, *Traumnovelle* (Berlin: S. Fischer, 1926), final paragraph. All translations from the German are the author's own unless otherwise stated. The standard English translation is Arthur Schnitzler, *Dream Story*, trans. J. M.00a0Q. Davies (Harmondsworth: Penguin, 1999).

7. The Schnitzler–Pollaczek relationship is extensively documented in Clara Katharina Pollaczek's unpublished diaries, held at the Wienbibliothek im Rathaus, Vienna. On Hedy Kempny (born 21 December 1895; died 16 May 1986), see Hedy Kempny, *Das Mädchen mit den dreizehn Seelen: Eine Charakterstudie von Arthur Schnitzler in Briefen, Notizenund Tagebuchaufzeichnungen aus den Jahren 1918–1929* (Reinbek: Rowohlt, 1984). On the divorce from Olga Gussmann (m. 26 August 1903; div. 26 June 1921), see *Schnitzler-Tagebuch*, 26.6.1921.

8. Karl Scheuermann, „Old Vienna Goes American," *New York Herald Tribune*, repr. in Müller (ed.), *Das Zeitlose*, vol. 1, pp. 279–283 (here p. 281). The interview probably dates to 1928, when Schnitzler was in his mid-sixties and had recently lost his daughter.

9. Frederic Raphael, *Eyes Wide Open*, passim. On the rights acquisition in 1968, see Michael Herr, *Kubrick* (New York: Grove, 2000), p. 53. Note: some sources mention Jay Cocks as an early screenplay collaborator on the project (in the early 1990s), but Cocks was not involved in the 1968 rights acquisition. The draft should not conflate the two.

Chapter 21

1.   THE SPRING/SUMMER 1926 MEETING with Cappellini is placed in Venice on the basis of Schnitzler's diary entries for that period; see *Schnitzler-Tagebuch*, ACDH-CH, https://schnitzler-tagebuch.acdh.oeaw.ac.at. Arnoldo Cappellini was a Capitano in the fascist militia, not, as sometimes reported, an Italian nobleman; the error originates in Pierre Loving's 1929 account (see note 15) and is corrected by Johannes Müller in his editorial apparatus: see Johannes Müller, ed., „*Das Zeitlose ist von kürzester Dauer*", 2 vols. (Göttingen: Wallstein, 2019), vol. 1, p. 410 (note to p. 284, line 35).

2.   Schnitzler's gradual reconciliation with the match is recorded across diary entries for March 1927; see *Schnitzler-Tagebuch*, March 1927 passim. His revised estimate of Cappellini's character is noted in the entry for the visit to Sternwartestrasse.

3.   Schnitzler's diary, April 1927; see *Schnitzler-Tagebuch*, April 1927.

4.   The ceremony date of 30 June 1927 is confirmed by the diary; see *Schnitzler-Tagebuch*, 30.6.1927. Cappellini's parting words are recorded there. Lili was born 13 September 1909, making her seventeen years and nine months old at the time of the wedding.

5.   The July Revolt (Justizpalastbrand) of 15–16 July 1927 resulted in 89 deaths and approximately 1,057 injured. See Gerhard Botz, *Gewalt in der Politik*, 2nd ed. (Munich: Fink, 1983). Schnitzler's diary records the events at a notable emotional remove: see *Schnitzler-Tagebuch*, 15–16.7. 1927.

6.   [O.V.], „Arturo Schnitzler di passaggio per il Molo Bersaglieri," *Il Piccolo*, Jg. 6, Nr. 2.614, 1.5.1928, p. VI; repr. in Müller (ed.), *Das Zeitlose*, vol. 1, pp. 273–276. The German rendering reads: "Er lebte einsam und abgesondert mit seiner Tochter Fräulein Lilly ... und mit seinem Schwiegersohn, Kap. Cappellini, die ihn begleiteten." This is the last dated public sighting of Lili Schnitzler prior to her death.

7.   Lili's state of mind is reconstructed from her diary (see note 8) and from Schnitzler's correspondence and diary entries. The word *todunglücklich* is attested in correspondence cited in Renate Wagner, *Arthur Schnitzler: Eine Biographie* (Vienna: Molden, 1981). On the anorexia and pregnancy fears, see also Michaela Perlmann, *Arthur Schnitzler* (Stuttgart: Metzler, 1987), pp. 198–200.

8.   Lili Schnitzler, *Tagebuch*, ed. Max Haberich (Vienna: Bread & Games Publishing, 2025). Full bibliographic details should be confirmed before final submission. The diary was sealed by testamentary instruction and withheld from scholars for over ninety years.

9.   Lili Schnitzler, *Tagebuch*, entry of 12 December 1927. Original German: "Zuerst weine ich, dann will ich mich erschießen, dann spreche ich ruhig, dann will ich mich wieder erschießen, dann versöhnen wir uns."

10.   The circumstances of the shooting are recorded in *Schnitzler-Tagebuch*, 25–26.7.1928. The pistol had been taken by Cappellini from a dead Austrian soldier during the war. Whether the shot was intentional cannot be established with certainty; see note 13.

11.   Time of death: 22:15 on 26 July 1928. See *Schnitzler-Tagebuch*, 26.7.1928. Lili was born 13 September 1909, making her eighteen years and ten months old at her death.

12.   Schnitzler, *Tagebuch*, 26.7.1928. German original: "DiesMal trat das Pathologische ihres Wesens leider in einer Weise hervor, die nicht mehr gut zu machen war – eine Minute später wäre es nicht passiert."

13.   Müller (ed.), *Das Zeitlose*, vol. 1, p. 410 (note to p. 284, line 36): "Im Zuge eines Ehestreits spielte Lili Schnitzler am 26.7.1928 mit einem Revolver, doch ob der Schuss absichtlich oder unabsichtlich gefeuert wurde, bleibt ungeklärt." Müller also corrects the "chartered plane" claim: Schnitzler flew, but on a scheduled flight.

14.   The dictation of Lili's diary to Frieda Pollak („Kolap") is recorded in *Schnitzler-Tagebuch*, August 1928 passim. Frieda Pollak had served as Schnitzler's secretary since 1909 and remained with him until his death in October 1931.

15.   Pierre Loving, „Time Robs Schnitzler of Anatole," *New York Evening Post*, 7.12.1929, Section M, p. 3; repr. in Müller (ed.), *Das Zeitlose*, vol. 1, pp. 283–288 (here pp. 284–285). Loving incorrectly identifies Cappellini as "an Italian nobleman" and states that Schnitzler "chartered a special plane" (both errors corrected by Müller). His observations of Schnitzler's physical and emotional state in late 1929 are consistent with other contemporary accounts. For the Hofmannsthal parallel—Hofmannsthal's son Franz died by suicide in July 1929, the shock contributing directly to the elder poet's fatal heart attack days later—see Loving, ibid., p. 287.

Chapter 22

1.   *Therese. Chronik eines Frauenlebens* was published by S. Fischer Verlag, Berlin, in 1928. The twenty-year gap from *Der Weg ins Freie* (1908) is confirmed by the Band 2 index in Johannes Müller, ed., „*Das Zeitlose ist von kürzester Dauer*", 2 vols. (Göttingen: Wallstein, 2019), vol. 2, Register, sub *Therese*. The novel's genesis is traced back to the short story *Der Sohn* (1892); see Müller (ed.), *Das Zeitlose*, vol. 2, p. 315 (note to p. 314).

2.   On Therese Fabiani's trajectory and Schnitzler's formal intentions, see Michaela Perlmann, *Arthur Schnitzler* (Stuttgart: Metzler, 1987), pp. 188–200; Renate Wagner, *Arthur Schnitzler: Eine Biographie* (Vienna: Molden, 1981), pp. 299–307. On the chronicle form, see also the subtitle's generic implications discussed in Konstanze Fliedl, *Arthur Schnitzler: Poetik der Erinnerung* (Vienna: Böhlau, 1997).

3.   Schnitzler began dictating *Therese* in 1925 and completed the dictation by October 1927 (the first full reading is confirmed in April 1929: see Müller (ed.), *Das Zeitlose*, vol. 2, p. 399 (note to p. 279)). The novel was therefore written across the period of Lili's engagement, marriage, and descent into unhappiness—and was complete before her death on 26 July 1928.

4.   Suzanne Clauser (born Suzanne von Adler, 16 May 1898, Vienna; died 11 September 1981, Paris; pen name Dominique Auclères) was a writer and translator. Her French translation of *Therese* appeared in 1931. Müller's editorial note confirms that Schnitzler was *partnerschaftlich verbunden* with Clauser during this period (Müller (ed.), *Das Zeitlose*, vol. 1, p. 412 (note to p. 308, line 28)). Schnitzler's will, as reported by Müller (ed.), *Das Zeitlose*, vol. 2, afterword, bequeathed all French royalties to Clauser.

5.   Franz von Hofmannsthal died by suicide on 13 July 1929, aged twenty-five. See Müller (ed.), *Das Zeitlose*, vol. 1, p. 410 (note to p. 287, line 126): "Franz von Hofmannsthal starb am 13.7.1929 im Alter von 25 Jahren."

6.   Hugo von Hofmannsthal died on 15 July 1929 of a stroke (*Schlaganfall*), not a heart attack as sometimes reported. Müller's note is unambiguous: "Hugo von Hofmannsthal starb zwei Tage nach dem Suizid des Sohnes, am 15. 7. 1929, an einem Schlaganfall" (Müller (ed.), *Das Zeitlose*, vol. 1, p. 410, note to p. 287, line 128–129). The romantic attribution of the cause to the son's death is consistent with contemporary accounts,

including Pierre Loving's 1929 article, but medically it was a stroke, not cardiac arrest.

7.   The Café Griensteidl circle is discussed in several interviews in Müller (ed.), *Das Zeitlose*, vol. 1; see pp. 24, 138, 363 (index sub „Café Griensteidl"). Schnitzler's letter of congratulation to Felix Salten on the occasion of Salten's sixtieth birthday (Müller (ed.), *Das Zeitlose*, vol. 2, pp. 536–538, dated July 1929) offers a view of the circle and its surviving members from the very weeks of the Hofmannsthal deaths.

8.   *Flucht in die Finsternis* was serialized 13 May–0 May 1931; see Müller (ed.), *Das Zeitlose*, vol. 2, Register, sub *Flucht in die Finsternis*: "[13.5.1931–30.5.1931]". Published in book form by S. Fischer, Berlin, 1931.

9.   Arthur Schnitzler, *Tagebuch 1879–1931*, 10 vols., ed. Werner Welzig et al. (Vienna: Österreichische Akademie der Wissenschaften, 1981–2000). The final entry is dated 19 October 1931; death followed on 21 October. Digital edition: *Schnitzler-Tagebuch*, ACDH-CH, https://s chnitzler-tagebuch.acdh.oeaw.ac.at.

10.   Reuben Brainin (1862–1939), dean of Hebrew letters and a personal friend of Schnitzler since their first meeting on 2 October 1903 (per Müller (ed.), *Das Zeitlose*, vol. 1, p. 415, note to p. 320, line 6), published „Schnitzler" in *The Jewish Chronicle*, vol. 21, Nr. 14, 26 June 1931, p. 2; repr. in Müller (ed.), *Das Zeitlose*, vol. 1, pp. 320–322. The tribute appeared four months before Schnitzler's death.

11.   The NSDAP received 18.3 percent of the vote in the Reichstag elections of 14 September 1930, rising from 2.6 percent in 1928 to become the second-largest party in the Reichstag behind the SPD. See Richard J. Evans, *The Coming of the Third Reich* (London: Allen Lane, 2003), pp. 263–270.

12.   Schnitzler died on 21 October 1931 of a cerebral haemorrhage (*Gehirnblutung*). He was born 15 May 1862, making him sixty-nine years and five months old at his death. See *Schnitzler-Tagebuch*, 21.10.1931.

13.   Clara Katharina Pollaczek (born 15 January 1875; died 22 July 1951), *Tagebücher*. Wienbibliothek im Rathaus, Vienna. Pollaczek's diaries for the final years of Schnitzler's life constitute a significant primary source for the period; the quoted phrase is from the entry for 21 October 1931. See also Friedrich Witz, ed., *Arthur Schnitzler–Clara Katharina Pollaczek: Ein Briefwechsel* (for reference; exact edition details to be confirmed before submission).

14.   The last will („Die letzten Verfügungen Artur Schnitzlers") was published in *Arbeiter-Zeitung*, Jg. 44, Nr. 292, 23 October 1931, p. 8; repr. in Müller (ed.), *Das Zeitlose*, vol. 2, pp. 543. The will is dated 29 April 1912. The text in the original has emphasis markings on „Herzstich" (heart puncture, to verify death), „Keine Kränze" (no wreaths), „Keine Parte" (no death notice), and „Keine Reden" (no speeches). The instruction „Begräbnis letzter Klasse" (funeral of last class) was a deliberate rejection of the ceremonial excess Schnitzler associated with bourgeois self-regard.

15.   Burial in the Israelitische Abteilung (Old Israelite section) of the Wiener Zentralfriedhof (first gate) is confirmed by the *Arbeiter-Zeitung* notice of 23 October 1931 (Müller (ed.), *Das Zeitlose*, vol. 2, p. 543): the body was to be taken from Sternwartestrasse on Friday at 11:30 a.m. Johann Schnitzler (the father) is buried in the same section. The Burgtheater memorial is confirmed by Müller's Band 2 index entry („WienerBurgtheater"), p. 674; the date of 15 November derives from standard biographical sources (Wagner, Perlmann).

16.   The Nazi book burnings took place on 10 May 1933, organized by the Deutsche Studentenschaft; Schnitzler's works were among those burned in Vienna and Berlin. The interval between his death (21 October 1931) and the burnings (10 May 1933) was approximately nineteen months—not "nine months" as sometimes stated. On the scope of the burnings, see Matthew Fishburn, *Burning Books* (Basingstoke: Palgrave Macmillan, 2008). The claim that *Der Weg ins Freie* was exempted from burning on account of a Nazi misreading has not been verified against pri-

mary documentation and should be treated as anecdotal unless confirmed by an archival source before final submission.

Chapter 23

1.   On the critical reception at the time of Schnitzler's death, see W. E. Yates, *Schnitzler, Hofmannsthal, and the Austrian Theatre* (New Haven: Yale University Press, 1992); and Konstanze Fliedl, *Arthur Schnitzler: Poetik der Erinnerung* (Vienna: Böhlau, 1997), ch. 1. The memorial service is noted in standard biographies; see Renate Wagner, *Arthur Schnitzler: Eine Biographie* (Vienna: Molden, 1981), pp. 319–321.

2.   On the state of the archive at Schnitzler's death, see Martin Anton Müller and Gerd-Hermann Susen, „Nachwort" in Johannes Müller, ed., *„Das Zeitlose ist von kürzester Dauer"*, 2 vols. (Göttingen: Wallstein, 2019), vol. 2, pp. 662–681. The diary was eventually published in 10 vols. by the Austrian Academy of Sciences (1981–2000) and digitized at *schnitzler-tagebuch.acdh.oeaw.ac.at*.

3.   The book burnings of 10 May 1933 were organized by the Deutsche Studentenschaft (German Students' Union); the number of cities involved is variously given in the secondary literature as twenty or more, with the main coordinated burnings occurring at universities across Germany. The claim that they took place in "thirty-four university towns" requires verification against primary documentation; the more commonly cited figure is around twenty university cities for the single night of 10 May. See Matthew Fishburn, *Burning Books* (Basingstoke: Palgrave Macmillan, 2008), ch. 5.

4.   The claim that *Der Weg ins Freie* was exempted from burning due to a Nazi misreading is repeated in several biographical accounts but has not been confirmed against primary documentation in the course of this research. It should be treated as anecdotal until verified against the Deutsche Studentenschaft's blacklists or equivalent archival sources.

On the novel's exploration of Jewish identity, see above, Chapter 9; and Steven Beller, *Vienna and the Jews, 1867–1938* (Cambridge: Cambridge University Press, 1989), pp. 212–220.

5.   The rescue of the archive is documented in Lorenzo Bellettini and Christian Staufenbiel, "The Schnitzler Nachlass: Saved by a Cambridge Student," in *Schnitzler's Hidden Manuscripts*, ed. Lorenzo Bellettini and Peter Hutchinson (Oxford etc.: Peter Lang, 2010), pp. 11–21. The coding of messages and diplomatic seal detail derives from this source. The specific individual named in the chapter draft as "Eric Blackall" is consistent with the scholarship on the rescue; the Bellettini/Staufenbiel chapter refers to a Cambridge student, and Blackall later became a Cambridge-trained Germanist. Full details of his role should be confirmed against Bellettini/Staufenbiel before final submission.

6.   On the divided archive, see Müller, ed., *Das Zeitlose*, vol. 2, pp. 663–64 (afterword notes): the Cambridge University Library had "zuvor die Überlassung abgelehnt" (previously rejected the handover). The press clippings collection was donated by Olga Schnitzler to the Germanist Henry B. Garland, who taught at the University of Exeter; after Garland's retirement and death, the collection passed to the University of Exeter Library, where it is held today. The main manuscript archive is at Cambridge University Library. In the 1980s, some 26,000 pages were preserved on microfiche as a result of paper acid deterioration; a digitized version has been available at *schnitzler-zeitungen.acdh.oeaw.ac.at* since 2019.

7.   Clara Katharina Pollaczek (15 January 1875–22 July 1951), *Arthur Schnitzler und ich*, typescript memoir, Wienbibliothek im Rathaus, Vienna. The page count of approximately 990 pages is noted in published descriptions of the manuscript; see the Austrian Academy of Sciences digital edition (2025). Frieda Pollak (Kóláp; 8 December 1881–13 July 1937), Schnitzler's secretary from 1909, died in Vienna in 1937. If Pollaczek's memoir was produced in the years immediately following Schnitzler's death (1931–33), Frieda Pollak could have assisted in typing it before her

own death; any role she played would have ended by mid-1937 at the latest (Müller (ed.), *Das Zeitlose*, vol. 2, register, sub „Pollak, Frieda").

8.   Clara Katharina Pollaczek died in Vienna on 22 July 1951. Date confirmed in Müller (ed.), *Das Zeitlose*, vol. 2, register, sub „Pollaczek, Clara Katharina." The digital edition of *Arthur Schnitzler und ich* was published by the Austrian Academy of Sciences; publication date [2025, details to be confirmed before submission].

9.   Olga Schnitzler (born Olga Gussmann, pseudonym Dina Marius; 17 January 1882 Wien–13 January 1970 Lugano), Schauspielerin und Sängerin. The date and place of death are confirmed by Müller (ed.), *Das Zeitlose*, vol. 2, register.

10.   On the self-imposed *Reigen* ban and its lifting, see Michaela Perlmann, *Arthur Schnitzler* (Stuttgart: Metzler, 1987); and Edward Timms and Ritchie Robertson, eds., *Vienna 1900: From Altenberg to Wittgenstein* (Edinburgh: Edinburgh University Press, 1990). Heinrich Schnitzler authorized the lifting of the ban in 1982. The date of his son Michael's birth in Berkeley, California, requires confirmation; the Register of Müller (ed.), *Das Zeitlose*, vol. 2 confirms Heinrich's own dates (born Hinterbrühl 9 August 1902; died Vienna 12 July 1982) but does not detail Michael's birth.

11.   Heinrich Schnitzler died in Vienna on 12 July 1982. He was born 9 August 1902, making him seventy-nine years old at his death—not "eighty" as stated in the draft. Date and place confirmed in Müller (ed.), *Das Zeitlose*, vol. 2, register, sub „Schnitzler, Heinrich."

Chapter 24

1.   *La Ronde* (France, 1950), directed by Max Ophüls, screenplay by Ophüls and Jacques Natanson, based on *Reigen*. Produced by Sacha Gordine; cinematography by Christian Matras. Cast: Anton Walbrook, Simone Signoret, Serge Reggiani, Simone Simon, Danielle Darrieux. Nom-

inated for two Academy Awards (Screenplay; Art Direction). On Ophüls'
national origins: he was born in Saarbrücken, then part of Germany, on
6 May 1902.

2.   The rights situation was distinctive: as noted in the Wikipedia article on *La Ronde* (citing the Criterion Collection), Schnitzler had bequeathed the rights to the French translation of *Reigen* to his French translator, who was able to grant permission to Ophüls even while Heinrich
Schnitzler was maintaining his father's ban on performance. This meant
the film was not technically in breach of the family's wishes with respect
to the German-language text. The New York censors initially classified the
film as immoral; it was approved for exhibition in New York after a U.S.
Supreme Court appeal in 1954.

3.   The shift in critical assessment from the 1960s onward is traced
in W. E. Yates, *Schnitzler, Hofmannsthal, and the Austrian Theatre* (New
Haven: Yale University Press, 1992); and Konstanze Fliedl, *Arthur Schnitzler: Poetik der Erinnerung* (Vienna: Böhlau, 1997), Introduction. On the
"linician's eye" as interpretive framework, see also Michaela Perlmann,
Arthur Schnitzler (Stuttgart: Metzler, 1987), ch. 1.

4.   On the feminist critical reassessment, see Dagmar Lorenz, *Wiener
Moderne* (Stuttgart: Metzler, 1995); and Linda C. Demeritte, "Gender
and Class in Schnitzler's Late Fiction," in *A Companion to the Works of
Arthur Schnitzler*, ed. Dagmar Lorenz (Rochester: Camden House, 2003).
On the antisemitism dimension, see Steven Beller, *Vienna and the Jews,
1867–1938* (Cambridge: Cambridge University Press, 1989).

5.   Arthur Schnitzler, *Tagebuch 1879–1931*, 10 vols., ed. Werner
Welzig et al. (Vienna: Österreichische Akademie der Wissenschaften,
1981–2000). Digital edition: ACDH-CH, *schnitzler-tagebuch.acdh.oeaw
.ac.at* (since 2019).

6.   On the acquisition of rights in 1968 and Jay Cocks' role, see the
Wikipedia article on *Eyes Wide Shut*: "Kubrick was interested in adapting
the story, and with the help of journalist Jay Cocks, bought the filming

rights to the novel." The Wikipedia account is consistent with Nathan Abrams, *Eyes Wide Shut: Stanley Kubrick and the Making of his Final Film* (New York: Oxford University Press, 2019), which traces the acquisition to the late 1960s.

7.   The casting wish list is documented in David Mikics, *Stanley Kubrick: American Filmmaker* (New Haven: Yale University Press, 2020). Wikipedia on *Eyes Wide Shut* lists Steve Martin, Woody Allen, Tom Hanks, Bill Murray, Dustin Hoffman, Warren Beatty, Albert Brooks, Alan Alda, and Sam Shepard at various stages; the draft's list (Steve Martin, Woody Allen, Dustin Hoffman, Warren Beatty) is accurate though not exhaustive. The 1994 revival and hiring of Raphael: Wikipedia, *Eyes Wide Shut*, confirmed. Frederic Raphael subsequently published his account of the collaboration in *Eyes Wide Open: A Memoir of Stanley Kubrick* (London: Orion, 1999).

8.   Principal photography began in late 1996 at Pinewood Studios, England; post-production began in early 1998. The entire production ran approximately 400 days—a Guinness World Record for the longest continuous film shoot (confirmed in multiple sources including the Letterboxd story feature and Moviefone). The Cruise–Kidman casting: it was Tom Cruise who suggested Nicole Kidman for the role; both signed open-ended contracts. See Wikipedia, *Eyes Wide Shut*.

9.   Kubrick submitted his final cut to Warner Bros. on 1 March 1999; he died of a heart attack six days later, on 7 March 1999. He was born 26 July 1928 and was therefore 70 years old at his death. The draft's phrase "died in his sleep" should be noted: while some accounts emphasize that his death was sudden and unexpected, the confirmed cause was a heart attack (Wikipedia, *Eyes Wide Shut*). The film's world premiere was in Los Angeles on 13 July 1999; general US release was 16 July 1999.

10.   The Scorsese observation is widely cited in critical literature on *Eyes Wide Shut* but requires a precise primary source before final submis-

sion—interview or published statement. On the film's reception, see the critical survey in Abrams, *Eyes Wide Shut* (2019), ch. 8.

11.   Schnitzler died 21 October 1931; *Eyes Wide Shut* was released July 1999: an interval of approximately 67 years and 9 months, which the draft rounds to "sixty-eight years." Technically accurate by rounding. *Traumnovelle* was serialized December 1925–March 1926 and published as a book by S. Fischer, Berlin, 1926; at approximately 90 pages (in standard editions), the length figure in the draft is correct.

12.   Florian Frerichs, *Traumnovelle* (aka *Dream Story*; Germany, 2024). Premiered as opening night film of the 31st Oldenburg Film Festival, 11 September 2024. Starring Nikolai Kinski and Laurine Price. Screenplay: Florian Frerichs and Martina van Delay. Production: Studio Babelsberg / Warnuts Entertainment. The film's critical reception was mixed; see the Hollywood Reporter review (14 September 2024) and the Film Verdict (September 2024). The draft's framing that the film "confirmed" the novella's enduring relevance is an editorial judgment; whether the Frerichs adaptation itself successfully demonstrates this is contested in the reviews.

Chapter 25

1. *Fräulein Else* (Berlin: S. Fischer, 1924). Schnitzler wrote the novella in early 1923 in an uninterrupted stretch; Olga Schnitzler recalled he completed the first draft in three weeks. For the interior-monologue technique, see Note 5 below.

2.   The 2024 anthology reference requires a full citation before final submission—title, editor, publisher, and page range—as it is unverified in the PDFs or web sources consulted. Mark as [TBC].

3.   *Professor Bernhardi* was written between 1910 and 1912 (Schnitzler worked on it over two years); the premiere was 28 November 1912 at the Kleines Theater, Berlin. It was banned in Austria until the end of the

Habsburg Empire. The draft's phrase "written in 1912" oversimplifies: the composition spanned 1910–12 and the work was published in 1912. Robert Icke's adaptation at the Almeida Theatre, London, opened in 2019 (subsequently transferring).

4.   The "quality of seeing" framing is the author's critical synthesis, not a direct quotation. For scholarly versions of this argument, see Swales (1971), pp. 1–10; and Fliedl (1997), Introduction.

5. *Leutnant Gustl* was published in *Neue Freie Presse* on 25 December 1900 (book edition 1901). *Ulysses* appeared in February 1922. Source: Wikipedia, "Stream of consciousness"; Mahler Foundation biography; E ncyclopedia.com on *Leutnant Gustl*. Note also that Schnitzler's technique is termed "interior monologue" rather than "stream of consciousness" in scholarship: the two terms are related but not identical, and Schnitzler's narration is somewhat more ordered.

6.   Tom Stoppard's *Dalliance* (adaptation of *Liebelei*) premiered at the Lyttelton Theatre, National Theatre, London, 27 May 1986, directed by Peter Wood; cast included Tim Curry, Brenda Blethyn, and Sally Dexter. Published: Faber and Faber, 1986. Note: Stoppard also adapted Schnitzler's *Das weite Land* as *Undiscovered Country* (National Theatre, 1979)—an earlier and equally significant Schnitzler adaptation by Stoppard that may warrant mention in the main text. David Hare's *The Blue Room* (freely adapted from *Reigen*): Donmar Warehouse, 10 September 1998, directed by Sam Mendes; starring Nicole Kidman and Iain Glen. Moved to Broadway (Cort Theatre) 13 December 1998. Published: Faber and Faber, 1998. London critic Charles Spencer's phrase "pure theatrical Viagra" became widely quoted.

7.   The draft states "forty thousand pages" for the Cambridge archive. The figures from Chapter 23 of this biography established: (a) the diary runs to "nearly eight thousand pages" (confirmed by Wikipedia and the Austrian Academy of Sciences); (b) approximately 26,000 pages were preserved on microfiche in the 1980s (from Müller's PDF sources); (c) the

press-clippings collection runs to approximately 30,000 items. The figure "forty thousand pages" does not correspond to any verified single figure and conflates multiple portions of the archive. The text has been revised to "tens of thousands of manuscript pages" pending a specific verified total from the Cambridge University Library catalogue.

8.   Martin Swales, *Arthur Schnitzler: A Critical Study* (Oxford: Clarendon Press, 1971), p. 1 (Introduction). The exact wording as cited in Encyclopedia.com's Schnitzler entry (itself drawing on Swales): "his understanding of human nature and his skill as an interpreter of the individual consciousness lend his works the quality of universality."

9.   The "love and death" quote is widely attributed to Schnitzler in response to a critic who observed that his works treated the same subjects repeatedly. The Mahler Foundation biography and ReadListenLearn give the context as a response to an interviewer.

Bibliography of Sources

Primary Sources

Works by Arthur Schnitzler

Schnitzler, Arthur. "Von Amsterdam nach Ymuiden." Wiener Medizinische Presse 20 (1879).

Schnitzler, Arthur. Anatol. Berlin: Verlag des Bibliographischen Bureaus, 1893 [published autumn 1892]. Verse prologue ("Einleitung") by Hugo von Hofmannsthal ("Loris").

Schnitzler, Arthur. Das Märchen. Premiered Deutsches Volkstheater, Vienna, December 1893.

Schnitzler, Arthur. Sterben. Berlin: S. Fischer, 1895.

Schnitzler, Arthur. Liebelei. Schauspiel in drei Akten. Berlin: S. Fischer, 1896. Premiered Burgtheater, Vienna, 9 October 1895.

Schnitzler, Arthur. "Arthur Schnitzler an Marie Reinhard (1896)." Modern Austrian Literature 10, nos. 3/4 (1977): 23–68.

Schnitzler, Arthur. Der grüne Kakadu. Paracelsus. Die Gefährtin. Drei Einakter. Berlin: S. Fischer, 1899.

Schnitzler, Arthur. Reigen. Zehn Dialoge, geschrieben Winter 1896/97. Private printing, 200 copies, 1900. Public edition: Vienna: Wiener Verlag, 1903. Berlin premiere: Kleines Schauspielhaus, 23 December 1920.

Schnitzler, Arthur. Leutnant Gustl. First published in Neue Freie Presse, 25 December 1900; book edition Berlin: S. Fischer, 1901.

Schnitzler, Arthur. Der Weg ins Freie. Roman. Berlin: S. Fischer Verlag, 1908. Full text available at Projekt Gutenberg-DE: https://www.projekt -gutenberg.org/schnitzl/wegfreie/

Schnitzler, Arthur. Das weite Land: Tragikomödie in fünf Akten. Berlin: S. Fischer, 1911.

Schnitzler, Arthur. Professor Bernhardi. Komödie in fünf Akten. Berlin: S. Fischer, 1912. Premiered Kleines Theater, Berlin, 28 November 1912.

Schnitzler, Arthur. "Zum 'Professor Bernhardi.'" Der Merker, Jg. 4, Nr. 4, 2. Februar-Heft 1913, S. 135.

Schnitzler, Arthur. Frau Beate und ihr Sohn. Berlin: S. Fischer, 1913.

Schnitzler, Arthur. Doktor Gräsler, Badearzt. Berlin: S. Fischer, 1917.

Schnitzler, Arthur. Casanovas Heimfahrt. Berlin: S. Fischer, 1918.

Schnitzler, Arthur. Letter to Stefan Großmann. Published in Das Tage-Buch, Jg. 2, Nr. 8, 26 February 1921, pp. 252–253.

Schnitzler, Arthur. Letter to an unnamed correspondent regarding Reigen, 13 September 1912. Published by Max Epstein in B. Z. am Mittag, 21 February 1921.

Schnitzler, Arthur. Fräulein Else. Novelle. Berlin/Vienna/Leipzig: Paul Zsolnay Verlag, 1924.

Schnitzler, Arthur. Traumnovelle. Berlin: S. Fischer Verlag, 1926.

Schnitzler, Arthur. Dream Story. Translated by J. M. Q. Davies. Harmondsworth: Penguin, 1999.

Schnitzler, Arthur. „Die letzten Verfügungen Artur Schnitzlers." Arbeiter-Zeitung, Jg. 44, Nr. 292, 23 October 1931, p. 8. [Repr. in Müller (ed.), Das Zeitlose, vol. 2, p. 543.]

Schnitzler, Arthur. *Jugend in Wien: Eine Autobiographie*. Edited by Therese Nickl and Heinrich Schnitzler. Vienna/Munich/Zurich: Fritz Molden, 1968.

Schnitzler, Arthur. Später Ruhm. Edited by Wilhelm Hemecker and David Österle. Vienna: Zsolnay, 2014. [Written c. 1894–95; published posthumously.]

Diaries, Letters, and Edited Collections

Schnitzler, Arthur. Tagebuch 1879–1931. 10 vols. Edited by Peter Michael Braunwarth et al. for the Kommission für literarische Gebrauchsformen der Österreichischen Akademie der Wissenschaften (Director: Werner Welzig). Vienna: Verlag der Österreichischen Akademie der Wissenschaften, 1987–2000. Digital edition (CC license): https://schnitzle r-tagebuch.acdh.oeaw.ac.at. Data repository: https://github.com/arthur -schnitzler/schnitzler-tagebuch-data.

Schnitzler, Arthur. Briefe 1875–1912. Edited by Therese Nickl and Heinrich Schnitzler. Frankfurt am Main: S. Fischer, 1981.

Schnitzler, Arthur, and Hugo von Hofmannsthal. Briefwechsel. Edited by Therese Nickl and Heinrich Schnitzler. Frankfurt am Main: S. Fischer, 1964.

Schnitzler, Arthur, and Hermann Bahr. Briefwechsel, Aufzeichnungen, Dokumente (1891–1931). Edited by Kurt Ifkovits and Martin Anton Müller. Göttingen: Wallstein, 2018. https://schnitzler-bahr.acdh.oeaw.a c.at/

Fliedl, Konstanze, ed. Arthur Schnitzler – Richard Beer-Hofmann. Briefwechsel 1891–1931. Vienna/Zurich: Europaverlag, 1992.

Kempny, Hedy, and Arthur Schnitzler. Das Mädchen mit den dreizehn Seelen: Eine Korrespondenz ergänzt durch Blätter aus Hedy Kempnys Tagebuch sowie durch eine Auswahl ihrer Erzählungen. Edited by Heinz P. Adamek. Reinbek bei Hamburg: Rowohlt, 1984.

Müller, Martin Anton, ed. Arthur Schnitzler: "Das Zeitlose ist von kürzester Dauer." Interviews, Meinungen und Proteste 1891–1931. 2 vols. Göttingen: Wallstein, 2023. CC BY 4.0. DOI: https://doi.org/10.46500/83535471. Digital edition: https://schnitzler-interviews.acdh.oeaw.ac.at.

Schnitzler press clippings collection. University of Exeter Library. Digitized edition: ACDH-CH, https://schnitzler-zeitungen.acdh.oeaw.ac.at.

Other Primary Sources

Bahr, Hermann. Die Überwindung des Naturalismus. Dresden/Leipzig: Pierson, 1891.

Freud, Sigmund. Letter to Arthur Schnitzler, 14 May 1922. https://www.freudedition.net. CC BY-NC-ND 4.0. Also published in Letters of Sigmund Freud, edited by Ernst L. Freud. New York: Basic Books, 1960.

Kraus, Karl. "Die demolirte Literatur." Wiener Rundschau 1, no. 1 (1897).

Pollaczek, Clara Katharina [as "Bob"]. "Mimi: Schattenbilder aus einem Mädchenleben." Szenenfolge mit einem Prolog von Hugo von Hofmannsthal. Neue Deutsche Rundschau 8, no. 4 (1 April 1897): 396–413.

Pollaczek, Clara Katharina. Arthur Schnitzler und ich. Typescript memoir, c. 900 pages. Handschriftensammlung der Wienbibliothek im Rathaus, Vienna. Digital edition: Austrian Centre for Digital Humanities, 2025. https://pollaczek.acdh.oeaw.ac.at/

Pollaczek, Clara Katharina. Unpublished diaries. Wienbibliothek im Rathaus, Vienna.

Wertheimer, Paul. "Begegnung mit Artur Schnitzler." In Brüder im Geiste: Ein Kulturbilderbuch. Wien/Leipzig: Deutsch-Österreichischer Verlag, 1923. Pp. 88–94.

Stage Adaptations

Hare, David. The Blue Room. Freely adapted from Arthur Schnitzler's La Ronde. London: Faber and Faber, 1998.

Stoppard, Tom. Undiscovered Country. London: Faber and Faber, 1980.

Stoppard, Tom. Dalliance and Undiscovered Country. London: Faber and Faber, 1986.

Wolf, Susanne Felicitas. Der Weg ins Freie. Stage adaptation, Theater in der Josefstadt, Vienna, 2021. https://www.susannewolf.at/theaterstuecke/der-weg-ins-freie

Films

Frerichs, Florian, dir. Traumnovelle [Dream Story]. Studio Babelsberg / Warnuts Entertainment, 2024.

Kubrick, Stanley, dir. Eyes Wide Shut. Warner Bros., 1999.

Ophüls, Max, dir. La Ronde. Sacha Gordine Productions, 1950.

Secondary Sources — Books and Chapters

Abrams, Nathan. Eyes Wide Shut: Stanley Kubrick and the Making of his Final Film. New York: Oxford University Press, 2019.

Alewyn, Richard. Probleme und Gestalten: Essays. Frankfurt am Main: Insel Verlag, 1974.

Beier, Nikolaj. "Vor allem bin ich ich...": Judentum, Akkulturation und Antisemitismus in Arthur Schnitzlers Leben und Werk. Göttingen: Wallstein, 2008.

Beller, Steven. Vienna and the Jews, 1867–1938. Cambridge: Cambridge University Press, 1989.

Bellettini, Lorenzo, and Christian Staufenbiel. "The Schnitzler Nachlass: Saved by a Cambridge Student." In Schnitzler's Hidden Manuscripts, edited by Lorenzo Bellettini and Peter Hutchinson, 11–21. Oxford: Peter Lang, 2010.

Beniston, Judith. "Professor Bernhardi. Komödie in fünf Akten (1912)." In Schnitzler-Handbuch: Leben – Werk – Wirkung, edited by Christoph Jürgensen, Wolfgang Lukas, and Michael Scheffel. Stuttgart: J. B. Metzler, 2022.

Bülow, Ulrich von. "Sicherheit ist nirgends": Das Tagebuch von Arthur Schnitzler. Marbacher Magazin 93. Marbach am Neckar: Deutsche Schillergesellschaft, 2001.

Calasso, Roberto. Afterword to La signorina Else (Italian translation of Fräulein Else). Milan: Adelphi, Piccola biblioteca series.

Denk, Rudolf. "Das weite Land: Tragikomödie in fünf Akten (1911)." In Schnitzler-Handbuch, edited by Christoph Jürgensen, Wolfgang Lukas, and Michael Scheffel. Stuttgart: Metzler, 2022.

Evans, Richard J. The Coming of the Third Reich. London: Allen Lane, 2003.

Farese, Giuseppe. Arthur Schnitzler: Ein Leben in Wien, 1862–1931. Translated by Karin Krieger. Munich: C. H. Beck, 1999.

Fishburn, Matthew. Burning Books. Basingstoke: Palgrave Macmillan, 2008.

Fliedl, Konstanze. Arthur Schnitzler: Poetik der Erinnerung. Vienna: Böhlau, 1997.

Fliedl, Konstanze. Arthur Schnitzler. Stuttgart: Reclam, 2005.

Fliedl, Konstanze. "Arthur Schnitzler." In Kindlers Literatur-Lexikon, 3rd ed. Stuttgart: Metzler, 2009.

Gaugusch, Georg. Wer einmal war: Das jüdische Großbürgertum Wiens 1800–1938. Vol. 2. Vienna: Amalthea, 2016.

Gillman, Abigail. Viennese Jewish Modernism: Freud, Hofmannsthal, Beer-Hofmann, and Schnitzler. University Park: Penn State University Press, 2009.

Herr, Michael. Kubrick. New York: Grove Press, 2000.

Hubmann, Gerhard. "Schwankende häusliche Stimmung: Mit Arthur Schnitzler beim Villenkauf." In So schön kann Wissenschaft sein!, edited by Marcel Atze. Vienna: Amalthea, 2017. Pp. 220–236.

Jacobi, Jutta. Die Schnitzlers: Eine Familiengeschichte. St. Pölten/Salzburg/Wien: Residenz, 2014.

Janz, Rolf-Peter, and Klaus Laermann. Arthur Schnitzler: Zur Diagnose des Wiener Bürgertums im Fin de Siècle. Stuttgart: Metzler, 1977.

Jürgensen, Christoph, Wolfgang Lukas, and Michael Scheffel, eds. Schnitzler-Handbuch: Leben – Werk – Wirkung. Stuttgart: J. B. Metzler, 2014. 2nd ed. 2022.

Kurz, Stephan. "Im Schatten Schnitzlers: Leben und Werk von Clara Katharina Pollaczek (1875–1951)." In "A. ist manchmal wie ein kleines Kind": Clara Katharina Pollaczek und Arthur Schnitzler gehen ins Kino, edited by Michael Rohrwasser and Stephan Kurz, 10–33. Vienna: Böhlau, 2012.

Kurz, Stephan, and Michael Rohrwasser, eds. "A. ist manchmal wie ein kleines Kind": Clara Katharina Pollaczek und Arthur Schnitzler gehen ins Kino. Unter Mitarbeit von Daniel Schopper. Vienna: Böhlau, 2012.

Lacher, Rolf-Peter. Der Mensch ist eine Bestie: Anna Heeger, Maria Chlum, Maria Reinhard und Arthur Schnitzler. 2014.

Le Rider, Jacques. Arthur Schnitzler oder Die Wiener Belle Époque. Vienna: Passagen, 2007.

Lesky, Erna. Die Wiener medizinische Schule im 19. Jahrhundert. Graz: Böhlau, 1978.

Lukas, Wolfgang, and Michael Scheffel, eds. Fräulein Else: Kommentierte Studienausgabe. Göttingen: Wallstein Verlag, 2025.

Markus, Georg. Wenn's euch nur gefällt: 100 Jahre Kammerspiele, 1910–2010. Vienna: Amalthea, 2010.

Mikics, David. Stanley Kubrick: American Filmmaker. New Haven: Yale University Press, 2020.

Müller, Karl. Das Zeitlose und der Zeitgeist: Arthur Schnitzler—Leben und Werk. 2 vols. Vienna, 2022.

Pankau, Johannes G. "Das weite Land: Das Natürliche als Chaos." In Interpretationen: Arthur Schnitzler. Dramen und Erzählungen, edited by Hee-Ju Kim and Günter Saße. Stuttgart: Reclam, 2007. Pp. 134–147.

Perlmann, Michaela L. Arthur Schnitzler. Stuttgart: Metzler, 1987.

Perlmann, Michaela L. "Traumnovelle." In Arthur Schnitzler: Kommentar zu den erzählerischen Schriften und dramatischen Werken. Munich: Winkler, 1987.

Pole, K. F. M. Two Halves of a Life. Gillingham, Kent, 1982.

Raphael, Frederic. Eyes Wide Open: A Memoir of Stanley Kubrick. London: Orion, 1999.

Robertson, Ritchie. "Schnitzler in Britain: Authorship, Translation and Finding a Place at the National Theatre." Project MUSE, 2022.

Saxer, Sibylle. "Fräulein Else (1924)." In Schnitzler-Handbuch: Leben – Werk – Wirkung, edited by Christoph Jürgensen, Wolfgang Lukas, and Michael Scheffel. Stuttgart: J. B. Metzler, 2022.

Scheible, Hartmut. Arthur Schnitzler in Selbstzeugnissen und Bilddokumenten. Reinbek bei Hamburg: Rowohlt, 1976. 13th ed. 2003.

Scheffel, Michael. "Der Weg ins Freie (1908)." In Schnitzler-Handbuch, edited by Christoph Jürgensen, Wolfgang Lukas, and Michael Scheffel. Stuttgart: J. B. Metzler, 2022.

Schorske, Carl E. Fin-de-Siècle Vienna: Politics and Culture. New York: Knopf, 1980.

Schwarz, Egon. "1921: The Staging of Artur Schnitzler's 'Reigen' in Vienna Creates a Public Uproar." In Yale Companion to Jewish Writing and Thought in German Culture, 1096–1996, edited by Sander L. Gilman and Jack Zipes, 412–419. New Haven: Yale University Press, 1997.

Simon, Anne-Catherine. Schnitzlers Wien. Vienna: Pichler, 2002.

Sprengel, Peter. Geschichte der deutschsprachigen Literatur 1900–1918. Munich: Beck, 2004.

Swales, Martin. Arthur Schnitzler: A Critical Study. Oxford: Clarendon Press, 1971.

Tacke, Alexandra. Schnitzlers "Fräulein Else" und die nackte Wahrheit: Novelle, Verfilmungen und Bearbeitungen. Cologne/Weimar/Vienna, 2017.

Titzmann, Michael. "Frau Beate und ihr Sohn (1913)." In Schnitzler-Handbuch, edited by Christoph Jürgensen, Wolfgang Lukas, and Michael Scheffel. Stuttgart: Metzler, 2022.

Torberg, Friedrich. "Schnitzler." In Das fünfte Rad am Thespiskarren. Wien: Georg Müller Verlag, 1966. Pp. 218–231.

Wagner, Renate. "Der fünfte Akt: Clara Katharina Pollaczek." In Frauen um Arthur Schnitzler, 145–159. Vienna and Munich: Jugend & Volk, 1980.

Wagner, Renate. Arthur Schnitzler: Eine Biographie. Vienna: Fritz Molden, 1981.

Weinzierl, Ulrich. Arthur Schnitzler: Lieben Träumen Sterben. Frankfurt am Main: S. Fischer, 1994.

Wisely, Andrew C. Arthur Schnitzler and Twentieth-Century Criticism. Rochester: Camden House, 2004.

Worbs, Michael. Nervenkunst: Literatur und Psychoanalyse im Wien der Jahrhundertwende. Frankfurt: Europäische Verlagsanstalt, 1983.

Yates, W. E. Schnitzler, Hofmannsthal, and the Austrian Theatre. New Haven: Yale University Press, 1992.

Secondary Sources — Articles and Reviews

Braunwarth, Peter Michael. "Worte sind alles: Beobachtungen am Vokabular von Arthur Schnitzlers Tagebuch." Dissertation excerpt, Kommentar 1925. Austrian Academy of Sciences. https://shared.acdh.oeaw.ac.at/schnitzler-briefe/2001_Braunwarth_Dissertation-Exzerpt_Kommentar-1925.pdf

Haberich, Max M. W. "Arthur Schnitzler's Professor Bernhardi: Anti-Semitism on the Stage and in Reality." Central Europe 10, no. 2 (2012): 126–146.

Klimaschka, Christine. "Spurensuche Frieda Pollak—Portrait einer Unbekannten." myGiulia, May 2022. https://www.mygiulia.de/post/spurensuche-frieda-pollak-mit-brigitte-karner-und-brita-kettner

Rey, William H. "'Arthur Schnitzler und ich': Das Vermächtnis der Clara Katharina Pollaczek." The Germanic Review 41, no. 1 (1966): 120–135.

Robertson, Ritchie. "Schnitzler in Britain: Authorship, Translation and Finding a Place at the National Theatre." Project MUSE, 2022.

Schinnerer, Otto P. "Schnitzler and the Military Censorship: Unpublished Correspondence." Germanic Review 5 (1930): 238–246.

Sheridan, K. "The Ethics of Empathy and the Correspondence Culture in Arthur Schnitzler's Der Weg ins Freie." ResearchGate, 2010.

Weber, Eugene. Review of Briefwechsel 1891–1931 (Schnitzler/Beer-Hofmann). Modern Austrian Literature 6, no. 3/4 (1973): 40.

Contemporary Accounts

Brainin, Reuben. "Schnitzler." The Jewish Chronicle, vol. 21, Nr. 14, 26 June 1931, p. 2. [Repr. in Müller (ed.), Das Zeitlose, vol. 1, pp. 320–322.]

[O.V.]. "Die letzten Verfügungen Artur Schnitzlers." Arbeiter-Zeitung, Jg. 44, Nr. 292, 23 October 1931, p. 8. [Repr. in Müller (ed.), Das Zeitlose, vol. 2, pp. 542–543.]

Wertheimer, Paul. "Begegnung mit Artur Schnitzler." In Brüder im Geiste: Ein Kulturbilderbuch. Wien/Leipzig: Deutsch-Österreichischer Verlag, 1923. Pp. 88–94.

Online Sources

Digital Editions and Archives

Arthur Schnitzler. Tagebuch 1879–1931. Digitale Edition. Austrian Centre for Digital Humanities (ACDH-CH), Austrian Academy of Sciences. https://schnitzler-tagebuch.acdh.oeaw.ac.at. Accessed March 2026.

Arthur Schnitzler. Chronik. ACDH-CH. https://schnitzler-chronik.acdh.oeaw.ac.at/. Accessed March 2026.

Arthur Schnitzler / Hermann Bahr. Briefwechsel. ACDH-CH. https://schnitzler-bahr.acdh.oeaw.ac.at/. Accessed March 2026.

Arthur Schnitzler. Interviews, Meinungen, Proteste 1891–1931. Digital edition. ACDH-CH. https://schnitzler-interviews.acdh.oeaw.ac.at. Accessed March 2026.

Schnitzler press clippings (digitized). ACDH-CH. https://schnitzler-zeitungen.acdh.oeaw.ac.at. Accessed March 2026.

Clara Katharina Pollaczek. Arthur Schnitzler und ich. Digital edition. ACDH-CH. https://pollaczek.acdh.oeaw.ac.at/. Accessed March 2026.

Freud, Sigmund. Letter to Arthur Schnitzler, 14 May 1922. Freud Edition. https://www.freudedition.net. Accessed March 2026.

Reigen Digitization Project. Binghamton University / University of Freiburg. https://omeka.binghamton.edu/omeka/collections/show/34. Accessed March 2026.

Reference and Research Sites

Arthur Schnitzler Portal (English). Biographical Sketch. https://www.arthur-schnitzler.org/bio-bibliography/biographical-sketch/. Accessed March 2026.

Arthur Schnitzler Portal (German). Biographische Skizze. https://www.arthur-schnitzler.de/biobibliographika/biographische-skizze/. Accessed March 2026.

Arthur-Schnitzler-Forschungsstelle, University of Vienna. https://www.univie.ac.at/schnitzler. Accessed March 2026.

Braunwarth, Peter Michael. "Worte sind alles: Beobachtungen am Vokabular von Arthur Schnitzlers Tagebuch." Dissertation excerpt. Austrian Academy of Sciences. https://shared.acdh.oeaw.ac.at/schnitzler-briefe/2001_Braunwarth_Dissertation-Exzerpt_Kommentar-1925.pdf. Accessed March 2026.

Cambridge University. "Saved from the Nazis in 1938: Schnitzler archive to remain in Cambridge." University of Cambridge Research News. https://www.cam.ac.uk/research/news/saved-from-the-nazis-in-1938-schnitzler-archive-to-remain-in-cambridge. Accessed March 2026.

"Das Wien des Fin de Siècle in Arthur Schnitzlers Weg ins Freie." ENS de Lyon, Clé des langues. https://cle.ens-lyon.fr/allemand/litterature/mouvements-et-genres-litteraires/tournant-du-xxe/das-wien-des-fin-de-siecle-in-arthur-schnitzlers-weg-ins-freie-. Accessed March 2026.

Freud Museum London. "Sigmund Freud & Arthur Schnitzler: A Doppelgänger Relationship?" https://www.freud.org.uk/. Accessed March 2026.

Gustav Klimt-Datenbank. Entries on Arthur Schnitzler, Hermann Bahr, Hugo von Hofmannsthal, Clara Pollaczek, and Café Central. https://www.klimt-database.com. Accessed March 2026.

Haus der Geschichte Österreich (hdgö). "1918: Arthur Schnitzlers Professor Bernhardi in Österreich." https://hdgoe.at/professor-bernhardi. Accessed March 2026.

Hollywood Reporter. Review of Traumnovelle (dir. Frerichs, 2024). https://www.hollywoodreporter.com/movies/movie-reviews/traumnovelle-review-1236001771/. Accessed March 2026.

litkult1920er.aau.at. "Pollaczek, Clara Katharina." https://litkult1920er.aau.at/litkult-lexikon/pollaczek-clara-katharina/. Accessed March 2026.

Mahler Foundation. Arthur Schnitzler. https://mahlerfoundation.org/mahler/contemporaries/arthur-schnitzler/. Accessed March 2026.

Museum of Contraception and Abortion. "Das ungeheure Unrecht in der Welt." https://muvs.org/en/topics/termination-of-pregnancy/das -ungeheure-unrecht-in-der-welt-en/. Accessed March 2026.

NÖ Landesarchiv. "Arthur Schnitzler, Professor Bernhardi." http:/ /www.noel.gv.at/noe/Landesarchiv/Schnitzler_Bernhardi.html. Accessed March 2026.

"Professor Bernhardi, a play by Arthur Schnitzler, M.D." Hektoen International, 2022. https://hekint.org/2022/02/08/professor-bernhar di-a-play-by-arthur-schnitzler-m-d/. Accessed March 2026.

Sheridan, K. "The Ethics of Empathy and the Correspondence Culture in Arthur Schnitzler's Der Weg ins Freie." ResearchGate, 2010. Accessed March 2026.

Arthur Schnitzler and Jakob Wassermann: Jewish Identity in Vienna. Doctoral thesis, University of Cambridge. https://api.repository.cam.ac.uk/server/api/core/bitstreams/73c e9ba6-1223-41b8-b99e-d063f90ad908/content. Accessed March 2026.

Wien Geschichte Wiki. "Arthur Schnitzler." https://www.geschichtew iki.wien.gv.at/Arthur_Schnitzler. Accessed March 2026.

Wien Geschichte Wiki. "Schnitzlervilla." https://www.geschichtewiki. wien.gv.at/Schnitzlervilla. Accessed March 2026.

Wien Geschichte Wiki. "Hedwig Bleibtreu." https://www.geschichtew iki.wien.gv.at/Hedwig_Bleibtreu. Accessed March 2026.

Wien Geschichte Wiki. "Kammerspiele." https://www.geschichtewiki .wien.gv.at/Kammerspiele. Accessed March 2026.

ww1.habsburger.net. "12 November 1918 as a Site of Memory." https:/ /ww1.habsburger.net/en/chapters/12-november-1918-site-memory. Accessed March 2026.

Wikipedia and General Reference

"Adele Sandrock." Wikipedia. https://en.wikipedia.org/wiki/Adele_Sa
ndrock; IMDB: https://www.imdb.com/name/nm0762277/. Accessed
March 2026.

"Anatol (Schauspiel)." German Wikipedia. https://de.wikipedia.org/w
iki/Anatol_(Schauspiel). Accessed March 2026.

"Arthur Schnitzler." Wikipedia. https://en.wikipedia.org/wiki/Arthur
_Schnitzler. Accessed March 2026.

"Bauernfeld Prize." Wikipedia. https://en.wikipedia.org/wiki/Bauernf
eld_Prize. Accessed March 2026.

"Der einsame Weg." German Wikipedia. https://de.wikipedia.org/wik
i/Der_einsame_Weg. Accessed March 2026.

"Der Weg ins Freie." Wikipedia. https://en.wikipedia.org/wiki/Der_W
eg_ins_Freie. Accessed March 2026.

"Die Gefährtin." Wikipedia. https://en.wikipedia.org/wiki/Die_Gef%
C3%A4hrtin. Accessed March 2026.

"Dalliance." Wikipedia. https://en.wikipedia.org/wiki/Dalliance. Accessed March 2026.

"Eyes Wide Shut." Wikipedia. https://en.wikipedia.org/wiki/Eyes_Wi
de_Shut. Accessed March 2026.

"Franz Grillparzer Prize." Wikipedia. https://en.wikipedia.org/wiki/Fr
anz_Grillparzer_Prize. Accessed March 2026.

filmportal.de. Entry for Fräulein Else (1929). https://www.filmportal.
de/en/movie/fraulein-else. Accessed March 2026.

"Fräulein Else (1929 film)." Wikipedia. https://en.wikipedia.org/wiki/
Fr%C3%A4ulein_Else_(1929_film). Accessed March 2026.

"Der grüne Kakadu." German Wikipedia. https://de.wikipedia.org/wi
ki/Der_gr%C3%BCne_Kakadu. Accessed March 2026.

"General Polyclinic Vienna." Wikipedia. https://en.wikipedia.org/wiki
/General_Polyclinic_Vienna. Accessed March 2026.

"Interior monologue / Stream of consciousness." Wikipedia. https://e
n.wikipedia.org/wiki/Interior_monologue. Accessed March 2026.

"Johann Schnitzler." Wikipedia. https://en.wikipedia.org/wiki/Johann _Schnitzler. Accessed March 2026.

"La Ronde (play)." Wikipedia. https://en.wikipedia.org/wiki/La_Ron de_(play). Accessed March 2026.

"La Ronde (1950 film)." Wikipedia. https://en.wikipedia.org/wiki/La _Ronde_(1950_film). Accessed March 2026.

"Lessing Theater." Wikipedia. https://en.wikipedia.org/wiki/Lessing_ Theater. Accessed March 2026.

"Liebelei (play)." Wikipedia. https://en.wikipedia.org/wiki/Liebelei_(play). Accessed March 2026.

"Maria Reinhard." German Wikipedia. https://de.wikipedia.org/wiki/ Maria_Reinhard. Accessed March 2026.

"Paracelsus (Schnitzler)." German Wikipedia. https://de.wikipedia.org /wiki/Paracelsus_(Schnitzler). Accessed March 2026.

Paul Schnitzler. Wikidata. https://www.wikidata.org/wiki/Q1252457 39. Accessed March 2026.

"Süßes Mädel." German Wikipedia. https://de.wikipedia.org/wiki/S% C3%BC%C3%9Fes_M%C3%A4del. Accessed March 2026.

"Tagebuch (Schnitzler)." German Wikipedia. https://de.wikipedia.org /wiki/Tagebuch_(Schnitzler). Accessed March 2026.

"The Blue Room (play)." Wikipedia. https://en.wikipedia.org/wiki/T he_Blue_Room_(play). Accessed March 2026.

"Young Vienna." Wikipedia. https://en.wikipedia.org/wiki/Young_Vi enna. Accessed March 2026.

Arthur C. Rauscher is an author, essayist, and Argentine tango instructor from Atlanta, Georgia. He studied journalism at the University of Georgia and film studies at Georgia State University, where his education reflected an early recognition that stories—whether on the page or screen—were windows into lives and worlds beyond his own experience.

Born in Milledgeville, Georgia, the same small town that produced Flannery O'Connor, Rauscher moved to Atlanta in his mid-teens. The contrast between these two environments—rural South and urban South, provincial and cosmopolitan, past and present—shaped his understanding of the region's complexities and contradictions, and gave him what he considers the essential education of his formative years: an insider's knowledge of two very different ways of being Southern, and an outsider's perspective on both.

His literary interests range from the Southern Gothic of O'Connor and Faulkner to the psychological realism of Chekhov, Tolstoy, and Arthur Schnitzler, from the hardboiled clarity of Truman Capote and Daniel Woodrell to the social consciousness of Barbara Kingsolver, Eudora Welty, and James McBride. He admires writers who render the interior life with precision, who take social structures seriously as forces that shape individual destinies, and who refuse to look away from what seeing clearly costs.

When not writing, he teaches Argentine tango, an art form that shares with literature the requirement that one pay very close attention to another person while maintaining the formal structure that makes genuine connection possible. He lives in Atlanta, Georgia.